ANDREY BELY

EDITED BY

GERALD JANECEK

ANDREY BELY

A CRITICAL REVIEW

THE UNIVERSITY PRESS OF KENTUCKY

ISBN: 0-8131-1368-7

Library of Congress Catalog Card Number: 77-75449

Copyright © 1978 by The University Press of Kentucky

A statewide cooperative scholarly publishing agency
serving Berea College, Centre College of Kentucky,
Eastern Kentucky University, The Filson Club,
Georgetown College, Kentucky Historical Society,
Kentucky State University, Morehead State University,
Murray State University, Northern Kentucky University,
Transylvania University, University of Kentucky,
University of Louisville, and Western Kentucky University.

Editorial and Sales Offices: Lexington, Kentucky 40506

CONTENTS

LIST OF FREQUENTLY CITED WORKS

To minimize the number of notes, the following works will be referred to in parentheses in the text by the English titles below.

WORKS BY ANDREY BELY

PROSE

(*First Symphony*) *Severnaya simfoniya (1-aya, geroicheskaya)*. Moscow: Skorpion, 1904.

(*Second Symphony*) *Simfoniya (2-aya, dramaticheskaya)*. Moscow: Skorpion, 1902.

(*Third Symphony*) *Vozvrat. III simfoniya*. Moscow: Grif, 1905.

(*Fourth Symphony*) *Kubok meteley. Chetvyortaya simfoniya*. Moscow: Skorpion, 1908.

(*The Silver Dove*) *Serebryanny golub*. Moscow: Skorpion, 1910.

(*Petersburg*) *Peterburg, roman v vosmi chastyakh s prologom i epilogom*. (1) St. Petersburg: Almanakh Sirin, 1916, cited from the reprint: Bradda, 1967; (2) Berlin: Epokha, 1922; (3) Moscow: Nikitinskie subbotniki, 1928.

(*Kotik Letaev*) *Kotik Letaev*. Petrograd: Epokha, 1922.

(*Notes of an Eccentric*) *Zapiski chudaka*. Moscow-Berlin: Gelikon, 2 vols., 1922.

(*The Baptized Chinaman*) *Kreshcheny kitaets*. Moscow-Leningrad: Nikitinskie subbotniki, 1927.

(*Moscow*) I: (*The Moscow Eccentric*) *Moskovsky chudak*. Moscow: Krug, 1926. II: (*Moscow in Jeopardy*) *Moskva pod udarom*. Moscow: Krug, 1926.

(*Masks*) *Maski*. Moscow: GIKhL, 1932.

VERSE

(*Gold in Azure*) *Zoloto v lazuri.* Moscow: Skorpion, 1904.

(*Ashes*) *Pepel, stikhi.* St. Petersburg: Shipovnik, 1909.

(*The Urn*) *Urna.* Moscow: Grif, 1909.

("The First Encounter") *Pervoe svidanie.* St. Petersburg: Alkonost, 1921.

(*Poetry*) *Stikhotvoreniya i poemy,* Biblioteka poeta, bolshaya seriya, ed. Tamara Yu. Khmelnitskaya. Moscow-Leningrad: Sovetsky pisatel, 1966.

CRITICISM; THEORY

(*Symbolism*) *Simvolizm.* Moscow: Musaget, 1910.

(*Arabesques*) *Arabeski.* Moscow, 1911.

(*Rhythm as a Dialectic*) *Ritm kak dialektika i 'Medny vsadnik,' issledovanie.* Moscow: Federatsiya, 1929.

(*Gogol's Craft*) *Masterstvo Gogolya.* Moscow-Leningrad: Ogiz, 1934.

MEMOIRS

(*At the Boundary of Two Centuries*) *Na rubezhe dvukh stolety.* Moscow-Leningrad: Zemlya i fabrika, 1930.

(*The Beginning of the Century*) *Nachalo veka.* Moscow-Leningrad: GIKhL, 1933.

(*Between Two Revolutions*) *Mezhdu dvukh revolyutsy.* Leningrad: Izd. Pisateley, 1934.

OTHER

(Mochulsky) Konstantin V. Mochulsky, *Andrey Bely.* Paris: YMCA Press, 1955.

GERALD JANECEK

INTRODUCTION

The sad fact is that Andrey Bely (1880 – 1934) is not well known in the West in spite of his being one of the most important innovators in prose and literary theory of the twentieth century. This is in part due to the difficulty of translating his works, but the lack of translations into English and other languages is gradually being remedied (see Struve's survey). It is also due to the inherent difficulty of the works themselves; Bely will probably never become a "popular" writer like Tolstoy or Dostoevsky. And, unlike James Joyce, he has not become the property of academic circles in his native language because his ideas are still considered politically unacceptable.

Recent years have shown a steadily increasing upsurge of interest in Andrey Bely (at least in the West) that seems to indicate that reassessment and renewed appreciation of his work are under way in the scholarly world. With a view to providing widely scattered scholars with a forum for exchanging fresh ideas on Bely and for formalizing this reassessment, the International Symposium on Andrey Bely was held at the University of Kentucky during 27–29 March 1975. Rumor has it that this event inadvertently turned out to be the first such gathering on a topic related to Russian Symbolism. This anthology of the selected papers, though not the first book in English on Bely, is the first collective work on him and is representative of the broad spectrum of topics and approaches to Bely now being adopted among Slavists.

The papers of the symposium have been divided here into two groups, based roughly on whether they focus more on criticism and analysis of Bely's works (Part I) or on extrinsic matters such as personal relationships and broad philosophical issues (Part II). Several of the papers could have been placed in either category.

I

Russian Realism, in a manner typical of all successful movements in art, had run its course by the 1880s. Nearly all the major Realists were dead, and the movement was largely in the hands of secondary talents and hacks who went on repeating its devices and themes ad nauseam. Realism appeared to be bankrupt, having failed to achieve the social progress and reforms that were the goal of its liberal theoreticians. Even the abolishment of serfdom ended up causing further problems rather than being a solution. Russian society was in turmoil, with encroaching industrialization, the shift of power to the merchant classes, assassinations and general unrest, coupled with governmental reaction and refusal to move with the times. This turmoil produced a growing tension over the approach of catastrophe and at the same time a sense of present stagnation.

Realism had emphasized the concrete, observable aspects of "this world" to the virtual exclusion of considerations of the "other world," except as these could be empirically observed. By the 1880s the prevailing philosophy in intellectual circles was materialism or positivism. Programmatically, Realism had made literature not an end in itself, but a tool for social change, a means for exposing social evils in order to effect reform. A lack of emphasis on the literary craft per se led to significant lowering of artistic standards, since it was the message and not the medium that was important. It had been a time of prose. The movement had not produced a major poet since Nekrasov, and poetry was often reduced to pamphleteering in verse. In the hands of hacks, the literary culture easily slid to a low level of artistic achievement.

The decline of Realism cleared the way for a swing toward areas that had been neglected: a mysticoreligious orientation and verse craftsmanship. For our purposes, the most important figures in this reaction were Dmitry S. Merezhkovsky and his wife Zinaida N. Gippius, Valery Ya. Bryusov, and Fyodor Sologub (F. K. Teternikov). This first generation of Symbolists was often called "decadent," perhaps because of their interest in the French Symbolist poets, their inclination to black arts and Baudelairean sensualism, and their generally pessimistic outlook. This is an oversimplified view, but the term served to distinguish them from the second generation to which Bely, Vyacheslav Ivanov, and Aleksandr Blok belonged, which was initially more optimistic and displayed greater interest in German idealism and especially in the ideas of Vladimir Solovyov.

While three of the "decadents" (Merezhkovsky excluded) were models of verse craftsmanship and insisted on skillful use of language and poetic devices, the influence of Gippius and Merezhkovsky on Bely was mainly in their emphasis on the importance of a mysticoreligious consciousness; in Bely's words, they influenced "the style of my relationship to life" (*Between Two Revolutions,* p. 325). Sologub, the pessimist par excellence, went so far as to believe that decay, death, and corruption were positive values, since they hastened destruction of the material world and thus made the way to the "other world" easier; but his influence on Bely seems to have been mainly in the area of prose style (see the article by Rabinowitz). Bryusov, though younger than the others in this early group, is included in it because of some of his typically "shocking," "decadent" behavior and his lack of a fervent ideological position. Having decided, upon finishing school, that his ambition was to become a literary coryphaeus and that Symbolism was the logical wave of the future, he proceeded to write in the requisite style and to achieve the position of influential publisher, critic, and poet. Bryusov was closer than the others to being more a colleague than a mentor to Bely. Nevertheless Bryusov's own skillfully wrought poetry and his critical and theoretical writings were important in Bely's literary education. Bryusov also provided Bely with vigorous constructive criticism of his early efforts in verse.

The "decadence" of this older generation, their tendency to escape, derived from a belief that a synthesis between the corrupt material world and eternal values was not only not around the corner, but not possible at all. The younger generation based their early, unguarded optimism chiefly on Solovyov's prediction that the seemingly eternal conflict between Christ and Antichrist might soon give way to a synthesis of the two worlds brought about by the manifestation of the "Woman Clothed with the Sun," Sophia—Holy Wisdom in a palpable form—who would resolve the conflicts between nations, religions, matter and spirit, and issue in an age of universal brotherhood and communion. Clearly it was the poetic image of this Eternal Feminine that was influential rather than the theological arguments supporting the concept, and much has been said about the matter of the Beautiful Lady in relation to Blok's and Bely's personal and creative lives. 1905 was a year of disillusionment for them both, but while Blok's view took a tragic turn, Bely continued to believe in the possibility of a synthesis and to seek it in new realms. Thus his fascination with Anthroposophy which began in 1912 and which, in spite of an official break with its founder Rudolf Steiner in 1922, may have in fact continued to the end of Bely's life. Steiner, in his formulation of a blend of Christianity and eastern occult religion, insisted that to those who followed the path of initiation the spiritual realm would become as knowable as the material world. The intimate relationship between the two worlds was described by Steiner in such minute detail that this "Spiritual Science" must have seemed to Bely to be the longed-for synthesis.

There was also a concurrent mode of synthesis for Bely—the word. The theurgic, mystic (Word-Logos-Christ) aspects aside, the word (and by extension, all art) provided a means of synthesizing the material and the spiritual. Relevant here, of course, is the theory of the symbol as an inseparable intersection of the material image and the abstract form or idea. But Bely went beyond this to investigate every word as a quasi-symbol having material properties (sound, graphic image, physical "gestures" of the vocal apparatus) and spiritual properties ("meaning" in all possible definitions of the word).

II

Andrey Bely is the pen name of Boris Nikolaevich Bugaev, who was born in Moscow on October 14, 1880 (Old Style), the only child of Nikolay Vasilevich Bugaev, a well-known Moscow University mathematician, and Aleksandra Dmitrievna née Egorova, a society woman renowned for her beauty. Without siblings, Bely had the privilege of serving as the third and most passive member of a familial triangle. Bely's memoirs and also *Kotik Letaev* describe how he was caught in a constant conflict between his parents in their warring over attitudes toward art (the mother was a musician) and intellectual pursuits (the father emphasized empirical sciences). As Samuel Cioran points out, the dichotomy was not as neatly drawn as this in fact.[1] But one cannot help sensing the ongoing division in Bely's perception of the world which caused him to be ever seeking a principle upon which to achieve a solid and lasting synthesis between art and science, reason and the emotions. Bely was the younger classmate of Valery Bryusov at the Polivanov Gymnasium, which provided Bely with educational and formative experiences that he recalled gratefully in later years. Evidently more to please his father than out of any self-motivation, he pursued and successfully achieved a degree in the natural sciences at Moscow University.

While a student at the gymnasium Bely had begun to write poetry, and he continued to do so as a university student. It was under the influence of Mikhail Sergeevich Solovyov, a neighbor of the Bugaevs and younger brother of the famous philosopher, that Bely published his first work, the *Second Symphony*, in 1902. Bryusov, editor of the Skorpion publishing house, agreed to issue the work when Mikhail Sergeevich provided the financial backing needed. Mikhail Sergeevich was reportedly also responsible for Bely's choice of pseudonym: when Bely first proposed the name Boris Burevoy, Mikhail Sergeevich quipped that some negatively disposed critic would be bound to see Burevoy as "Bori voy" (Boris's howl), and he suggested the alternative of Andrey Bely (Andrew White) (*Beginning of the Century*, p. 128). From 1893 until his death in 1902, Mikhail Sergeevich and his wife and son, Seryozha, provided a congenial and encouraging environment for the insecure young author. It was at the Solovyovs's that Bely several times met the philosopher and came under his influence.

On the evening of the spring day in 1903 when Bely's father, by then dean of the university, had signed his son's diploma, he died in his son's presence. Bely decided not to pursue a career in science and became a full-time writer. The years 1903–10 were stormy ones for Bely. He was a major contributor to Bryusov's journal *Vesy* (*The Scales*), which had become the major organ of the Symbolist movement. This was a time of disarray in the movement and much creative energy was spent on internal and external polemics and squabbles. Bely was in the thick of things, busy quarreling with just about everyone in and out of Symbolism, but also deeply involved in trying to synthesize from the disparate strains of theory a coherent philosophy of Symbolism. Probably only Vyacheslav Ivanov succeeded better in giving the Symbolist world view a structure. Bely's articles of this period, written under the pressure of publishing deadlines and in the heat of bitter dispute, are on the surface quite disorganized and seemingly contradictory. However, beneath the surface there is a system to Bely's thought, and this has recently received a suitable analysis and evaluation.[2] 1905 was a crucial year, since the revolution, seen as a harbinger of the manifestation of V. Solovyov's Beautiful Lady and the initiation of the Final Times, failed miserably, issuing in a period of repression, disorganization, and disillusionment. In 1905, Bely's relationship with Aleksandr Blok, which had begun so auspiciously and mystically in 1903, began to fall apart due to Bely's involvement with Lyubov Dmitrievna Blok, the poet's wife. With the encouragement of Serezha Solovyov, Ellis, and other friends, Bely had come to see in Lyubov Blok the embodiment of Sophia, and he proceeded to fall in love with her. She was at times flattered and receptive to this attention; at times coldly distant and repelled. Blok, initially indulgent, became more and more upset and jealous. (Blok seems to have been inclined to accept her position as Sophia and to spiritualize their union, feeling that Bely's attitude was justified; but at the same time he was unable to support his generous ideas emotionally.) More than once a duel between the poets was in the offing but was averted. In 1905–06, Bely escaped from all this turmoil by going abroad to Munich, where he met Sholom Asch, Stanislav Przybyszewski, and Frank Wedekind. From there he went to Paris, where he managed to establish a friendship with Jean Jaurès, the socialist leader. He returned to Russia for further disputes and agonies. In spite of the difficulties of this period, it was extremely prolific. Bely's publications included two more *Symphonies*, three major collections of verse, and over 200 articles, reviews, and polemical essays.

By the end of the decade, Bely had arrived at no satisfactory solution for his personal, artistic, and philosophical dilemmas; and he had completely exhausted himself in the process of attempting to find one. In 1909 he had begun a relationship with Asya Turgeneva, and in 1910 they went abroad together, having become unofficially married. After traveling around Europe and the Middle East they settled in Brussels, where Asya resumed her art lessons. At this time, 1912, they had mysterious experiences, such as unexplained aromas of flowers and strangers who seemed to be leading them somewhere, all of which resulted in their being drawn to a house that turned out to be the Anthroposophical Lodge. The head of the movement, Dr. Rudolf Steiner, was in residence. Although the subordinates guarding access to the doctor were dutifully stern, he

intervened from behind the scenes to afford Bely and Asya the unusual honor of being allowed to attend several lectures "for the
initiated only," even though they had not been initiated. Steiner's
personal magnetism and his choice of subjects struck a responsive
chord in Bely, and the couple decided to become actively involved
in Anthroposophy. Bely seems to have been ripe at this time for re-
leasing responsibility for the direction of his life to others, and
Steiner filled the bill as the needed preceptor and father figure.
After more than a year of attending Steiner's lectures in various
cities around Europe, receiving occult instruction and lessons in
German, Bely settled in Dornach, Switzerland in February 1914.
Dornach had recently been selected as the headquarters of the
Anthroposophical movement and Steiner was in the process of
erecting the Johannesbau, or Goetheanum, the Anthroposophical
temple, of which Steiner himself was the architect and builder.
Bely and Asya both participated in the manual labor involved in
constructing the Johannesbau, while they continued their occult
training. In 1916, Bely was called up for military duty by the Russian government, and he returned to Russia. Asya Turgeneva remained in Dornach, having become completely and permanently
immersed in Anthroposophy.

After returning to his homeland, Bely did not serve in the military but spent the next several years lecturing, chiefly in connection with the Free Philosophical Society (Volfila) of which he was a
founder. He also worked in various archives to earn a meagre liveli-
hood under the severe conditions of the Revolution. Bely welcomed
the Revolution at the start but saw for it distinctly different goals
than the Bolsheviks had in mind, and he soon became more a "fellow traveler" than an active supporter (see the papers by Levin and
Rosenthal for a more detailed picture of Bely's attitudes). As early
as 1916, Bely's mental state had begun seriously to weaken. In the
peculiar *Notes of an Eccentric* (1922) he describes his sickness as he
made his way back to Russia from Dornach as a form of paranoia.
Overwork, difficult physical circumstances, and separation from
Asya had only worsened his condition; and in November 1921, he
managed to make his way by a difficult and circuitous route to
Berlin. He was near nervous collapse. His two-year stay there did
not alleviate his problems, since not only did Asya refuse to resume
their relationship but Steiner, too, received him coldly. In the
period of his return to Russia Bely had made himself the leading
spokesman for Anthroposophy in Russia and had even written a

book, *Rudolf Steiner and Goethe in the Contemporary Worldview* (1917), defending Steiner against the attacks of Bely's erstwhile friend Emily Metner. Steiner's reasons for his seeming ingratitude remain to be discovered, but they probably have to do with Bely's tendency to interpret Anthroposophy in an improperly independent fashion. It is also likely that Steiner perceived Bely's mental imbalance. Bely spent the time in Berlin (by eyewitness accounts, of which there are many) acting strangely, erratically, and occasionally violently. In the end he succeeded in alienating nearly all his comrades in émigré circles. Nevertheless, this period was extremely productive of publications (seven volumes of new editions of earlier works and the first publication of nine new works). In October 1923, Bely decided to depart again for Russia in little better condition than when he had gone there in 1916, but this time with a substitute for Asya in the person of Klavdiya Nikolaevna Vasileva, an Anthroposophist and old acquaintance. Vasileva was perhaps the ideal companion: she was stable, steady, intelligent, and yet very devoted to Bely. She ultimately divorced her husband to marry Bely and remained his loyal helper and, after his death, the chief guardian of his literary legacy.

The details of Bely's last decade of life are simple, as far as is known at present. But much work remains to be done, and an important contribution to our knowledge of Bely in the later period is made here in the essay by Keys. Evidently, Bely spent most of his time outside the capital quietly writing the Moscow novels, his memoirs, a new defense of his theory of rhythm in verse, a book on Gogol, and an unpublished (and apparently unfinished) history of culture. His death on 8 January 1934, in Moscow seems to have been due to a cerebral hemorrhage which occurred on 17 July 1933, at Koktebel on the Crimea (where he had been spending his summers at the estate of Maksimilian Voloshin) rather than to a sunstroke, as originally assumed. The sunstroke legend resulted from Bely's fanatical, systematic, program of sunbathing, and also from the fact that it would have conveniently fulfilled his own prophecy:

> He believed in the golden sparkle,
> But died of the solar arrows.
> His thought measured the ages,
> But he did not manage to live out his life.
> (1907; *Poetry*, p. 249)

III

Although Bely's earliest surviving published work, "Prishedshy" ("He Who Has Come") is a drama (see the essay by Yurieff), he spent little further creative energy in this area, except for later dramatizations of his novels *Petersburg* and *Moscow*. However, a great deal of his early theorizing and literary criticism concerned contemporary dramaturgy, most importantly the works of Chekhov and Ibsen. Bely's goal for drama was connected with the theory of the mystery play as a link between art and life. The significance of drama for Bely is now coming under scholarly examination (see the essay by Kalbouss).

Bely concentrated his artistic activities on verse during the first decade of the twentieth century (the *Symphonies*, also important in this decade, will be discussed below). Considering Bely's importance as a poet, it comes as something of a surprise to realize that very little scholarly attention has been devoted to his verse. The only two extensive treatments of it to date are Tamara Yu. Khmelnitskaya's introductory essay to the 1966 Soviet edition of the poetry (*Poetry*, pp. 5–66) and the comments and analyses included by K. Mochulsky in his biography of Bely.[3] With the exception of the statistical survey of Bely's iambic tetrameter by K. Taranovski, and two articles on "The First Encounter" (1922)[4] the article by Herbert Eagle in the present volume is the first that analyzes a Bely poem. Interest in the verse has been eclipsed by Bely's prose and possibly also by comparison with the verse of some of Bely's contemporaries, in particular Blok's, with which it was so closely associated. Of Bely's six original volumes of verse—*Gold in Azure*, 1904, *Ashes*, 1909, *The Urn*, 1909, *The Princess and the Knights* (*Korolevna i rytsari*), 1919, *Star* (*Zvezda*), 1922, and *After Parting* (*Posle razluki*), 1922—it is in the initial three plus the later "The First Encounter" that we find his most important poetry.

Gold in Azure is a brightly colored and fairly optimistic expression of expectation at the imminent arrival of Sophia and is a mixture of Solovyovian mysticism and Balmontian sensuality. The volume's title was obviously a reference to several passages in Solovyov's famous poem "Three Encounters" ("Tri svidaniya"), where the image is directly associated with the "Woman Clothed with the Sun" who had manifested herself to the philosopher on three occasions described in the poem. Also, Balmont's book *We Will Be Like the Sun* (*Budem kak solntse*) was admittedly a model.

The predominant image in Bely's book is the sunset, which was seen as a medium for mystical communion with the absolute world beyond. Thus Bely filled his lyrics with descriptions of sunset colors and shifting shapes of clouds structured in an elaborate system of color symbols, precious stones and fabrics (see Cioran's essay for an explanation of specifics). Even this most exuberant collection of poems is not, however, without its self-satirical moments. Bely was immediately dissatisfied with this first book of poems, in part because it did not compare favorably with Vyacheslav Ivanov's book *Transparency* (*Prozrachnost*) which came out at approximately the same time, but also because the book had been somewhat sloppily composed.

The second book, *Ashes*, was much more somber in mood as a result of Bely's disillusionment of the past several years (the 1905 Revolution and the difficulties with the Bloks). There is an ongoing image in the titles of these volumes. This book, at one point to be entitled "Sunset Ashes," is meant to describe the hue of twilight after the sunset has been extinguished, or alternately the ashes of the Icarian poet whose body has been scorched and burnt out by a flight too near the sun. In any case, the poet is now earthbound in more ways than one and the prevailing images and colors are gray dust, coldness, storm clouds, and destruction. The dream has failed and the poet must look to the painful aspects of reality. The chief subject here is Mother Russia and her people, and the collection is dedicated to Nekrasov. Bely, in associating himself with the catastrophic fate of the nation, pours out some of the most moving expressions of emotion to be found anywhere in his writings. His experiments with new forms of versification, already evident in *Gold in Azure* in the fragmentation of lines into small groups of words, take further steps in the introduction of visual components.

The Urn, containing poems written at the same time as those in *Ashes* has a different emphasis. As indicated by the title of the collection, the sufferings involved are made into an object of contemplation. The title of one of the sections of this collection, "Philosophical Melancholy," is indicative of the mood involved.

The later collections continue experimentation in rhythm, soundplay, and typography, but do not contain much important poetry. Perhaps because from 1909 on Bely's interest in versification took a decidedly theoretical turn, his preoccupation with theory replaced the energy of sincere expression that imbues art with life force. In any case, the later poetry is more interesting from a technical standpoint than from an emotional one. Typical of this period is the volume *Poems (Stikhotvoreniya,* 1923) in which Bely included selections from all his earlier collections but often in radically revised form. Some of these new versions date from as far back as 1914 and seem more to reflect Bely's theoretical principles than a genuine need to alleviate inadequacies in the earlier poems. At best the later versions can be seen as brilliant verbal manipulations.

Bely in retrospect noted his problem with theory in comparing himself to Blok: "he himself [Blok] never engaged in the analysis of verse, maintaining that for a poet this was dangerous; later he constantly pointed out: 'Look, Andrey Bely had been a poet, he engaged in the study of rhythm, and he stopped writing himself' " (*Between Two Revolutions*, p. 403).

Nevertheless, Bely's best single poetic achievement, the long narrative "The First Encounter," dates from the late period. The poem is a fascinating verse memoir containing Bely's reminiscences from the turn of the century and his relationship with Mikhail Solovyov and family and through them with Vladimir Solovyov. The quadripartite work, which has similarities to the structure of the *Symphonies*, reaches a peak in the third part in the re-creation of a concert performance at the *Nobility Assembly Hall* during which the poet encounters the lovely Sophia-like society lady Zarina—in real life Margarita K. Morozova, the wife of the Moscow philanthropist. Bely has here relaxed his theoretical concerns in favor of a seemingly effortless poetic improvisation, the work reportedly of only a few days of intensive writing, which nevertheless displays his poetic craftsmanship and full scope of skills. Bely's resources for rhythmic inventiveness within the framework of regular iambic tetrameter, rich sound orchestration, and brilliant imagery are used to their best advantage. It is probably because "The First Encounter" was backward-looking in subject that Bely released himself from theoretical and personal involvements. Nevertheless, in it he managed to combine his best achievements in verse, philosophy, literary theory, and even prose.

There is probably an understandable explanation for the noted neglect of Bely's poetry in literary criticism. The fact is that Bely was basically not a miniaturist, not comfortable in a work of small compass. Bely's fundamental compositional process is one of repetition of words and phrases and a building of complexities by developing associations with these units as they intertwine themselves in the fabric of a text. For this process to achieve its full effectiveness and depth of significance a certain amount of space is needed, more, certainly, than the length of a page-long lyric poem. "The First Encounter" succeeds because it is long enough to allow the necessary development of the units of material. It has been pointed out that even Bely's books of verse are not intended to be read as collections of individual self-sufficient poems, but rather as carefully structured mosaics which form a total, unified picture in which each poem has its particular place and function and is dependent on the whole for its full meaning.[5] This is true of other Symbolists as well, and for Bely it became an increasingly important consideration with each succeeding collection. It is therefore not surprising that the poems often strike one as fragments of some larger work. Perhaps it remains for scholars and readers to read the collections as those "larger works" in order to arrive at the complete measure of Bely's poetic achievement.

IV

Bely's four *Symphonies* are one of the most remarkable beginnings in twentieth-century prose. From the very start Bely was an innovator. For Bely prose was not essentially distinct from verse, and it was in his ornamental, lyrically oriented prose that he seemed to be most seriously striving for the "new form" that the Symbolists sought. As the titles of the works suggest, it was by experimenting with the possibility of incorporating a musical structure into a work of literature that Bely first sought this new form. Music had been for Bely and other Symbolists a sort of ideal which they strove to approximate in poetry (see Hughes's essay for a further discussion of this topic), so that it is natural that he should have chosen this path. The "symphonic" structure of these works involves a four-part arrangement in three of the works (the *Third* has only three parts) suggesting the standard four movements of the classical symphony, and it involves a fairly regular repetition of important phrases and longer passages that resembles not so much the development of symphonic themes as the use of leitmotifs in a Wagner opera. Of course, significant internal details of symphonic form, such as contrasting tempos and keys, are missing, since they are unrealizable in a literary medium.

The *Northern Symphony, 1st, Heroic,* completed in 1900, but not published until 1903 with an imprint date of 1904 depicts a fairy-

tale kingdom in which a pure princess, daughter of a king who has
fled his regal responsibilities and retreated into isolation, saves the
kingdom by assuming control. In the process she subdues and re-
deems a sensuous knight of demonic origins. The next in the series,
Symphony, 2nd, Dramatic (1902) is, as mentioned above, Bely's
first published work. While the first symphony is charming in its
directness and simplicity, the second is more complex and contemporary in subject. It involves a stylishly mystic intellectual who
identifies a certain society woman as the embodiment of "The
Woman Clothed with the Sun." He is distressed by her indifference
to his prophetic stance, and in the end he is embarrassed by being
told that the "male child" of this woman is in fact a girl that they
like to dress in boy's clothing. Combined with mundane details
and a mystical atmosphere is a strong tone of satire, which touches
not the mystical ideas themselves but rather the ridiculous mani-
festations of them fashionable at the time. Later Bely liked to brag
that he was truly prophetic here, since many of the incidents which
he had only imagined soon became reality and in some cases the
reality "surpassed my caricature" of them (*Beginning of the
Century,* p. 122). In *The Return. III Symphony* (1905) we see a
mentally unbalanced graduate student in chemistry have a dream
and then find the dream filtering into real life. In the end he becomes so unable to distinguish dream from reality that he dives into
a still lake thinking he is diving into the "other world" of the sky,
and thus he is drowned. The tripartite structure is very neatly
(some might say too neatly) arranged: Part I is the dream, Part II
reality, and Part III dream and reality intertwined. The circular
pattern of "return to the dream" is carefully maintained. Although
perhaps suffering from a schematic structure, the work is nevertheless one of the most clear-cut artistic expressions of the Symbolist
orientation. *Goblet of Blizzards. Fourth Symphony* (1908) was the
product of several years of writing and revision and is much more
elaborate in its thematic development and more precise in its
"symphonic" structure than the preceding three. Yet the upshot
of this work was that Bely decided to abandon the overt imitation
of musical form, although he retained the principles of motival
repetition and development that he had worked out for use in the
Symphonies. The *Fourth* has points of contact with each of its three
predecessors in that it depicts a man who sees in the heroine a
manifestation of Sophia, but he perishes at the hand of a jealous
husband; at the death of the woman, their mystical union in heaven

is described. These works immediately established Bely's importance as a modernist and leading member of the literary avant-garde in Russia, and they are still of considerable literary worth.

Intermittently between the *Symphonies* Bely wrote several short prose works, the best of which, "Adam," is definitively analyzed herein by Charlotte Douglas.

Bely's first work to qualify as a full-length novel is *The Silver Dove,* 1910. This is the tale of a young "decadent" poet, Daryalsky, who is disenchanted with urban intellectual life and seeks spiritual renewal in a rural environment. He becomes involved with a sect of "Doves," the leader of which had decided that the poet is the man destined to give birth to the new Savior by one of the sect's women. This plan fails when no child is conceived and the sect proceeds to murder Daryalsky to prevent their being exposed. The most striking feature of the novel is its narrative manner, which is couched in a quasi-Gogolian style. This novel was to be the first of a trilogy on the theme of "East or West," the Solovyovian conflict of irrational and rational cultures.

The projected second volume of this trilogy, *Petersburg,* soon departed from the original plan and assumed an independent status. Generally considered Bely's most important work (Nabokov has even called it one of the four greatest prose works of the twentieth century), *Petersburg* went through four editions during Bely's lifetime: 1913-14, 1916, 1922, and 1927 (there was also a posthumous edition of 1935). Although Bely had initial difficulty getting the novel published, it was immediately recognized as a masterpiece and has retained that status. The 1916 edition was radically revised for the edition of 1922. The later version is usually preferred, though the earlier one has arguments in its favor. (A more detailed discussion of the versions of *Petersburg* is contained in my survey of Bely's prose rhythm.) The plot of the novel, the most tense situation in Bely's fiction, centers on the relationship between a father, who is an important government figure (Senator Ableukhov), and his son, who is a radically inclined intellectual and Neo-Kantian. The son had once incautiously promised to cooperate with a revolutionary group and they now give him a bomb with which to assassinate his own father (Flyer's essay deals with the bomb image). The assassination attempt fails, but along the way Bely manages to add layers of meaning and subplots that involve areas ranging from linguistic relationships to broad philosophical issues (see Berberova's essay). The atmosphere of the novel, which is set in the time of the 1905 Revolution, combines Pushkinian, Gogolian, and Dostoevskian moods in relation to the image of the city of Petersburg; and the work is a brilliant culmination of the career of that multivalent symbol in Russian literature. The central theme, one well-rooted in the literary tradition, consists of the duality (symbolized by the city) of rationality and irrationality, illusion and reality, and of the boundaries of consciousness, their instability and relativity.

Of all Bely's works, *Petersburg* has the largest critical literature connected with it, but *Kotik Letaev,* his next major prose work, has been receiving an equivalent amount of attention recently. Since it was unfortunately not the subject of a special study at the symposium, it is perhaps fitting to devote more attention to it in this introduction. *Kotik Letaev,* the first volume of another unrealized trilogy, *Epopeya,* is an autobiographical work only slightly fictionalized. It deals with the author's childhood achievement of self-consciousness from ages three to five. The novel was begun in Dornach in 1915 under the direct influence of Anthroposophy and has a definite Anthroposophical level of meaning.[6] Although it describes perceptions from the point of view of a young child, the language and imagery are sophisticated and in no way reduced to a child's range of expression. In fact, the dialectic between child's view and adult language is a particularly interesting aspect of the novel. The author's ability to re-create the universal experiences of childhood is nothing short of remarkable, and his intuitions about child psychology are astounding, considering that they predate most scientific work in this field. Many of the novel's symbols and images, which are presented as a kind of individual mythology, might well be illuminated by a Jungian approach, but such a study has not yet been made.

Kotik Letaev employs the full range of Bely's structural and verbal techniques (*Petersburg* is rather more conservative in this area). The overall pattern of the work is circular (like the *Symphonies*), or rather spiral, since, while it does return to the beginning, there is a concomitant expansion process in which larger and larger areas of experience are encompassed. Bely uses rhythmic devices (which I discuss in my survey) and soundplay. There are even disguised verses (couplets and quatrains) with rhymes and hidden line structures incorporated into the text. Yet everything is flexible, fresh, and constantly varied, so that, though one senses the poetic nature of the text, there is no monotony of the sort that a lengthy work in verse would almost surely produce. At the same time, utilizing his techniques of repetition and development of motifs, Bely has built a structure in which by accretion of associations the material seems to grow organically, until the web of associations is so complex and thoroughgoing that virtually everything in the novel is related to everything else. Furthermore, Bely has so perfectly integrated all the levels and parts of the novel that, for instance, the conflict between parents over the education of the child is reflected in the sounds and images associated with the parents long before it is evident in the plot. In these respects it is in *Kotik Letaev* that Bely has achieved his "new form," a perfect blend of verse and prose seemingly independent of all that has gone before it in literature. No doubt because of the difficulty of the subject (the rise of self-consciousness in a child too young to understand his experiences) and the complexities of the style (in places it is extremely opaque) and perhaps also due to historical circumstances, *Kotik Letaev* did not gain the fame afforded to *Petersburg.* However, it is certainly worthy of placement beside the latter on a twin pinnacle of achievement.

The sequel to *Kotik Letaev* in *Epopeya,* ultimately issued as a separate book under the title *The Baptized Chinaman* (*Kreshcheny kitaets,* 1927) depicts the emergence of the Oedipus complex in the child. Unfortunately, perhaps because it was not originally intended to be an independent volume, this work is not as carefully structured as its predecessor and many of the techniques used so successfully in *Kotik Letaev* have become ossified and monotonous.

Since in his essay John Elsworth ably characterizes the Moscow novels, Bely's last major prose fiction, there is no need to do so here. Similarly, I refer you to Beyer's essay for discussion and evaluation of Bely's other noteworthy contribution, his theory of verse rhythm.

The more one studies Bely, the more one feels secure in the belief that Bely's unique contribution to Russian literature, and indeed to world literature, is the full depth of his understanding of the human phenomenon of language and his appreciation and use of the manifold properties of words. His poetry is, for the most part, not emotionally engaging, his philosophical ideas are indebted to others, the plots of his novels are not astoundingly original; yet he continues to fascinate us by his powerful verbal creativity. The variety and inventiveness of his verbal pyrotechnics is such that to call Bely a great stylist is to do an injustice to the scope of his imagination. Perhaps only Khlebnikov, in his own way, comes close to

Bely in this, but even the extremely word-oriented Futurist movement is a pale successor. It is clear that Bely's work will continue to provide a fertile field for investigation by many different scholars for many years to come, and to enthrall and challenge readers indefinitely.

V

I would like to express my gratitude to the University of Kentucky for making its resources available to sponsor the symposium; to the Research and Development Committee of the American Association for the Advancement of Slavic Studies and Professor George W. Hoffman, the committee chairman, for important financial support; to Professor Vera Dunham, the committee's representative at the meeting, for her moral support and spirit of good humor; and to the International Research and Exchanges Board for their willingness to fund the Soviet participation which failed to materialize. Special thanks to Professor Roger Anderson for his advice and encouragement, and to Mrs. Penny Cox and Mrs. Ann Buckner for skillfully managing the sizable secretarial work generated by the symposium. Finally, my immense appreciation must go to all the participants, without whose enthusiasm and cooperation the project would have been stillborn.

NOTES

1. Samuel Cioran, *The Apocalyptic Symbolism of Andrej Belyj* (The Hague: Mouton, 1973), pp. 37–38.
2. John Elsworth, "Andrei Bely's Theory of Symbolism," *Forum for Modern Language Studies* 2, no. 4 (October 1974): 305–33.
3. Konstantin Mochulsky, *Andrey Bely* (Paris: YMCA Press, 1955).
4. K. Taranovsky, "Chetyryokhstopny yamb Andreya Belogo," *International Journal of Slavic Linguistics and Poetics* 10 (1966): 127–47; O. Ilinsky, "O poeme Andreya Belogo 'Pervoe svidanie,' " *Novy Zhurnal,* no. 90: 98–111; S. Karlinsky, "Symphonic Structure in Andrej Belyj's 'Pervoe svidanie,' " *California Slavic Studies* 6 (1971): 61–70.
5. John E. Malmstad, "The Poetry of Andrej Belyj: A Variorum Edition" (Ph.D. diss., Princeton University, 1968), pp. lviii–lxi.
6. See Gerald Janecek, "Anthroposophy in *Kotik Letaev,*" *Orbis Litterarum* 29 (1975): 245–67.

PART I

BELY'S LITERARY LEGACY

GLEB STRUVE

ANDREY BELY REDIVIVUS

I am not exactly a specialist on Andrey Bely. At least I do not regard myself as such, and I have not written or published anything about him for quite a long time. I did not know Bely well personally, as did, for instance, Nina Nikolaevna Berberova among those who are here. It is true that I did have one very short meeting and conversation with him in Berlin in 1922. I may be the only one here who had seen Bely *before* the Revolution. It must have been early in 1917 that I attended a lecture by him in Saint Petersburg. I have a fairly clear visual and auditory recollection of Bely as a speaker, but I do not recall what he spoke about.

It was my father who rejected Bely's *Petersburg* when it was more or less accepted by Bryusov for publication in *Russkaya Mysl*. Perhaps the organizer of the symposium expected me to throw some new light on this episode. Unfortunately, I cannot. I was very young then and knew or heard nothing about it. And I never talked to my father about it in later years. When I first read *Petersburg* (I think it was in *Sirin* in 1914) I was fascinated by it. (My interest in Bely had been aroused somewhat earlier by his studies in Russian versification in his book *Symbolism*. I was then beginning to write poetry myself.)

Bely was one of those writers who, on the whole, "accepted" (as the phrase went at the time), and even welcomed—some people would even go so far as to add "enthusiastically"—the Bolshevik October Revolution. By 1921, however, he came to feel neglected and surrounded by a hostile atmosphere (not the first time that he suffered from something which bordered on persecution mania);

and towards the end of that year he left Russia and became a sort of semiémigré. He spent one day in Riga, the capital of Latvia, where he was not allowed to stay any longer (he later devoted a few bitingly satirical pages to this stay in a little, nasty skit which he published upon his return to Russia).[1] Then he went on to Lithuania and spent about a month in Kaunas, awaiting a German entry permit. There his reception was much more friendly than in Riga. Late in 1922 he reached Berlin, then the center of Russian émigré literary life and publishing activities. He remained there for about two years. Toward the end of 1923, all of a sudden, Bely went back to Russia. His return certainly came as a surprise to some of his friends, especially as there was at the time some talk of his moving to Prague, another important Russian émigré cultural center, and Marina Tsvetaeva was expecting to welcome him there. Bely's future second wife and Anthroposophic friend, Klavdiya Nikolaevna Vasileva, was later said to have influenced his decision to return.

During Bely's stay in Berlin several of his works were reissued there. They included his two major pre-Revolution novels, *The Silver Dove* and *Petersburg,* the latter in a revised version. Both were printed in the old spelling, which implied that they were not meant to be imported into Soviet Russia. (In fact, *The Silver Dove* was never republished there again.) It was in Berlin also that Bely's earlier-written *Notes of an Eccentric* was published, never to be reissued again. This would-be autobiographical work, a mixture of fiction and memoirs dealing mainly with one critical episode in Bely's personal life, is his most debatable, wildest, and weirdest piece of writing. Bely's new works continued to be published in Russia, among them his long autobiographical poem "The First Encounter," one of Bely's most rewarding works in verse and in a way his swan song (there was also, in 1922, an émigré reprint of it). Also published then was *Kotik Letaev,* now regarded as one of his three best novels.

While abroad, Bely also worked on his memoirs. He had started writing them while still in Russia, as a story of his very complex personal and literary relationship with Aleksandr Blok. One version of his reminiscences about Blok appeared in *Zapiski Mechtateley* while he was still in Russia. Another was published in his Berlin journal *Epopeya.* In Berlin he wrote still another, expanded version, which he seems to have left behind when he went back to Russia, but which is now preserved in Soviet archives. Part of this

Berlin version, dealing with Blok and the Merezhkovskys, was published recently in a Soviet periodical.[2] Bely resumed working on these memoirs after his return to Russia, while at the same time revising what he had written earlier. The work was to be a memoir of the whole era of Russian Symbolism, one of the most interesting periods in the history of Russian culture in general and of Russian literature in particular, often referred to now as "the Silver Age," though I, at one with the late D. S. Mirsky, prefer to call it "the second Golden Age." But as Bely's friend, Vladislav Khodasevich, was to say later, under Bely's pen this work degenerated from a memoir or a history of Russian Symbolism into a sort of autobiographical diatribe. At times it is an extremely bitter and venomous, though highly fascinating, pamphlet. It grew eventually to three volumes, and the last volume, *Between Two Revolutions,* was published soon after Bely's death.

After his return to Russia, Bely also wrote several new novels: *The Baptized Chinaman* and the three novels forming part of the Moscow trilogy. In fact, Bely continued until his death as a very prolific writer, even if he did not produce any prose or verse— with the exception of "The First Encounter"—equal to his pre-Revolution work.

In 1934, when Bely died, Soviet Russian literature had not yet reached its nadir, and even though Bely more than once said that he had been placed "behind the threshold of Russian literature" (*za porogom russkoy literatury*), especially after the attack made on him by Trotsky, his new works continued for some time to be published in Russia.[3]

In the 1920s Bely's work was still quite often discussed, and some interesting things were written about him by the Russian Formalists, Viktor Shklovsky, Boris Eichenbaum, and others. There was also a very interesting article about his early, innovatory *Symphonies* by the well-known philosopher Sergey Askoldov. In 1928, Bely's *Petersburg* was reissued in the same version as the Berlin (1922) edition. A reissue of *Kotik Letaev* was also planned at this time, and Bely wrote a new introduction to it; but that edition never materialized. The introduction was for the first time published in Russian in the New York *Novy Zhurnal* (*New Review*), no. 101 (December, 1970). A French translation of it, from a slightly different manuscript version, will be found in an appendix to Georges Nivat's French translation of *Kotik Letaev*. In 1935 there was another edition of *Petersburg,* with an introduction by Kornely

Zelinsky, a well-known poet and critic who had once belonged to the Soviet literary avant-garde. Zelinsky expressed the view that, even though Bely had revised the novel after the October Revolution, this revision did not reflect any change in his attitude to the Revolution or in his general philosophy. The novel nevertheless deserved reissue, said Zelinsky, because of its literary qualities. He spoke of it as Bely's greatest and most significant work, masterfully written. Bely's lexical deformation, which had shocked so many old-fashioned critics, he ascribed to the fact that with Bely words were subordinated to all the twists of his "cerebral game." Bely's verse-oriented prose he saw not as a defect—not at least in *Petersburg*—but as something that enabled Bely to give free rein to his play on the meanings of words.

Two of Bely's new works about literature, which he wrote in the last years of his life, were published soon after his death. One, *Gogol's Craft,* dealt with Gogol as a literary craftsman and was full of brilliant insights. The other, entitled *Rhythm as a Dialectic,* was a study of Pushkin's "The Bronze Horseman." Both are now very highly valued outside Russia and have been reprinted there. Of Bely's poetry, only his second volume, *Ashes,* was reissued in 1928.

Although after Bely's return from Berlin Soviet critics liked to refer to him as someone who became a Soviet writer, his death did not evoke much general response, though there was an obituary published in *Pravda* and signed by three well-known poets, one of whom was Boris Pasternak. There were, on that occasion, no worthwhile overall appraisals either of his work or of his fascinating personality. Still, in 1937, in a special volume of *Literaturnoe Nasledstvo* devoted to Symbolism, the surviving fragment of a sequel to Bely's memoirs was published. It took up the story where Bely had interrupted it at the end of the third volume. The same issue of *Literaturnoe Nasledstvo* contained a valuable survey of Bely's entire literary legacy. It was compiled by Bely's widow, K. N. Vasileva-Bugaeva, and his friend, A. S. Petrovsky. Bely's name also figured quite prominently in the essays published in that volume, which dealt with the philosophy of Symbolism (by V. Asmus) and with the Symbolists' language (by V. Gofman).[4]

Soon after that began a long period of almost complete neglect of Bely. The one and only exception was the publication, in 1940, of a little volume of Bely's collected poetry in the minor series of *Biblioteka poeta.* Since then and to this day there have been, in the

Soviet Union, no reprints of any of Bely's novels or of his critical and theoretical works. Nor were his memoirs reissued. But in 1966 a volume of his poetry, which included all his published volumes of verse plus numerous variants and some unpublished poems, appeared in the major series of *Biblioteka poeta*. For students of Bely's poetry it was a most welcome edition. It was prepared for publication by Tamara Khmelnitskaya. Its publication testifies, at least, to the revival of an interest in Bely's poetry. In the last ten years or so, in connection with a great revival of interest in the problems of versification and of poetics in general among Soviet scholars, there have been many references to Bely's contribution in that field, and even a few specialized studies. As for the novels, there has been some talk for some time about the possible reissue of *Petersburg* in the series "Literaturnye pamyatniki"; and there was, not so long ago, an article in one of the Soviet periodicals about Bely's work on the novel, which may have been connected with this project.[5]

The situation has been quite different most of this time among the Russian émigrés in the West. A great many of Bely's literary contemporaries and friends emigrated in the first postrevolutionary years. Some of them were banished by Trotsky in 1922, when Bely himself was already living in Berlin. Had this not been the case, he might have easily found himself among their number and thus might have remained an émigré. During his semiémigré stay in Berlin he was in constant touch with the émigrés. His works of the Soviet period aroused invariable interest, even though the novels (with the exception of *Kotik Letaev*) were received very critically by many of his former admirers. The greatest interest was aroused by his memoirs in which he spoke—often most disparagingly—of so many of his former friends who were now émigrés.[6] His death gave rise to a number of very interesting articles, both reminiscences and critical appraisals. A few of these critical appraisals, especially those of adverse nature, I shall discuss later. Here let me mention some of the more interesting reminiscences of Bely by those who knew him personally at one time or another. The place of honor among them belongs to Marina Tsvetaeva's essay "The Captive Spirit," in which she describes mainly her meetings with Bely in Berlin.[7] It is one of the best pieces of her memoir prose. Of course, in it we see Bely through Tsvetaeva's eyes, and he appears to us rather different from some other portraits of him. The same period in Bely's life was much later described, from a different angle, by Nina Berberova (who was then Khodasevich's wife) in her autobiography *The Italics Are Mine*. There were also interesting reminiscences of Bely by Khodasevich himself, Fyodor Stepun, Boris Zaytsev, Nikolay Otsup, and Ilya Ehrenburg, all of whom knew Bely quite well, while some of them were, at one time or another, bound by ties of friendship to him. Of these essays the one by Stepun is perhaps the most interesting. It is built around the fascinating though disturbing notion that Bely simply "did not exist" as a human being. No one has put this so bluntly as Stepun, but Bely's "spectral" nature can be read into much of what was written about him by those who knew him well.

A place apart in the memoir literature about Bely belongs to what Nikolay Valentinov-Volsky had to say about his numerous meetings and long conversations with Bely in 1908 – 1909. They often talked long into the night of Symbolism and its philosophy, as well as of other philosophical issues, and a great variety of other matters. After Volsky's death (in 1964) his reminiscences, originally serialized for the most part in various periodicals, were brought out in a volume entitled *Two Years with the Symbolists*.[8] Their fascination comes, in part, from the fact that they were written by a man who came from an entirely different background. A Marxist, a former companion of Lenin (about whom he also wrote very interestingly), Volsky had no use for either the poetry or the literary doctrine of the Symbolists, but was nonetheless hypnotized, held spellbound by what he heard from Bely, and greatly impressed by his multifaceted, polyphonic personality. (In fact, this polyphonic character of Bely's personality—approached from a somewhat different standpoint, it could perhaps be described as Protean— echoes the polyphonic nature of his novels, noted by so many critics.) On top of everything else, Volsky possessed a remarkable memory, as attested by all those who knew him, which enabled him to record Bely's astounding perorations in great detail.

The culminating point of the Russian émigré contribution to the study of Bely was the book about him by Konstantin Mochulsky (1892 – 1948), one of the best émigré critics and literary scholars, who was also the author of books on Vladimir Solovyov, Aleksandr Blok, Dostoevsky (also translated into English), and Bryusov. Left somewhat unfinished, it was published in Paris in 1955. To this day it remains the only monograph in Russian about Bely. To illustrate Mochulsky's attitude to Bely, let me quote just one passage from his book:

No other Russian writer has experimented so boldly with words as did
Andrey Bely. His narrative prose has no equivalent in Russian literature. Bely's "stylistic revolution" may be considered a catastrophic
failure, but its great significance cannot be denied. The author of *The
Silver Dove* and of *Petersburg* left no stone unturned in the old "literary
language." He stood Russian prose on end, turned the syntax upside
down, flooded the vocabulary with a torrent of newly coined words.
Bely's audacious experiments, sometimes bordering on madness, left
their imprint on all new Soviet literature: he created a school.

"The verbal revolution," prepared by the lyrical prose of the *Symphonies,* found its expression in *The Silver Dove.* Bely begins by
imitating Gogol as a pupil. He adopts all the devices of Gogol's
style, straining them to an extreme emotional tension. The lyricism,
the grotesque, the hyperbole, the piling-up, the contrasts, the verbal
puns, the intonation, the coloring, and the rhythm of Gogol's prose
are shown by Bely as if through a magnifying glass.[9]

There was, of course, nothing new in this parallel between Bely
and Gogol: it had been noted many times before, and Bely himself
was perfectly aware of his affinity with Gogol, as may be seen in
his *Gogol's Craft.* D. S. Mirsky in his *History of Russian Literature*
also spoke of Bely's debt to Gogol. This is what he wrote, in 1926, of
The Silver Dove:

It is closely modelled on the great example of Gogol. It cannot be
called an imitative work, for it requires a powerful originality to learn
from Gogol without failing piteously. Bely is probably the only Russian
writer who succeeded in doing so. The novel is written in splendid,
sustainedly beautiful prose, and his prose is the first thing that strikes
the reader in it. It is not so much Bely, however, as Gogol reflected in
Bely, but it is always on Gogol's highest level, which is seldom the case
with Gogol himself.[10]

Incidentally, Mirsky, unlike some other, and especially later,
critics, seemed to assess *The Silver Dove* particularly highly. And
he motivated this evaluation as follows: *"The Silver Dove* is somewhat alone . . . in being the one of Bely's novels which has most
human interest in it, where the tragedy is infectious and not merely
puckishly ornamental." To this Mirsky added that *The Silver Dove*
had more narrative interest than most Russian novels, and a complicated and excellently disentangled plot, as well as wonderful
evocations of nature. "All this, together with the splendidly orna-

mental style," concluded Mirsky, "makes *The Silver Dove* one of the works of Russian literature that are most full of the most various riches." [11] Today few people, I think, will accept the preference, implied in that judgment, for *The Silver Dove* over *Petersburg* and *Kotik Letaev*. Though not many people would subscribe perhaps to the view which stands at opposite poles to Mirsky's and sees *The Silver Dove* as a "childish and cheap (*lubochnaya*) book." This latter view was voiced by none other than Boris Zaytsev, the well-known writer and Bely's friend.[12]

In more recent times the interest in Bely has switched to the West. This was one of the clear and welcome signs of the rapid growth, both quantitative and qualitative, of Western interest in the study of Russian literature, especially of modern Russian literature. It was in sharp contrast to the picture we, the first post-October émigrés, found and observed on our arrival in the West in the early 1920s. One of the novel elements in the situation more recently has been the appearance of a number of younger scholars, be it in Europe, in the Americas, or in other parts of the world, with such interests. We can have no better illustration of this than a symposium like this one. Let me now survey briefly the growth of the interest in Bely in the West.

The only language into which Bely's two major, pre-Revolution novels were translated soon after their publication in the original was German (in those days Germany, in general, was in the forefront in keeping watch on what was going on in Russian literature). *The Silver Dove* was translated as early as 1912 (a second edition of that translation appeared in 1920). *Petersburg* was published in German in 1919. (Had it not been for the First World War, this translation would probably have appeared even earlier; incidentally, this was the first somewhat revised version of the novel.) A partial Italian translation of *The Silver Dove* appeared in 1920, and later there was a complete one. England and France, unfortunately, lagged behind, and for a long time Bely remained virtually unknown in English-speaking countries and in France. In fact, this situation persisted until after World War II. In England Bely's name was for years known only to the readers of D. S. Mirsky's book on modern Russian literature. In 1933 there appeared the Slonim-Reavey anthology of Soviet literature, and into it were smuggled George Reavey's translations of an excerpt from *Kotik Letaev* and of one short poem (they were not, strictly speaking, part of Soviet literature). The translation from *Kotik Letaev* was preceded by a short note on Bely. Marc Slonim spoke of Bely in his introductory article, treating him, along with Remizov, as one of the precursors of the new trends in Russian literature.[13] A little earlier, in 1932, George Reavey had published in *Novy Zhurnal* a short article on Bely, comparing him with James Joyce. This parallel was later, in connection with Bely's death, taken up by other critics, including Evgeny Zamyatin and myself, in my obituary of Bely. This obituary was published in the London *Times*, and I think it was probably the only one to appear in the British press. Somewhat later, I published a longer article on Bely in the *Slavonic and East European Review*.

There were, of course, mentions and brief discussions of Bely's work in general surveys of modern Russian literature written in Western languages: Mirsky's in English; Vladimir Pozner's in French; Nikolay Arsenev's, Nikolay Otsup's, and Arthur Luther's in German; and Ettore Lo Gatto's in Italian. There were also some articles in special Slavistic publications. But as far as the Western reading public at large was concerned Bely still remained a name barely known.

The major pioneering study of Bely in the West came much later, after World War II. This was the book by my late colleague at the University of California at Berkeley, Oleg Maslenikov. Called *The Frenzied Poets* and subtitled *Andrey Biely and the Russian Symbolists*, it grew out of Maslenikov's Ph.D. dissertation, written in the mid-forties. It was published in book form in 1952. The book concentrated on Bely's early work and touched only briefly on his novels. Even if Professor Maslenikov did have the intention of writing a sequel to that volume, his attention switched later to other poets of the period, and he was, in any case, more interested in Symbolist poetry in general. He did, however, write an article on Bely's *Third Symphony*, and toyed with the idea of translating it. Some translations of Bely's poems were included in his anthology of Russian poetry, prepared not long before his death and published posthumously.[14]

Bely is now also represented in several other anthologies, including those of Yarmolinsky and Babette Deutsch and of Markov and Sparks, to mention the English-language ones only. In his preface to their anthology Vladimir Markov passes the following retrospective judgment on Bely the poet: "Andrei Biely, Blok's friend and foe, was no less the soul of Russian Symbolism, but his poetry proved to be of less lasting merit, probably because Biely was too much of a Proteus and lacked inner unity to his verse. Thus the fantastic visions of his early verse do not carry one away any more, his bewailing of Russia in *Ashes* does not stun, and his later anthroposophic verse leaves one cold. But he was a virtuoso of rhythm and still influences young poets in Russia." To this Markov adds: "Biely's real achievements, however, are in his sometimes unbelievably penetrating literary criticism (especially his Gogol studies) and in his epoch-making novels." [15]

One of the earliest pieces about Bely to be published in this country was a short note on him by Nina Berberova in the *Russian Review* in 1951. The real upsurge of interest in Bely came later, beginning with the mid-fifties. The first English translation of a major Bely novel appeared in 1959. This was John Cournos's translation of *Petersburg*, published with an introduction by George Reavey, himself an old Bely enthusiast. Unfortunately, the translation leaves much to be desired, though it must be borne in mind that the task of rendering Bely into any language is almost insuperably hard. It is not without interest that John Cournos was the man who, more than forty years earlier, had provided an English version of another notable Symbolist novel, Sologub's *The Petty Demon*, to which Sologub himself wrote a special preface. There is at present some talk of a new English translation of *Petersburg*, and two participants in this symposium are involved in this project.[16]

New German versions of *The Silver Dove* and *Petersburg* appeared in the early 1960s. Strangely enough, there is to this day no German translation of *Kotik Letaev*, though I hear that one may be on the way now. There was in Germany a reprint of the original Russian text of *Kotik Letaev*, with a preface in German by Professor Dmitrij Tschizewskij. Both *Petersburg* and *Kotik Letaev* are now available in French translations. *Petersburg* was translated by Georges Nivat and Jacques Catteau in 1967; and *Kotik Letaev*, by Nivat alone in 1973.

The French translation of *Kotik Letaev* was anticipated by an American one. It was done by the initiator and organizer of this symposium, Gerald Janecek. And last year a belated English translation of *The Silver Dove* by George Reavey was published in this country. This translation has been criticized rather severely. Thus, all Bely's major novels, that is, all the pre-Revolution ones, are now available at least in some of the principal Western languages (there is as yet no German translation of *Kotik Letaev*, no French translation of *The Silver Dove*, and no Italian translation of either *Peters-burg* or *Kotik Letaev*). There are, of course, translations into other Slavic languages, and they are probably among the best. I shall mention here only the recent (1974) translation of *Petersburg* into Polish by Seweryn Pollak, with a long postface by the translator.

There are now also several books on Bely in languages other than Russian. In listing them, I shall confine myself to books in Western languages. Here again, the Germans led the way. As far back as 1957, a whole chapter was devoted to Bely's *Petersburg* by Johannes Holthusen in his book *Studien zur Ästhetik und Poetik des russischen Symbolismus*. In 1965 appeared a book entitled *Andrej Belyjs Romane: Stil und Gestalt* by Anton Hönig; and in 1966, a book by Lily Hindley (incidentally, an American or half-American), *Andrej Belyjs Neologismen*, a detailed analysis of various types of Bely's word coinings. Both of these studies grew out of dissertations written at the University of Heidelberg under Professor Tschizewskij, who has been very active in promoting the knowledge of Bely in Germany. In English there are two recent books on Bely: a book on Bely's "apocalyptic symbolism," by Samuel Cioran, a Canadian student of Bely, and a little book of more general nature on Bely's life and work by John D. Elsworth, who teaches at the University of East Anglia. In French there seems to have been, so far, no separate book-length study of Bely, but both translations of his novels are provided with interesting postfaces by Georges Nivat. Especially interesting and good is the one to *Petersburg*. It also has a preface by the senior French Slavist Professor Pierre Pascal.

There have been, I understand, several Ph.D. dissertations on Bely in recent years in American universities. There was also an interesting dissertation on the relationship between music and words in Bely's work in the Hebrew University in Jerusalem. Written in Russian, it is now being translated into English.

There have also been, in recent years, several reprints of Bely's original texts in various Western countries. These reprints included *Petersburg* (both 1916 and 1928 editions) and *Kotik Letaev,* as well as Bely's memoirs, the original version of his reminiscences about Blok, and some theoretical and critical writings.

I should now like to present some of the judgments passed on Bely by his fellow writers. In doing so, I intend to dwell on some of the adverse judgments, acting as a devil's advocate, without necessarily subscribing to all the opinions I shall quote. Though most of these opinions concern Bely as a writer in general or Bely the novelist, I should like to begin with something that has to do with Bely's poetry. I have in mind an intriguingly mysterious review of Bely's third volume of verse, *The Urn,* by Nikolay Gumilyov. It was written in 1909 for the Petersburg newspaper *Rech* before the launching of *Apollon,* to which Gumilyov then began to contribute regular "Letters on Russian Poetry." Gumilyov began his review by saying that of the entire generation of Russian Symbolists Bely was "the least cultured" (*naimenee kulturen*). Realizing obviously that such a statement would sound amazing to many of his readers, Gumilyov hastened to explain that he did not mean the bookish culture of scholarly people, which is something like a Siamese order, valued because it is difficult to get and those who have it are but few. That kind of culture, said Gumilyov, was Bely's strong point: he can write about the Marburg philosophers and Hiram's golden triangle. What Gumilyov meant was general human culture, which teaches one respect and self-criticism, permeates one's flesh and blood, and lays its imprint on man's every thought and movement. To which Gumilyov added, apparently by way of elucidation, but, if anything, rather confusing the matter still further: "Somehow one does not imagine him [i.e., Bely] having been to the Louvre or read Homer."

Gumilyov then spoke of Bely the poet who has been quick in assimilating all the subtleties of modern verse technique. "This is how a barbarian learns at once not to eat fish with a knife, wear colored collars in winter, or write sonnets of nineteen lines (as did recently a fairly well known poet)." "Bely," said Gumilyov, "makes use of free verse, of alliterations, of inner rhymes, but he cannot write a regular poem with clear and vivid images and without the ballyhoo of superfluous words. In this he stands below even the third-rate poets of the past century." Gumilyov then went on to say that one could argue very strongly against Bely's conception of the iambic tetrameter in which nearly the whole of *The Urn* was written. Bely's practice seemed to Gumilyov to go against the grain of the Pushkin tradition.

This intriguingly negative appraisal of Bely the poet was followed by a no less intriguing juxtaposition of some positive ele-

ments. Wherein then, asked Gumilyov, lay the charm of
Andrey Bely; why did one feel like talking and thinking about
him? Gumilyov's own answer to these questions was as follows:

> Because his poetry has motives, and because those motives are
> truly profound and unusual. He has enemies: they are time and space.
> And he has friends: eternity, the ultimate goal. He makes those abstract
> concepts concrete, he confronts them with his own "I"; they are, to him,
> real creatures of his world. Combining the too airy colors of the old
> poets with the too heavy and sharp ones of the modern ones, he attains
> some wonderful effects which prove that the world of his dreams is
> indeed magnificent.[17]

Gumilyov wound up this tongue-in-cheek review—so unlike all his
other reviews of contemporary poetry—with an even more tongue-
in-cheek statement: "The reader will not be satisfied with my
review. He will certainly want to know whether I am praising or
disparaging Andrey Bely. I won't answer this question. The
time for summing up has not come yet." This time never came
for Gumilyov: for all practical purposes, Bely's *The Urn* was
his last significant collection of verse. It was certainly so within
Gumilyov's lifetime. It would be fascinating to know what
Gumilyov thought of "The First Encounter," if he had a chance
to read it. In all of Gumilyov's subsequent critical writings
Bely's name is mentioned only fleetingly. On only one occasion
did he refer to a poem by Bely in an almanac as "very fine." On
Bely's prose he left us no judgments. Gumilyov's friend Nikolay Otsup, who knew Gumilyov well and had many conversations
with him in the last years of his life, wrote once that Gumilyov
used to say of Bely: "This man was endowed with genius, but he
managed to ruin it." To me, Gumilyov's review of *The Urn* remains something of an enigma. Gumilyov had reasons for some
personal resentment against Bely after their meetings in Paris
in 1908, but I am not inclined to seek an explanation in that.
And in any case the review was ambiguous, not purely negative.

Gumilyov's disciple and friend, and one of those who are
sometimes described as "younger Acmeists," Georgy Ivanov, wrote about Bely in an article printed in the Berlin issue
of *Tsekh poetov* in 1923. This is what he said apropos of Bely's
reminiscences about Blok, then in the course of publication:

These memoirs continue to swell and swell. It is extremely un-
pleasant and difficult to read them because of their annoying manner,
but there is a great deal in them that is curious. The most curious thing
is, of course, Bely himself.

It would have been more correct to call these memoirs "Why nothing came of me," or something of that sort. Here is the picture that
emerges. In the forefront of Russian literature stands the gigantic
figure of Andrey Bely. He is conducting a verbal war against everybody,
rushing from Moscow to Paris, from St. Petersburg to Munich, quarreling, making peace, quarreling again, challenging people to duels, and
backing out of them. It is quite natural that all this hustle and bustle
goes against the grain of men who are of less choleric temperament
and lesser "diapason." So these men (Blok, Vyacheslav Ivanov) politely
but resolutely refuse to fight duels or to fraternize with Bely. Bely regards this as an "ideological challenge" and redoubles his attacks. . . .

And Ivanov concluded his article thus:

I repeat: the memoirs are very interesting. They are an excellent
key to numerous *Epopeyas,* "Partings," and *Notes of an Eccentric,*
which can only sadden all those who are disciplined in the slightest
degree. We see from them how it came that Andrey Bely descended so
low. We see how psychic laxity and neurasthenia progressed in him,
having now reached their very limit. Covering every day colossal quan-
tities of paper, as though he was out to set a world record, no longer
restrained by anybody or anything, this famous writer is a brilliant
confirmation of a sad truth which says that talent and graphomania
are not incompatible.[18]

Next, I shall quote from one more Acmeist and one near-
Acmeist. Perhaps it is not accidental that several of the adverse
judgments on Bely came from the Acmeists and their allies who felt
antagonistic to Symbolism. First, I refer to two quotations from
Osip Mandelstam. One is from his review of *Notes of an Eccentric.* One could hardly expect a positive review of that work
from anyone, but it may nevertheless be significant that Mandelstam chose to write about it. He began by making fun of Symbolism: "Russian Symbolism is alive. Russian Symbolism is not
dead. The python is swirling. Andrey Bely continues the glo-
rious tradition of that era when a waiter reflected by the double
mirrors of the *Praga* restaurant was seen as a mystical phenomenon, as a *Doppelgänger,* and a respectable man of letters was

ashamed of going to bed without accumulating, in the course of
the day, some five or six 'little horrors' (*uzhasiki*)."

Mandelstam then went on to say that in his postface to *Notes*
Bely remarked that he had written an obviously bad book—"an
admission," said Mandelstam, "which is nearly always insincere
in the mouth of a writer. And, indeed, what follows immediately is
the statement that 'on the other hand, my book is extraordinarily
truthful.' " The sincerity of Bely's book, said Mandelstam, was a
problem which lay outside literature and outside any area of general significance. A bad book was always a literary and social
transgression, a lie. The devices Bely used in *Notes of an Eccentric*
were by no means new; there was no revelation in them: they
represented a consistent and caricatural development of the worst
characteristics of Bely's early prose, of the vulgar, repellent musicality of a poem in prose (nearly the whole book was written in
hexameters), of the pompous, apocalyptic tone, of high-sounding
declamatory effects. It was crammed full of "astral terminology,
interlarded with hackneyed embellishments of the poetic jargon of
the 1890s." Mandelstam saw in the book "heaps of verbal rubbish,
of pseudoscientific charlatanism, lack of balance and tact, lack of
taste." He wrote: "If a man goes three times a day through colossal
psychic catastrophes, we cease to believe him, we are entitled not
to believe him—he looks ridiculous to us." But he hastened to add:

> One does not feel like laughing at Bely, and it would be a sin to do
> so: he wrote *Petersburg*. All the worse for Bely, if he has turned his
> human and literary style into an absurd and vulgar dance. The danc-
> ing prose of *Notes of an Eccentric* is the high school of literary self-
> infatuation: telling about oneself turning oneself inside out, showing
> oneself in the fourth, the fifth, the sixth dimension. Bely's prose shows a
> peculiar propensity towards elegance, towards pirouettes, a desire to en-
> compass, in dancing, the unencompassable.[19]

"Genuine prose," went on Mandelstam, "implies dissonance, dis-
harmony, polyphony, counterpoint; while *Notes of an Eccentric*
reads like a schoolboy's diary written in semi-verses." Mandelstam
saw that book of Bely's as a reversion to his early *Symphonies,*
while in the polyphonic prose of *Petersburg* he obviously saw the
genuine qualities he listed. It is interesting to note that a no less
negative view of *Notes of an Eccentric* was held by Bely's friend
and great admirer, Mikhail Gershenzon. This we know from Bely's

own memoirs, where he says that Gershenzon did not like *Notes* and after listening to Bely's reading of the work to him would snort (*fyrkal*): "Crude, physiological: you describe spiritual experiences, but the impression one gets is of the processes of digestion." To which Bely added: "Alas, this was true" (*Between Two Revolutions,* p. 292).

In a little booklet which Mandelstam published in Kharkov in 1922 he passed a more general negative judgment on Bely:

> Andrey Bely is a sick and negative phenomenon in the life of the Russian language for the simple reason that he drives the word (*gonyaet slovo*) mercilessly and unceremoniously, guided solely by the temperament of his own speculative thinking. Choking in his refined verbosity, he cannot sacrifice a single nuance, a single twist of his capricious thought, and he blows up the bridges which he is too lazy to cross. As a result, after momentary fireworks, all we have is just a pile of rubble, a desolate picture of destruction, instead of the fullness of life, of organic wholeness, and of active equilibrium. The cardinal sin of writers like Andrey Bely is their lack of respect for the Hellenistic nature of the word, their ruthless exploitation of it for their own intuitive ends.[20]

I am, of course, fully aware that these highly negative judgments do not represent the totality of Mandelstam's attitude. In his review of *Notes of an Eccentric* he made quite clear his admiration of *Petersburg*. And there are, of course, those poems which Mandelstam wrote after Bely's death. Nevertheless, *iz pesni slova ne vykinesh,* (you cannot leave a word out of a song) and we cannot dismiss Mandelstam's severe strictures on some aspects of Bely's art as accidental.

The same is true of Georgy Adamovich. Before Bely's death, in 1933, Adamovich published in a Paris newspaper a long article about Bely's *Masks.* He began with a few generalities about Bely— *pour prendre position*, as he put it:

> I visualize Bely in the shape of an enormous ruin, as someone who has succumbed under the weight of the terrible burdens he took upon himself. Something majestic was to come of it, but—nothing came. There was not enough staying power, enough firmness of mind and will. Blok was perhaps less endowed by nature, but Blok had a very great sense of responsibility for everything he did and said. . . . With Bely, everything was in the wind, and everything, like wind, blew through

his consciousness, without holding on, without taking root. It was consciousness of genius, no gainsaying that. There was hardly an equal of him in our literature in the generosity of his responses, in the acuteness of his receptivity to the music of the world, in the capacity to understand it on the wing, with half-a-sound, half-a-hint. . . . But his books retained only the glimmerings, the reflections of what he saw or understood; there was no continuation, no sense of life where a hint would be turned into a word, and word perhaps into a deed. Coupled with it, a changeability, almost feminine, bordering on treacherousness, on mendacity, and the invariable tendency to joke things off . . . [here Adamovich drew again a contrast with Blok], to dismiss things with a capricious grimace where this was least expected. On the whole, a "pathetic" sight: a veritable "failure" (*neudachnik*), and yet one of those by whom one can dimly guess what might have become of this man, if—it is really difficult to say: if what? If, I daresay, at the last moment the man had not been replaced by his own caricature. . . .

In the same article, speaking of *Masks* on a purely literary plane, Adamovich wrote:

It seems to me that Bely does not have a real great writer's talent, and that a certain dilletantism of his in all the fields of creative endeavor is not accidental, but compulsive. . . . Bely's genius is somehow vague, "deaf-mute." One feels it more in his themes than in their treatment. A poet? Yes, he has some unforgettable strophes which reach, to my ear, "beyond Blok," which sing with the same passion, sadness, and power as the best lines of Nekrasov. But just a few wondrous strophes in a welter of trash and rubbish. A novelist? On this score, there can hardly be a disagreement. *Petersburg* is a book which is extremely interesting to read; there is in it so much intelligence, wit, inventiveness. But people in it are of cardboard, and their emotions are thought up: nothing can hide this. The smell of printer's ink in this book is too strong. This is, of course, a remarkable, a most curious piece of literature, but a most subtle and fateful line divides it off from those areas in art in which greater effects are achieved more easily and more spontaneously.

Turning to *Masks* specifically, Adamovich said that "the only extraordinary thing in it is words, the unprecedented debauch and flood of words: of everything else it has but little." The preface to the novel was described by Adamovich as "a mixture, incredible in its weirdness, of haughtiness and timidity, of conceit and curtsies towards the Marxists, of perspicacity and blindness, of pathos and comedian's grimaces." Noting that in his conclusion Bely kindly informs his readers that he has been learning "verbal ornamentation from Gogol, rhythm from Nietzsche, dramatic devices from Shakespeare, gestures from the pantomime, music of the inner ear from Schumann, whereas he learned the truth from the nature of his impressions," Adamovich commented upon this as follows: "There are things, words, and statements at which it is embarrassing to laugh: it is too easy to do so." And he suggested that it would be more appropriate to repeat the words which once came to the mind of Turgenev as he was observing Gogol: "What an intelligent, strange, and sick creature!"[21]

After Bely's death Adamovich wrote a special article for the magazine *Vstrechi*, of which he was the coeditor. In it he developed some of the same themes: Bely was a remarkable novelist, a talented poet, a brilliant critic, a man who responded to everything, was interested in everything, caught everything on the wing. "But the best thing about him was that about which he kept silent, for that is the only true test of a poet." The praises bestowed by Adamovich on Bely were, as was often the case with this critic, offset by a number of reservations. To Adamovich, Bely would have been indeed a writer of genius ("as he was sometimes, not quite justifiably, described"), if the gift of speech and the gift of silence had been balanced in him. *Petersburg* was once again described as "a remarkable book," but it was also, "right through, down to the very last comma, invented and spectral, something which could not stand confrontation with reality." "In the final analysis," it was now dismissed as "an interesting, an amusing, a 'curious' book, no more than that." "Let us leave the legend about one of the greatest writers of our time to the literary soirées with debates and recitals of poetic fragments." Bely was once more described as "a failure." This was a persistent theme in many appraisals of Bely. To Adamovich this now was "the most precious thing" about him: "He had birth pangs through all the thirty years of his life as a writer, but he died barren." And yet, went on Adamovich, "we hear the music, even through the unenduring, dubious books. Nowadays we have to make an effort, in the past our hearing was sharper, more responsive. Yes, it is that, that very same thing, the most important one, the unforgettable. Yes, it is that which made our heads turn, and not for nothing, twenty years ago." In trying to pinpoint this "thing," Adamovich hit upon the phrase "transformation of the world," and decided that it was neither better nor worse than anything else. And he ended his article thus: "So, let us bow to the memory of Andrey Bely for the 'transformation of the world,' for a glimmer of that for the sake of which it is worth writing, thinking, hoping, remembering, and living."[22] In presenting Adamovich's final article on Bely at such length, I fully realize that it is full of ambiguities, self-contradictions, and evasions, so characteristic of this talented Protean critic. Were Adamovich to write on Bely much later, he might have written quite differently.

There are still two other fellow writers whose opinions on Bely I would like to quote. One of them is Boris Pasternak. That Pasternak had a high regard for Bely as a man and for his early work can be felt in the way he wrote about Bely in his *Safe Conduct*. It is also reflected in one of his letters to Jacqueline de Proyart, in which he speaks of Blok's poetry and of Bely's prose (with its "éléments du surnaturel et du mythologique ou du cosmique") as of two of the "keys" to the Russian realities of the beginning of the century. But in the same letter he says that Bely's later works, such as *Masks* for example, appeared to him "*mortes et schématiques.*"[23] His negative attitude to certain aspects of Bely's art was more clearly voiced in a conversation reported by Olga Andreyev Carlisle. To Pasternak, "Bely never came into contact with real life." Pasternak could not understand—at least, towards the end of his life—Bely's "fascination with new forms," his "dreams of a new language, of a completely original form of expression." To him, "because of this dream, much of the work of the twenties was merely stylistic experimentation and has ceased to exist," for "the most extraordinary discoveries are made when the artist is overwhelmed by *what* he has to say. In his urgency he then uses the old language, and the old language is transformed from within." And to this Pasternak added: "Even in those years one felt a little sorry for Bely, because he was cut off from the immediate, which alone could have helped his genius to blossom."[24] It looks thus that towards the end of his life Pasternak, the author of *Dr. Zhivago*, saw as Bely's weakness what so many others saw not only as the hallmark of his work, but also as his forte. This is indirectly confirmed by Pasternak's use of the word "even" in his reference to *Kotik Letaev* when in the above-quoted letter to Jacqueline de Proyart, in speaking of Bely's early prose, he refers to his *Symphonies, The Silver Dove,* and *Petersburg,* and adds: "*et même Kotik Letaev.*"

The most unreserved positive assessment of Bely as a writer came after his death from Yevgeny Zamyatin. He wrote it in Paris and it was intended for non-Russian readers, but I have been unable to ascertain whether it actually did appear in a French journal. Such a French publication is not mentioned in Alex Shane's very detailed bibliography in his book on Zamyatin. The Russian text appeared posthumously in *Litsa,* and an English translation of it will be found in Mirra Ginsburg's compilation of Zamyatin's essays, *A Soviet Heretic.*

To Zamyatin, Bely was above all "a writer's writer, a master, an inventor whose inventions have been used by many Russian novelists of the younger generations" (Zamyatin was himself one of them). Zamyatin saw one of the many paradoxes in Bely's personal and literary biography in the fact that "the books of this master, the theoretician of an entire literary school, remain untranslated and live only in their Russian incarnation." This was, of course, largely true when Zamyatin wrote his article. To this Zamyatin added: "I am not certain, however, whether one can properly say that they are written in Russian, so unusual is Bely's syntax, so full of neologisms his diction. The language of his books is Bely's language, just as the language of *Ulysses* is not English but Joyce's language."

Zamyatin regarded *Petersburg* as Bely's best work, and thought that in it the city found its true portrayer for the first time since Gogol and Dostoevsky. Of *Kotik Letaev,* Zamyatin said that it was "perhaps the only attempt in world literature to embody Anthroposophic ideas in a work of art. A child's psyche is chosen as the screen that is to reflect these ideas—at the age when the first glimmerings of consciousness stir within the child, when the child steps out of the world of four dimensions, into the solid three-dimensional world which wounds him painfully."

Of Bely's later novels, Zamyatin wrote:

> We no longer find here the fantastic, four-dimensional world of *Kotik Letaev* and *Petersburg*. These novels are built on real, partly autobiographical, material from the life of the Moscow intelligentsia during the crucial years of change in the early twentieth century. The clearly satirical approach taken by the author was a concession to the spirit of the time. But Bely's tireless formal experimentation, this time chiefly in the lexical area, continued in these last novels as well. Until the very end he remained a Russian Joyce.[25]

In most of what his fellow writers wrote about Bely we perceive two dominant notes. One is—but here Zamyatin is an exception—that Bely as a writer was, in the final analysis, a failure (*neudach-nik,* as Adamovich put it). The other was that in Bely genius and madness were closely interwoven. Perhaps this was put best by a non-Russian Slavic scholar, Pierre Pascal, who, in his introduction to Georges Nivat's translation of *Petersburg,* described Bely as "un cerveau où la folie et le génie se cotoient constamment et font ensemble bon ménage."[26]

I have the impression that among the present-day admirers of Bely who set the tone for the Bely studies in the West, *Kotik Letaev* is held in particular esteem and regarded perhaps as Bely's supreme achievement. I am still "old-fashioned" enough to place *Petersburg* above all the other novels. I doubt very much whether anyone today would be inclined to assign the first place to *The Silver Dove,* as Mirsky seemed to do fifty years ago.

There can be no doubt that Bely was an extremely uneven writer. I do not think there was another writer of the same caliber in Russian literature who was so uneven. Uneven within one and the same novel. Uneven as between the novels. There is no doubt that all Bely's novels after *Kotik Letaev* fall well below his earlier levels. Some of them are extremely irritating, as, for example, *The Baptized Chinaman,* with its artificial, obsessive verse rhythm. I confess to not having been able to read it through. The novels of the *Moscow* cycle are almost unbearable, too, because of the utter absurdity of their plots in combination with excessive lexical tricks.

Of *Notes of an Eccentric* even Mochulsky, who is, on the whole, very tolerant of Bely's "flops," says that there is in it so much "muddle," "delirium," "screaming," and "lunacy," that it is not easy to make one's way in it. Osip Mandelstam, as we saw, wrote a vicious review of it.

With the notable and marvelous exception of "The First Encounter," Bely's poetry of the postrevolutionary period also marked his decline as a poet. To this one must add some of the horrors perpetrated by him in revising, in his Berlin years, much of his earlier poetry. Nevertheless, Bely's contribution to poetics and literary criticism was of very great importance.

NOTES

1. Andrey Bely, "Odna iz obiteley tsarstva teney" (Leningrad, 1924). This little pamphlet was reprinted in England in 1971 by Bradda. It was hardly ever mentioned by Bely's émigré friends at the time of its publication.

2. Andrey Bely, "Iz knigi 'Nachalo veka' (Berlinskaya redaktsiya. 1924–1925 gody)," *Voprosy Literatury*, no. 6 (1974): 214–44.

3. The last time Bely seems to have used the phrase about "the threshold of Russian literature" was in 1931 in what appears to be an unpublished letter. But he used the same formula in his memoirs in speaking of the reception accorded him by fellow writers after his return from Paris in 1908.

4. K. N. Vasileva-Bugaeva, *Literaturnoe Nasledstvo* 27/28 (Moscow, 1937). More recently some interesting excerpts from Bely's widow's reminiscences of him were published outside Russia, in the New York *Novy Zhurnal*, nos. 102, 103 (1971), and 108 (1972).

5. L. K. Dolgopolov, "Andrey Bely v rabote nad 'Peterburgom,'" *Russkaya Literatura*, no. 2 (1972): 157–67.

6. See, for instance, the scathing description of Khodasevich in *Between Two Revolutions*, pp. 249–50.

7. Marina Tsvetaeva, "Plenny dukh (Moya vstrecha s Andreem Belym)." Originally published in *Sovremennye Zapiski* (Paris), it was reprinted in Marina Tsvetaeva, *Proza* (New York: A. Chekhov, 1953), pp. 286–352.

8. N. Valentinov, *Two Years with the Symbolists*, ed. Gleb Struve (Stanford, Calif.: Hoover Institution, 1969).

9. K. Mochulsky, *Andrey Bely* (Paris: YMCA, 1955), p. 157.

10. Prince D. S. Mirsky, *Contemporary Russian Literature: 1881–1925* (New York: Knopf, 1926), pp. 232–33.

11. Ibid.

12. Boris Zaytsev, "Andrey Bely," in *Dalyokoe* (Washington, D.C.: Inter-language Literary Associates, 1965), p. 31. *Petersburg* Zaytsev described as "an airless phantasmagory."

13. Marc Slonim and George Reavey, eds. and trans., *Soviet Literature: An Anthology* (London: Wishart & Co., 1933).

14. Oleg A. Maslenikov, trans., *Lyrics from the Russian: Symbolists and Others* (Berkeley, Calif.: University of California Press, 1972).

15. Vladimir Markov, "Introduction," in *Modern Russian Poetry*, Vladimir Markov and Merrill Sparks, eds. (New York: Bobbs-Merrill, 1967), p. lviii.

16. Since this talk was given an English translation of *Petersburg* by Robert Maguire and John Malmstad was published in 1977.

17. N. Gumilyov, "Review of Bely's *Urna*," in *Sobranie sochineny*

v chetyryokh tomakh, ed. G. Struve and B. Filippov, vol. 4 (Washington, D.C.: Victor Kamkin, 1968), pp. 205–6.

18. Georgy Ivanov, "Pochtovy yashchik," *Tsekh poetov* 4 (Berlin, 1923): 66–67.

19. Osip Mandelstam, "Andrey Bely *Zapiski chudaka,*" in *Sobranie sochineny v tryokh tomakh,* ed. G. Struve and B. Filippov, vol. 2 (New York: Inter-language Literary Associates, 1971), pp. 421–24.

20. Osip Mandelstam, "O prirode slova," ibid., pp. 246–47.

21. Georgy Adamovich, " 'Maski' Andreya Belogo," *Poslednie Novosti* (Paris), 1933, April 20, p. 3.

22. Georgy Adamovich, "Pamyati Andreya Belogo," *Vstrechi,* no. 2 (February 1934): 56–58.

23. Jacqueline de Proyart, *Pasternak* (Paris: Gallimard, 1964), pp. 238–39.

24. Olga Carlisle, *Poets on Street Corners* (New York: Random House, 1968), p. 301.

25. Yevgeny Zamyatin, *A Soviet Heretic: Essays by Yevgeny Zamyatin,* ed. and trans. Mirra Ginsburg (Chicago: University of Chicago Press, 1970), pp. 242, 244–45.

26. Pierre Pascal, "Aux lecteurs" in Andrei Biely, *Petersbourg,* trans. Georges Nivat (Lausanne: Editions l'Age d'Homme, 1967), p. 7.

ZOYA YURIEFF

PRISHEDSHY:
A. BELY AND A. CHEKHOV

Ideally, a study of Andrey Bely—and of Russian Symbolism—should start at the beginning, that is with the preceding transitional period, called by Bely "the boundary between two centuries," where the roots of Russian Symbolism are already discernible. During this period, when a war against tendentious literature was declared and the struggle for new art began, Russian Symbolists sought and found allies among their contemporaries as well as their predecessors. These were not exclusively foreign. During this time varying influences were clashing and merging: Baudelaire and Tyutchev ranked side by side; Gogol and Dostoevsky stood next to Nietzsche; Ibsen and Maeterlinck, next to Chekhov. Foreign influences on Russian Symbolism have been studied more thoroughly than the relationship between Russian Symbolists and the Russian classics. But the so-called second generation of the Russian Symbolists, to which Bely belonged, especially liked to stress their native roots. Bely pointed out his affinity to Gogol and outlined some interesting problems of his creative relationship with him in *Gogol's Craft*. These problems should be further explored.

I have taken up the subject of Bely and Chekhov and hope to develop it more fully in the future. At present I would like only to point to Bely's relationship to Chekhov as it existed in Bely's youth and as it was reflected in his articles on Chekhov, and particularly in a fragment of an unfinished mystery play *Antichrist*, published later under the title *Prishedshy* (*He Who Has Come*).[1]

This paper was delivered at the Bely Symposium in Russian.

In my opinion Chekhov's presence in *Prishedshy* is strongly evident, in spite of the fact that names such as Goethe, Maeterlinck, and Nietzsche have also been cited.

Prishedshy, dedicated to the theme of the coming of Antichrist in the guise of Christ, was written by Bely in 1898 (while he was still in high school), when Chekhov was at the height of his renown and popularity, especially with the new generation. Korney Chukovsky, reminiscing about his youth, testified:

> I divided all people into two warring camps; on the one side were those "sensitive" to Chekhov—on the other were the ones "insensitive" to Chekhov. Now I am ashamed to recall what naive hatred was actuated in me by that breed of people to whom Chekhov was alien. And there were many such people then, first of all the majority of old men. Those who were past forty, whose hair was graying, formed a solid opposition to Chekhov. In their view the wide success of Chekhov's writings amounted to public disaster. They maintained that "worst of all was the fact that he was talented." They regarded it their solemn duty to "save" the youth from him.[2]

According to Bely, his own father, Nikolay Bugaev, was just such an "old man" who read Chekhov "with a shrug of his shoulders" (*Beginning of the Century,* p. 13). In contrast, Mikhail Solovyov, brother of the famous philosopher Vladimir, and his family, who became Bely's spiritual family, valued Chekhov very highly. Suffice it to recall Mikhail Solovyov's remark after he had listened to the two first parts of Bely's *Second Symphony:* "In contemporary literature only Chekhov and Borya [diminutive of Boris Bugaev] are a consolation to me." Bely reacted: "I was in seventh heaven because of his words" (ibid., p. 123). Around the same time Bely insisted that "Chekhov is closer (to me) than Verlaine" (ibid., p. 330) and that "Chekhov is more a symbolist to me than Maeterlinck is" (*Between Two Revolutions,* p. 196). While still in high school Bely read Maeterlinck's works to his mother, but soon Chekhov, Ibsen, and Hauptmann became prominent in their readings together (*At the Boundary,* p. 389).

Bely's peculiar perception of a change "in the atmosphere" and "in the color-aura of years," which in his memoirs is dated 1896–97, is connected for him with Chekhov's *The Seagull,* Balmont's book of poetry *Stillness (Tishina)* and the dramatic works of Ibsen. In the years 1896–97 *The Seagull* was first performed (in Petersburg) and appeared twice in print.[3] We can safely assume that Bely was familiar with the published texts of the new drama when he started to work on his mystery play.

Why did young Bely decide to write a mystery play and not some other kind of drama? The problem of mystery plays is little explored, especially in Russia. We know, however, that both Russian Romanticists and Symbolists attempted to revive the mystery play. This was particularly difficult because the Russian theater did not evolve from the *mysterium*. New impulses for creating mystery plays at the turn of the century came from such influential sources as Nietzsche's *Die Geburt der Tragödie aus dem Geiste der Musik* (1872), Maeterlinck's dramas, and Wagner's music, with all of which Bely was conversant.

Bely has also left an interesting account of an unusual experience he had in a church which was perceived by him as a theater. The experience was colored by acute apocalyptic accents, his personal drama prefiguring the doom of the world. However, the parallel he draws *ex post facto* between the Temple of Glory (where the action of *Prishedshy* is located) and the Theosophical Temple of Saint John (in Dornach, Switzerland) is hardly convincing.[4] Apocalyptic expectations on the one hand and an ardent longing to transfigure life on the other—two all-important features in Russian literature according to Bely—probably also accounted most for the emergence of his own mystery play.

It is noteworthy that in Russian literature various parodies of mystery plays received greater renown than did the mystery plays themselves. Kozma Prutkov's parody of mystery plays entitled *Affinity of Universal Forces* (*Srodstvo mirovykh sil*) is much more popular than, for instance, V. Kuechelbecker's *mysterium* entitled *Izhorsky*. An excellent parody of Vladimir Pecherin's poem-*mysterium Triumph of Death* (*Torzhestvo smerti*) (1833) by Dostoevsky in *The Possessed* (which contains, however, also a real *mysterium*) is better known than is its model. In 1893 Vladimir Solovyov wrote a humorous mystery play *The White Lily* (*Belaya liliya*). In spite of being humorous, it remained a mystery play.

Treplev's play within Chekhov's *The Seagull* can also be considered a parody of a mystery play, or a mystery play which is on the very border of a parody. It is usually not referred to as a "mystery play," but is defined as a "miniature," "decadent scene," "allegory," even a "philosophical allegory," or "a play as a dream."[5] But how else is one to classify a play for which a monologue by the World Soul is all-important and in which "the father of eternal matter, the devil," appears for some cosmic combat, accompanied by the smell of sulfur?

The feelings of impending doom[6] and of universal gloom (*At the Boundary,* p. 400) were known to Chekhov and have found a vivid expression in Treplev's dramatic fragment. I cannot agree with B. A. Larin, who asserts that the symbols in Treplev's play are alien to Chekhov.[7] "The kingdom of beautiful harmony and of the world will" which will come in a distant future, the World Soul and "a captive thrown into a deep empty well" who suffer from loneliness and cannot communicate—an affliction which is common to Chekhov's characters—are recognizable even if they have a cosmic tinge or are dressed in abstraction. The image of a "captive" in an empty well, however, could be traced back to Balmont's poem "V bezvodnom kolodtse," where the following lines can be found: "Between damp walls covered with fungi, / in a waterless well, at the bottom, deep."[8] This would make Treplev's play even more steeped in the symbolism of the "decadent" movement.

Under these circumstances it would be only natural to suppose that Treplev's mystery play and its author captured the attention of young Bely. The question of what part of Chekhov was integrated into Treplev and in what manner remains largely unexplored: here too Trigorin was much luckier. However, we may assume that Chekhov valued Treplev's childlike freshness, and even naiveté (with which he endowed his most beloved heroines), his youthful Romantic idealism, his commitment to art, and his struggle for new forms in art, especially in drama. It is noteworthy that in early versions of *The Seagull* Chekhov gave even more prominence to Treplev's play: it was read not only in the first and fourth acts, as in its final form, but also in the second act. Thus the little mystery play could be considered a *sui generis leitmotif* of the entire Chekhov drama.[9]

I believe that Bely appreciated Treplev's attempt to find "new forms" for drama (throughout his life Bely fought for "new forms"), his taking a *sujet* from the realm of abstract ideas, his rejection of all external action, and his shifting of the emphasis to a special "musical" mood created by means of lyrical and rhythmical devices (e.g., threefold repetition of the key words). Moonlight over the "magic" lake with its reflection in the water must have appeared to the audience new and appealing. Actually Treplev attempted to create a "theater of the spirit" (*teatr dukha*); he might even be said to have anticipated "the theater-as-a-dream" (*teatr kak snovidenie*), advocated at a later time by Maksimilian Voloshin.[10]

The supposition that Treplev's mystery play, with its cosmic and eschatological theme, must have evoked a keen response on the part of young Bely is confirmed by the orchestration which Bely gave to the beginning and the end of the piece in his unfinished mystery play fragment *Prishedshy:*

In *The Seagull* we have at the beginning of the World Soul monologue:

Nina: . . . "Cold, cold, cold. Empty, empty, empty. Horrible, horrible, horrible. (Pause). . . ."

(*Nina:* . . . "*Kholodno, kholodno, kholodno. Pusto, pusto, pusto. Strashno, strashno, strashno.* [*Pauza*]. . . .")

And at the end of the monologue:

(Pause; on the background of the Lake appear two red dots.) This is my powerful opponent, the devil, approaching. I see his horrible, crimson eyes. . . .
Arkadina: It smells of sulfur. Is that necessary?
Treplev: Yes.
Arkadina (laughs): Yes, it's an effect.

(*Pauza; na fone ozera pokazyvayutsya dve krasnykh tochki.*) *Vot priblizhaetsya moy moguchi protivnik, dyavol. Ja vizhu ego strashnye, bagrovye glaza. . . .*
Arkadina: Seroy pakhnet. Eto tak nuzhno?
Treplev: Da.
Arkadina [*smeyotsya*]: *Da, eto effekt.*)[11]

In Bely's *mysterium* disciples at the Temple of Glory, who are in the state of expectation of the Second Coming and perceive various signs on land, on water, and in the sky, listen to their teacher Nikita who is "again prophesying. It is horrible, horrible, brethren . . ." (opyat prorochit. Strashno, strashno, bratya . . .).[12] This is a double repetition of the same word, that is repeated three times by Nina in the monologue of the World Soul. However, Bely added a two-syllable word "brethren" (*bratya*) in order to preserve the rhythm of his model. The fact that rhythmic adoptions—whether conscious or subconscious—are often more important than verbal ones has been well established. In Bely's case it is even more pronounced, since he composed verse parts of *Prishedshy* in iambic pentameter (as in Byron's mystery plays). Bely's prose in this early dramatic attempt quite naturally passes into verse, then reverts again, thus creating a unified musical mood. Nikita prophesies:

> Oh, woe to those who live on earth, woe . . . !
> Woe floats on the sea toward us and soon
> From the abyss the marked beast will come . . .
> He floats in the mist, with his red eye
> Rotating and threatening us with disaster . . .
> . . . Now here, now there among us abysses gape,
> And sulfurous smoke rises to the heavens. (p. 16)

And again after the disciples' cue and following the stage direction "on the horizon between the cliffs the red moon shows itself," Nikita says: "There the beast floats, rotating its red eye/ And thundering out threat after threat" (p. 16).

As in Treplev's play, so in *Prishedshy,* a menacing approach on water (there on the lake, here on the sea) is portrayed, a drawing closer of a "mighty foe"—the devil in *The Seagull,* and in Bely's play an apocalyptic beast whose eyes are red (crimson in *The Seagull*). The red eye and the red moon, which rises according to the stage direction in *Prishedshy,* merge, intensifying the mystical and cosmic coloring of an image that was always so important to Bely. The smell of sulfur in Treplev's play and sulfuric smoke rising to the sky in Bely's contribute to the similarity and underline it.

Another response to Treplev's mystery play can be found toward the end of Bely's fragment. After the stage direction containing the description of the "lingering sound, perhaps a child in tears, perhaps a cry of a night bird"—also very Chekhovian—the mood of Nina's monologue is again re-created by this exchange of cues:

First pupil: Cold . . .   *(Kholodno . . .)*
Second pupil: And horrible . . .   *(I strashno . . .)*
Dmitry: And sad . . .   *(I grustno . . .)* (p. 23).

Here the multiple dots substitute for the intensifying recurrence, the triple repetition in the World Soul monologue. A little further down in the text "cold" (*kholodno*) is repeated once more.

As is evident from the above, young Bely was not disturbed by accents of parody in Treplev's play and responded to it creatively in his early dramatic work. This response is an extremely rare example of a reaction to parody in a "high key."

It is possible, of course, to compare other devices of young Bely, as they are reflected in *Prishedshy,* and some devices of "Chekhov's theater." It would be difficult and perhaps even futile to attempt to establish the relative degrees of influence of Chekhov, Ibsen, Maeterlinck, and even Hauptmann. Ibsen and Chekhov entered the Russian theater simultaneously. Ibsen did not create any new tradition in the Russian dramaturgy; his influence upon young Russian dramatists was limited compared to that of Chekhov.[13] Ibsen was much more complicated than Chekhov. It seems that Bely took more after Chekhov in his *Prishedshy;* he felt much closer to him. Although seashore and cliffs in Bely's *mysterium* might be reminiscent of Ibsen's landscapes, Bely's scenery is much more symbolic. One finds seashore also in Maeterlinck's work, which is considered to be a model of the lyrico-static drama. In general in Ibsen's, Maeterlinck's, and Chekhov's drama static motifs predominate over dynamic ones. All three authors use symbolism, although in different ways. But comparing and contrasting them lies outside of the scope of this paper.

Melodiousness, the musical quality and melodic value of the word, were considered the important features of the new drama. Bely was inclined to consider "mood . . . the attunement . . . of the image as its musical harmony" (*Symbolism,* p. 172). In his article "Chekhov" (1904), Bely stressed the musicality and symbolism of Chekhov's "dramas with a mood" (*Arabesques,* p. 403). Bely claims that "every phrase of Chekhov's has a life of its own and all of the phrases are subordinated to a musical rhythm" (ibid., p. 399). He calls the dialogue in *The Three Sisters* and *The Cherry Orchard* music. Bely bestowed upon Chekhov the title of the "foremost master of stylistic instrumentation among Russian author-realists" (ibid.). However, according to Bely, Chekhov places his realistic devices around his central symbolic focus. "Everything Maeterlinck has said to us, we guess in Chekhov involuntarily" (ibid., p. 398). As to the symbolism, here too Bely prefers Chekhov to Maeterlinck, whose symbols are obvious to the point of being allegorical, whereas Chekhov's symbols are unpremeditated, growing involuntarily into reality. Perhaps this is why Bely suggests that the Symbolists should make Chekhov their master, since they are the only ones who can appreciate his unique talent (ibid., p. 400). As we have seen, Bely followed his own advice, even before he made it public. It remains to be established to what degree.

However, even now we can make some general remarks about *Prishedshy* and Chekhov's drama. The stationary and mysterial drama of *Prishedshy* partially coincided and merged with Chekhov's static lyrical drama. Bely's characters are still more passive than those of Chekhov. As in Chekhov's dramatic work, Bely's characters in *Prishedshy* are characterized by two or three external features, including clothing of symbolic color. The dramatic tension in Bely's play, as often in the plays of Chekhov, vacillates between sound and silence, thunder and stillness, light and darkness; but above all, between the high tide and the ebb of emotions, which often are collective, group emotions. Anticipation, an emotional background of *Prishedshy,* whose characters are referred to as "servants of anticipation," can be compared to that anticipation of a change in the whole structure of life and dissatisfaction with it which was found to be of such importance to Chekhov's drama.[14] This is particularly true of *The Seagull.*

Leitmotifs and pauses—novel dramatic devices—are often used by both Chekhov and Bely. In Bely's drama, as in Chekhov's, *leitmotifs* sometimes accompany the characters, reinforcing their characterization. At times they emphasize the most significant points, at times—as the pauses also do—they help to create a mood, the musical and expressive coloring of the play. Pauses in *Prishedshy* often perform the same function as in Chekhov's drama. They prepare us for the inevitable.[15] They serve as signals for anticipation, function as *"ein retardierendes Moment,"* or are an integral dramatic part of a scene.[16]

In Bely as in Chekhov the effects of light, color, sounds, music, and noise are used to create changes in the waves of emotions, to achieve a particular mood and atmosphere. It is possible that the moon, which played such an important part in Treplev's *mysterium,* was instrumental in elevating the moon in *Prishedshy* almost to the status of a personage: "The moon has risen not long ago. It rose and, rising, became fiery. And then something dark, dark, began to float over it" (p. 6). The significance of the role of the moon is emphasized by lyric repetitions and alliterations. The moon's changes predetermine the course of events.

It must be noted that a sea gull (and sea gulls) also play a part in *Prishedshy.* Their sad, shrill cries, intensified even into a "sorrowful sobbing," contribute to creating an intended atmosphere and a symbolic perception of the landscape:

A seagull with plaintive moaning   *(Chayka s zhalobnym rydanem,*
Harbinger of foul weather,   *Predvestnitsa nenastya,*
   in the distance   *vdaleke*
Diving among the white-capped   *Mezh voln sedykh nyryaya,*
   waves quickly darts . . .   *bystro mchitsya . . .) (p. 17).*

But that sea gull is not out of Chekhov; it is Balmont's famous "Chayka" ("Sea gull"), which together with Chekhov's *The Seagull* intimated for Bely the *fin de siècle:*

Previously the works of Chekhov had become established: Nina Zarechnaya declaimed a muddle, and "Uncle Vanya" was despondent with Balmont, who went off into mists of water-lilies and whispers of reeds; the seagulls soared:

"The seagull, gray seagull with   *("Chaykà,   seraya   chayka   s*
   pitiful cries dashes   *pechalnymi   krikami*
               nositsya
Above the plain which is   *Nad   ravninoy,   pokrytoy*
   shrouded with grief."   *toskoy.")*[17]

It would be worthwhile to find out when and how the sea gull became the bird of Russian modernism. The fact that Chekhov's "sea gull" became an emblem of the Moscow Art Theater is well known; less known is the popularity of a romance, inspired by Chekhov's play, which was set to music by four different composers.[18] Even Gorky's Malva compares herself to a sea gull. Characteristically Merezhkovsky, writing about Chekhov, concludes: "Sometimes, in the dead stillness before a storm, a single bird sings, literally moans, despondently, despondently and plaintively: thus is the song of Chekhov. . . . But no matter what the strength of the storm that sweeps away Chekhov's world,—we will never forget—upon the darkness of the storm cloud the white sea gull with its plaintively prophetic cry."[19]

For Bely the "crisis of life" and the "crisis of culture"—to which he addressed himself in his later writings—were expressed effectively in Chekhov's and Balmont's musico-impressionistic manner. Bely's apocalyptically attuned ear has caught rhythmic and emotional vibrations in Chekhov's poetical drama inaudible to other ears. Bely proved to be not only an incisive but even a perspicacious critic of Chekhov, who was misunderstood and undervalued by many a Russian Symbolist: D. Merezhkovsky, Z. Gippius, V. Bryusov, V. Rozanov, and others.

The "new forms" proclaimed by Chekhov-Treplev in 1896, which meant for Bely not only new forms for the theater and the arts but also new forms of life, can be much more closely related to Symbolism than is customarily admitted. In his *Notebooks* (*Zapisnye knizhki,* 1891–1904) Chekhov wrote: "Behind new forms in literature there always follow new forms of life (forerunners), and therefore they are so contrary to the conservative human spirit."[20]

Bely did not complete his mystery play. Very soon he placed himself in the opposition to the very form of *mysterium:* "If drama approaches a mystery play, returns to it, then it will inevitably descend from the stage and spread into life" (*Symbolism,* p. 172). In his article "Teatr i sovremennaya drama" (1908) Bely took an even more definite stand: "one must not forget that a temple presupposes a cult, and a cult the name of God, i.e., religion" (*Arabesques,* p. 29). Without it there can be no religious creativity, no discussion of a "theater as a temple, and of a drama as a religious rite" (ibid.).

One more explanation for *Prishedshy* is found in Bely's "Ya-epopeya" (1919), where the author comments: "I did not finish the drama; in my soul the drama-mystery took on very complex forms. Only now have I understood: I will never finish my drama-mystery because I myself am already a participant in events which are leading to catastrophe."[21]

In later periods the *mysterium* was used by Bely not as a genre, but as a trope. My list of these tropes is still incomplete. So is my elucidation of further creative contacts between Bely and Chekhov, for instance in the *Third Symphony,* which was published in 1905 and reprinted later as a *povest.* But I shall continue to pursue this topic.

NOTES

1. *Prishedshy* was published in the almanac *Severnye tsvety* for 1903. Another fragment of the mystery play *Antichrist* appeared in no. 2 of *Zolotoe runo* for 1906. I was unable to obtain the original manuscript of the play from Literaturny muzey in Moscow.

2. Korney Chukovsky, *O Chekhove.* (Moscow: Izd. Khud. Lit., 1967), p. 96.

3. In the December issue of *Russkaya mysl* and in Chekhov's collection of dramas *Pesy* in 1897.

4. "Ya-epopeya," *Zapiski mechtateley* 1 (1919): 57–59.

5. "Pesa-snovidenie" was coined by A. Roskin in A. P. Chekhov, *Stati i ocherki* (Moscow: Goslitizdat, 1959). I quote after G. Berdnikov, *Chekhov-dramaturg* (Moscow: Iskusstvo, 1972), pp. 151–52.

6. Dmitry Merezhkovsky, *Gryadushchy kham* (Petersburg: Izd. M. V. Pirozhkova, 1906), p. 52.

7. B. A. Larin, *Estetika slova i yazyk pisatelya* (Leningrad, 1974), p. 151.

8. This poem was written in 1894 and belongs to Balmont's collection *Pod severnym nebom*. It is known that Chekhov appreciated Balmont's poetry and knew him personally. He wanted Balmont to write a play for the Moscow Art Theater.

9. G. Berdnikov, *Chekhov-dramaturg*, pp. 158–59. Berdnikov relates a recent production of *The Seagull* by the Moscow Art Theater in which Treplev's play is in the foreground, and alienation is stressed. The comparison with a "captive thrown into a deep empty well" is repeated in the fourth act. It is interesting to note in this connection that Treplev in the fourth act says to Nina: "I am alone, not warmed by anyone's affection, I'm cold, as if in a dungeon . . . ," and echoes thus the image of his play, one not "alien" to Chekhov.

10. I. Dukor, "Problema dramaturgii simvolizma," *Literaturnoe nasledstvo* 27–28 (1937): 120.

11. A. P. Chekhov, *Sochineniya* (Moscow: Ogiz, 1948), 2: 151–52.

12. A. Bely, "Prishedshy," *Severnye tsvety* (1903): 15.

13. Nils Ake Nilsson, *Ibsen in Russland,* Acta Universitatis Stockholmiensis Etudes de Philologie Slave 7 (Stockholm, 1958), pp. 223–24.

14. A. Skaftymov, *Stati o russkoy literature* (Saratov: Kn. izd-vo, 1958), p. 332.

15. Ad. Stender-Petersen, "Zur Technik der Pause bei Cexov," in *Anton Čexov, 1860–1960: Some Essays,* ed. T. Eekman (Leiden: E. J. Brill, 1960), p. 198.

16. Ibid., pp. 202 and 203.

17. A. Bely, "Vospominaniya ob A. A. Bloke," *Epopeya* 1 (1922): 132. Balmont's line was: "nad kholodnoy puchinoy morskoy . . . " ("much less decadent . . ."). See the whole poem in *Bolshaya biblioteka poeta* edition (Moscow, 1969), p. 85.

18. E. A. Bulanina, "Pod vpechatleniem 'Chayki' Chekhova," *Pesni i romansy russkikh poetov* (Moscow-Leningrad: Bolshaya biblioteka poeta, 1965), pp. 867–68. See also note on p. 1062 and an illustration facing p. 849.

19. Merezhkovsky, *Gryadushchy kham,* p. 52.

20. *Iz arkhiva A. P. Chekhova. Publikatsii* (Moscow: Gos. ordena Lenina biblioteka SSSR im. V. I. Lenina. Otdel rukopisey, 1960), p. 46.

21. A. Bely, "Ya-epopeya," *Zapiski mechtateley* 1 (1919): 59.

CHARLOTTE DOUGLAS

"ADAM" AND THE MODERN VISION

The Russian modernists were obsessed with visions of the future. Futurism, which found its name only four years before the Revolution, had been a significant attitude of mind since the days when the Slavophiles dreamed of Russia's special destiny. In art the general trend to idealism at the end of the nineteenth century carried with it a particular appreciation for things illogical, supralogical, or unconsciously naive—folk art, Eastern religion, the language of mystics—and underlying all these interests can be found the idea that they were "more perfect" expressions of human nature, their very primitiveness proof of their fundamental truth. For all the arts the future implied changes in human nature and perception, an evolutionary movement toward perfection. From Solovyov's "Godmanhood" to Khlebnikov's universal utopia the coming revolution was visualized as spiritual in nature, a realization of the divine in man, and to be accompanied by an increase in man's sensual and psychic powers. The new art, often based on a mythology of mystified science, was to predict, portray, and even create such a future.

This magnificent obsession contributed to the abrupt and drastic change in artistic style. The necessity of giving expression to an interior life—either spiritual or psychological—inevitably involved experimentation in expressive form. Lack of a specific image of the coming age also tended to make more concrete and conventional representation difficult. This was especially true in Russia, where prior to the Revolution the avant-garde was much less attracted by machinery and other technological images than their counterparts further west. References to the physical and social environment became less obvious, objects disappeared from paintings, the fabula in prose writing became confused and obscured, and poetry was written in *zaum*. By 1913 the new art found itself completely free to reflect its author's understanding of the New Jerusalem unencumbered by references to apparent reality.

The subject of all Andrey Bely's prose is the mode of transformation of present into future. Like most of his contemporaries, Bely saw a millennium approaching, a time which would be at once the end of one era and the beginning of a significantly different one. His belief that man's movement toward perfection is of spiral form implies a ceaseless return to origins. Bely perpetually stands on the edge of a narrow gulf which separates the end and the beginning, and builds bridges. His works are not only prophecies of the new time, but experiences of his vision, imagistic voyages through time, which by the form of their prediction are self-fulfilling. And this is their primary function. The clear-sighted artist, Bely believed, was time's special instrument, self-sacrificed to lead men into the next round of the future. The artist is to induce in the perceiver a direct and intuitive apprehension of "reality," a supralogical understanding which may be his normal perception in time to come.

In "Adam," a short story published in *Vesy* in April, 1908, Bely attempted to give form to the artist-hero whose art is self-creation.[1] The story is his last fictional work before the major novel *The Silver Dove,* which began to appear in the same journal eleven months later, and is obviously related to it both in style and theme. Much could be said about the nature of the protagonist Adam as a Christ figure and a representative of the revolution, in particular the "revolution of the spirit" in which Bely so strongly believed. But the story's position at the onset of a spectacular novelistic career and early in what has since been recognized as a pervasive alteration in Western literary style makes it especially interesting as a subject of textual study. We therefore try here to characterize this point in the evolution of Bely's own narrative style and hope also that the discussion will contribute to the continuing task of contemporary criticism—the description and definition of modernism.

I

It is difficult to select the essential motifs of the fabula—according to Tomashevsky's formula—simply by retelling the story, because so many seem to be weighted equally that the distinction between those which are "free" and those which are "constrained" seems hardly to apply. The development of the fabula is sly and it is hidden behind the amazing array of devices and images that constitute the *sujet;* as with symbolist writing generally, precious little can be made out in the way of cause and effect. There is, in fact, only one cause—the Great Universal Works—and its effect is tricky and only partially manifest in a myriad of little bright glimpses, like reflections in the facets of some rotating cosmic crystal.

Nevertheless, an attempt must be made to relate the main "events," always keeping in mind that their selection is somewhat arbitrary, and their sum hardly speaks of "what happened." Directly beneath the title "Adam," we are referred to a footnote which explains that the story has actually been put together by a patient in an insane asylum from notes left by another patient, now dead. The remainder of the story is divided into six sections. In the first, entitled "In the Coach," some final time having arrived, and urged on by two friends, Adam boards a train for his father's country estate. The train, after making one stop along the way and experiencing some difficulty in crossing a bridge, arrives at Adam's station, where his father awaits him. The second section, "At Father's," consists mainly of dialogue between Adam and his father. Father, it seems, has remained at home all of his life, while the son has escaped to "new horizons." Father has had several women, a source of some satisfaction, and his estate abounds in livestock; he, himself, has gotten very fat. Adam says he has returned home for a cure, to acquire his father's health, even though in the past the two had been enemies. He is discouraged with his life in the city and has decided to begin again in his native region. Both men are drunk at dinner.

In the next section, "The Annex," father and son have finished dinner and sit talking while the cook, the father's mistress, washes dishes. When the father appears to leave the room the cook seduces Adam, but they are caught immediately by the father peeking from behind the door. He insists that Adam bathe in a tin tub, which he does; but then Adam, astride a dog, rides into the courtyard to announce some "new testaments." Convinced that Adam is about to take over the estate, Father has him flogged by the police and put to bed. "At Home—On Vacation," the fourth section, begins on the following morning as Adam goes to drink tea with his father. Father urges him to settle down at home and remarks that Adam, when he was drunk, said something "absurd." Adam anxiously tries to remember whether he has revealed the "secret." As Father is complaining about feeling ill Adam leaps from his seat and starts for the village. There in the fields he finds people blackened from fire sitting on the charred remains of their houses. Dressing himself in bast and wearing a grass wreath on his head, Adam begins to speak in biblical phrases. He attempts, unsuccessfully, to cure some blind men. In the meanwhile Father chokes on his supper and dies as his house burns down.

The fifth section is called "Lisichensk," the name of Adam's village. There he waits for a train back to the city. Adam carries his "kingly regalia" in a basket and still speaks in biblical language. After a look around the village, he boards the train for the city. "King Adam," the last section, is another dialogue, now between Adam's two friends who are cleaning up his room in the city. Adam, they say, has been gone three months and they do not expect him to return. They gather his clothes and other personal belongings and plan then to light candles and drink his wine. Suddenly someone knocks, the door swings back, and the two friends see Adam standing in a brilliant bast cloak, a birch sceptre in his hand. But the vision evidently does not materialize, for in the morning he is not there.

The story is told by an omniscient, at times ironic, narrator who undergoes abrupt changes in syntax and vocabulary, now speaking poetically in an archaic lexicon, now turning to the reader with questions and comments, and lapsing sometimes into coarse colloquialisms. The narrator's position as an omniscient reporter outside the action is not constant. For long periods—and this is not always made clear by the syntax—the narrator speaks with Adam's more limited vision, actually from inside Adam's head. The narrative continues to be in the third-person *"he"*—thus not really becoming "stream of consciousness"—and the syntax remains relatively linear and stable. In a dream sequence in the third section, for example, Adam's dream is reported as if from the objective point of view of an external narrator. There is no syntactic indication that the story has been taken up from a very different vantage point. Only later, when we are told that "it was only a dream" do we realize what happened. There are semantic clues. The importance of sound to the scene—the father's counting, the splash of the water, and the lashing—gives it a certain sensual quality. Simultaneously we see that Adam's intellectual grasp on things has become impaired: "Adam . . . dimly understood . . ."; "Now he stared stupidly. . . ." Lulled by "the sleepy muttering of streams" and overcome by the drinking and revelry after dinner, Adam loses consciousness as he goes through the motions of bathing. By the time the servants are called upon to finish bathing him by switching him with sticks, Adam is asleep, and this procedure becomes part of a dream about being lashed by the police. It is, naturally enough, the only event in this section of the text which seems to occur away from "the annex."

Thus, we witness the entire scene as Adam experienced it and not as an uninvolved narrator would have seen it. With the words "Afterwards they laid him in a bed . . . ," the narrator moves back to his position on the sidelines—though still with some poetic involvement—and immediately thereafter he withdraws still further from the action. For Adam, of course, before he becomes fully awake, the dream has the same weight of reality as the other events of this scene—that is, he is neither drunk nor asleep. The narrator's gradual withdrawal is simultaneous with Adam's awakening. This movement back from subjective to objective viewpoint is expressed nicely by his description of Adam's condition: when he first awakes he squints "as if he were drunk" (*"budto s perepoya"*). This expression leaves some doubt about his actual condition, but in the succeeding paragraph he hiccoughs "drunkenly" (*"s perepoya"*), dispelling all doubt. For the remainder of the scene the narrator moves back and forth between an internal and external position, at times actually approaching a kind of interior monologue. Whenever the emotional content intensifies the third-person pronoun disappears—although never to be replaced with "I," which would do away with the external narrator entirely. Sitting on his bed, for example, Adam becomes anxious about inadvertently revealing his secret; as his anxiety mounts the description moves from the third-person singular pronoun to an impersonal construction: "Last night he had arrived at his father's house and right away his father had made him drunk: Oh just to hide it, if only it doesn't get out! He knew what he was doing. . . ." The presence of the narrator is maintained because the exclamation is part of a sentence narrated in the third person and is not put between quotation marks, even though we are obviously inside Adam's head. We hear both Adam's voice and that of the narrator, who seems himself to be emotionally overwhelmed and to exclaim to us involuntarily.

A similar device occurs in the scene with the blind men in the following section. As the emotion of the scene mounts the narrator abandons his third-person description of Adam and reacts to the situation in his own voice: "Strange it was to see this mute procession in the stormy twilight. They made their way immutable, primordial, blind. Oh, if only they could open their eyes, oh if only they were not blind! Russian Land, awake!" At the critical moment as Adam is about to perform the miracle the narrator loses his detachment entirely and calls out to Adam—in the immediate and emotionally heightened present tense—addressing him as *"ty"* in archaic and Church Slavonic words. The three imperatives— *pomogi, verni, pridi* (*help, bring back, come*)—sounding the ecstatic long i sound three times—are both the narrator's appeal to Adam and Adam's calling of the Holy Spirit upon the blind. Again we are hearing the double voice. The narrator then immediately returns to the third person and past tense.

The narration is interrupted by two sections of dialogue written in dramatic form. Even here there is no attempt at verisimilitude. The characters are made to mouth a mixture of poetic oration and colloquial speech. This cannot be construed as the misplaced high-flown language of the *"skaz"* simpleton. In "At Father's" Adam and his father lapse from one linguistic mode to the other, but their usage is always correct and they are quite capable of functioning within either mode. Their language, rather, reflects their own double vision; they live in two distinct worlds simultaneously—the poetic, cosmically historic world, and the *"bytovoy"* world of their individual lives. Because they are keenly aware of both dimensions they can live wholeheartedly in neither, and no matter which language they speak, it is always with a kind of schizoid detachment, without committing emotion or self to their words. Their hold on either perspective is tentative and their conversation assumes a certain formality as they attempt to maintain balance in one world for the sake of communication. The effect is of a delicate verbal ballet above a psychic abyss:

Son: Father, you are my father. You sired me. I have sired no one because I left the primordial. . . .

Father: Yes, I am your father. I sired you and nowhere did I go. Where I was in the beginning there I remained. . . .

Son: But you are taking up even more room in these spaces, father, you've gotten fat. It's about time to tie up a wheelbarrow to your belly. . . .

Father: Yes, son, I am swelling, soon the whole world will fit in me and I shall become father to my world and you will be the son. But I will not give out information about my wealth, although the estate books are in order. . . .

II

Adam's journey is, at bottom, a migration in consciousness. The irreducible fact of the story, the bone behind its most intricately elaborated flesh, is the presence of two worlds. One, concrete, located in space, is ultimately *maya*. The other, the transcendent illusion, is the only reality and the only value. They exist interdependently, defining each other; and Adam, like every man, crawls between them. As the story unwinds he moves steadily away from the material world and becomes increasingly occupied with the transcendental. The consciousness becomes transfigured and eventually so also does the body, until finally he exists in a completely spiritual state. Adam suffers a death but will be reborn. In his new form, clothed in the "brilliant coal of dead worlds," he is undoubtedly a prefiguration of time and worlds to come.

Adam's transcendental universe is conjured partly of Christian mythological imagery, biblical style and vocabulary, even direct quotations from the Bible. The concrete world, on the other hand, is put together out of seemingly ordinary objects and activities: the train ride, the domestic routine, the kinds of things he leaves behind in the city, trousers, hat, cigar case. We, like Adam, often see both worlds simultaneously. Consider, for example, Adam's observation of his fellow passenger on the train: "A dark passenger somewhere sideways went up to the rack and stretched out his arms and stiffened and it seemed that pain nailed him, crucified, to the wall." In the world of common sense "dark" is accepted in the literal sense, and "rack" as a coat rack. "Crucified" may be understood as a metaphor (that is, "as if he were crucified"); there is overall a heavy dependence on the word "seem." For those with a transcendent perspective, however, "dark" is meant figuratively (that is, spiritually dark), and "sideways" seems physically to emphasize that "rack" is indeed an instrument of torture. "Crucified" is for one instant painfully real. "Somewhere" transports the whole scene from the train to the particular but unspecified location of the other world. That "crucified" is in fact meant literally in this perspective is demonstrated in two succeeding sentences when Adam with a shock realizes what he sees and creeps up for a closer look: " 'The passenger is crucified too,' he thought. Rising from his seat and pretending to look for the conductor he moved closer to the crucified man." This last use of "crucified" leaves no doubt as to its reality. The narrator here shares Adam's vision.

In "The Annex" Adam reenacts several biblical scenes: the revelation of the Testament, the washing of the master's feet, and the scourging and the death. At the end of the dream sequence, the narrator is not wholly separate from Adam, and his imagery is affected by his vision. The description of Adam being put to bed is given in images from Christian mythology:

> Afterwards they laid him in a bed as in a grave; they piled him with quilts like stones, colorless, deathly still. At the head of Adam's bed keened the cook, crooked, looking old, her frightened, orphan-silhouette drawn close to him. And he squinted as if he were drunk; but throwing back the quilts and stretching out his hands to the cook, he stood up swaying in his drawers and shirt: "I have risen from my pallet, my soul, don't be blind."

The metaphors produce the image of the burial and resurrection. The mourning cook plays the role of the mourning Virgin, the poetic and obsolete language reinforcing the mythological references.

From the beginning Adam has had considerable difficulty operating in the concrete world; in fact, his vision of it is very faint, even with the aid of his pince-nez. He makes a real effort at first to communicate with his father, who lives almost completely in the concrete dimension, to answer his questions, to do as he is told. But in spite of himself and in spite of the repeated adjusting of his glasses, he keeps slipping into the other perspective. His abstracted mind cannot focus on things so close at hand; he cannot remember what it was he said to his father; his eye, caught by a clod of dust outside the window, sees only the great gray universe speckled with rosy worlds. As the days are fulfilled and time approaches its cataclysmic end, Adam throws aside the pince-nez, abandons the filial mask, and simply gives up trying. Striding out into the fields, he surrenders himself completely to transcendent reality. Without the perspective of the concrete world, metaphor turns actuality and Adam seems indeed to be Christ and speaks with his voice: " 'I am the alpha and the omega, the beginning and the end. . . . ' " Dressed in symbolic, kingly clothing (he sees the purple pall, the wreath of wheat; we, still peering through prosaic eyes, see bast and field grass), Adam lays hands upon the blind. Again there is a discrepancy between our sight and his: we see he has not restored their sight; he sees he has. What appears to be ambiguity is a result of perspective. The narrator who has both visions sometimes reports them simultaneously, sometimes successively; but sometimes he gives only one or the other. In the scene on the train, for example, we saw both a crucified passenger and a coat on a rack. In this scene we are given the same image in the form of a scarecrow (*pugalo*). The image of the crucifixion which Adam must perceive is left implicit, although the semantic root of the word (*pug* = fright) does point toward the other perspective.

III

The heart of Bely's style and its most striking aspect is the enumeration and intimate revelation of the nature of "things." Like Proust's famous *madeleine,* which for the narrator elicited a flood of affective memories, Bely's objects do not have a wholly external existence. What exactly objects are must necessarily depend upon how they have been perceived, not only by particular individuals, as was the case with the madeleine, but by the sum total of human percipients since the origins of language. As Cassirer and others have pointed out, linguistic and psychological distinction between those qualities which reside outside ourselves and those which are inside is relatively recent. Before articulation of the ego the "objective and realistic" existence of an object was felt to contain inherent and equally-important abstract and emotional qualities: "The mythical world is concrete not because it has to do with sensuous, objective contents, not because it excludes and repels all merely abstract factors . . . it is concrete because in it the two factors . . . are undifferentiated, because they merge, grow together, concresce in an immediate unity." [2]

The evolution of consciousness is in large part inseparable from the inherent capacity of language to talk about things as well as to name them. Inevitably its syntactic discursive form informed and directed the development of logical and "scientific" exposition, which is concerned with the world "outside" the subjective consciousness. Bely's work returns the object to its original position. His use of language cannot even be said to be metaphorical, in that it is not a comparison that he is making between object and experience, but an identity. The object for Bely is coherent with the experience; it is the supposition or indeed the generation of the "prelogical" consciousness that makes the work "mythical."

Susanne Langer, in her ongoing series of works on the philosophy of art, considers the work of art as a whole to be a nondiscursive symbol of vital processes.[3] We find that Bely makes a closely similar use of objects within the story—i.e., the objects themselves function as nondiscursive symbols based on forms expressive of concepts fundamental to human life. The feeling so intimately associated with an object is exhibited symbolically by its abstracted shape. This is the way any feeling can be formulated most directly, since emotion alone is pure experience and can hardly be exhibited without an image: "the basic symbols of human thought are images, which 'mean' the past impression that begot them and also those future ones that exemplify the same form. . . . No human impression is only a signal from the outer world, it is always *also* an image in which possible impressions are formulated, that is, a symbol for the conception of *such* experience." [4]

The objects in "Adam" are islands of sentience in a sea of discourse; they are named but not discussed. In Tomashevsky's terms, they are static but constrained (*svyazannye*) motifs, their function being not to move the situation, but to define it. "The village tower stuck up stupidly"; "A scarecrow flapped before Adam Antonovich." They are simply there, with a kind of self-sufficient fullness of being. Bely names these objects and then proceeds to talk about something else. "Two friends leaned upon their canes. One had on a crushed bowler (why?). . . . Both were weary. . . ." The canes, the crushed hat, are not part of a description of the two friends— indeed, we get no real description of anyone in the story—they are objects associated with these two people as separate things with which they "have traffic" and which they carry as a kind of emblem. Such emblems do not necessarily characterize their bearers; indeed, the bearers may exist only to support the objects. In any case, the characters do not will to have these things. Father carries around his belly with a kind of superdetachment. The cook's gold braids do not really seem to be hers; they do not tell how she *looks* but what she is supposed to *be*. The narrator is very anxious that the reader understand this situation and keeps poking him in the ribs: "Did you get it?" and "Why?" he asks in direct address to the poor reader who is trying to make his way through the tangle of images.

There is such a profusion of images because no single appearance of an object in the story is of significance in itself. As they accumulate, as the objects one after another are named and laid down in the mind, their import gradually bodies forth. The symbolic "meanings"—that is, the emotional valences—become apparent when enough objects of similar shape make an abstracted form or a geometric relationship obvious and when such a form or relationship is associated with a particular concept by virtue of its universal value and its emotional environment in the text. An iconic symbol is meant to affect the reader unconsciously, conveying its import on such a level that it is actually sensed rather than understood.

To look more closely at how objects function within the text, let us go back to the two friends standing with Adam on the platform: "his two friends leaned upon their canes. One had on a crushed bowler. . . ." The narrator's vision, of course, has provided some initial selection—he mentions just the canes and the hats—but it is difficult to assign any other significance to them at this point. At the end of the same paragraph, however, there is another mention of the hats: "And then the bell rang, and then they waved their bowlers; three wooden arms swung in the air." Again the bowlers appear in conjunction with other objects, not with canes this time but with arms, which might be considered to have the same general shape. The arms, in fact, are wooden, and the reader may be caught wondering whether the men themselves are wooden. The wood makes even more explicit the similarity in shape between cane and arm. (Of course, one may go a step further and imagine that the hats are being waved atop the canes, so that the canes are indeed wooden "arms.") The contiguity—within the same sentence—of a bell, impels one to look for similarities. The ringing is obviously a sound that serves to emphasize the accompanying action, especially since a bell customarily denotes a significant time; but beyond this, the shape of the implied clapper or hammer and its oscillating motion, silently echo the shape and motion of the arm and bowler. Of course the fact that there are three arms creates a further ambiguity. There are only two "friends." One might suppose that Adam too was wearing a bowler, but this will not be substantiated by anything else in the story.

Because these images occur so prominently at the beginning of what is obviously to be a rather morbid affair—just at that moment "someone long and dark with the face of an ox and shoulders crooked as a cemetery cross" makes his appearance—they seem already to carry a sense of doom. This despite the fact that the objects themselves, if taken out of context, in no way carry a semantic, phonetic, or mythic connotation of disaster. The emotional freight is intensified when the image appears soon again, now as a hammer tapping beneath the train. "Beneath the coach a little man ran tapping his hammer *'ten-teren'* the broken heart beating beating and stopping." Here again the form is associated with a sound and with repetitive action, and the primary metaphor, hammer-heart, makes the subjective connotations of marking time and impending doom very explicit.[5]

The shape implied by the images, cane with bowler, arm with bowler, clapper, and hammer, is iconic of the biological fact either of the heart being pounded or the heart itself as an instrument knocking within the chest. The symbol is not arbitrary; it has a physical logic the reader must respond to because his own physical experience is connected with its emotion. Throughout the story it reappears at intervals as a reminder of the note rung on the first pages. The raising and lowering of the vodka glasses, the herdsman with his whip, and similar images flash by as the narrative proceeds, freezing for an instant an image of time, stopped action shots of the universal clock. At the end of the story, just prior to the appearance of the transfigured Adam before his two friends, the shape is again conjured up, as in the case of the bell, by a sound: "Lyogky stuk u dveri, lyogky stuk u dveri. Slushayte: lyogky stuk u dveri" ("A light tap at the door, a light tap at the door. Listen, a light tap at the door"). The sound of the words themselves reproduce the knocking and the excitement, but behind them looms the ghostly image of an arm and clenched fist.

The image examined above was a combination of two more fundamental shapes, the circle and the straight line. They also appear together—though never so attached to one another—in the royal regalia of Adam's transformed existence, the wreath and the staff: "A wreath of roadside field-grass he placed upon his brow. A staff, not a switch he pulled from the ground. . . . On the road he stood like a guard, the dust-gray road running into the sunset. And a crow perched there, perched and croaked, there where the celestial fire consumed the earth." Adam, as tokens of his new spiritual state, possesses the two controlling elements of both life and time. He holds them ceremoniously, aware that they are of fundamental significance, as he stands motionlessly at the beginning of time. At the train station in Lisichensk the image blooms again, an immobile emblem of Adam's transcendent state: "Gloomily a furbearer stood there, what for, the devil knows, but he had a saber and a high Caucasian hat. Somewhere the engine was complaining about the distance and at the buffet the fly-specked pies were drying up."

The overall geometry of the two scenes is strikingly similar; it is the spatial analogy of Adam's temporal position; both figures stand at a beginning on time's way. The sun sets and the earth disappears at the end of Adam's dusty road. Time is so apparent at the railroad station that pies dry up visibly. On both occasions a distant noise sounds the melancholy theme—the screech of a crow, the engine's moan. Both of the scenes are static; nothing and no one moves. They are presented as tableaux, perfect "living pictures" of spiritual concepts. But iconic significance is not necessarily static. In Adam's dream he "goes through the motions" of definitive events in the life of Christ—the washing of the feet, the scourging, the burial and resurrection. But Adam seems somehow uninvolved emotionally with what is happening. He certainly does not seem to have the consciousness befitting a new Christ. In fact the whole scene, instead of projecting a reality, has the appearance of pantomime, deliberate and self-aware. The same thing occurs when Adam leaves his father and walks out into the fields. He speaks Christ's words exactly—and sometimes not so exactly—but again without emotion. After leaving his father's house he never speaks simply again, but "recites" instead, in a detached and monotonous voice. By contrast, the voice of the narrator seems brash. Adam's actions, the ritual dressing, the attempted miracle, are potentially acts of refined passion, yet even at the magic moment when the Holy Spirit is implored to become manifest, there is a curious lack of feeling. The narrator becomes caught up with himself, but we are forced to move a step back from Adam. We see no evidence of his emotion; we cannot even be sure that the crucial words are indeed his own.

The power of these scenes comes specifically from their dynamic form. We *know* something is happening because of the care and solemnity with which the elaborate actions are conducted. Adam's emotion is turned inward. The concentrated carefulness of his gestures fastens our attention on their form and gives them great import. Adam, in fact, performs a kind of mime of the life of Christ, a sacred drama which he "walks through" to induce his rebirth. As his name indicates, Adam is not Christ; he is still merely a man. But having been "called," he must undergo a new birth wherein he transcends his earthly origins. Both Adam's dream and his subsequent excursion into the village are *dromena,* mimetic and ritualistic reenactments of the past and magical prefigurations of the future. They are the initiation of Adam into a new life and their power comes from the kinesthetic representation of what is desired; Adam's words are not strictly necessary.[6] The physical relationships acted out do not serve as mere "signs"; they are the essential part of the process they represent, the form. From a temporal point of view, "The now is filled and saturated with the future." [7] In anticipating his future, Adam gives it the shape it will later assume. The geometries do more than anticipate, they create; their trace upon this world lays down the seed of the next one. Their value consists in just this: they are the vital forms, the relationships of human experience.

For both writer and reader the story as a whole is a *dromenon.* Even as we experience it, its unstable content seems to collapse: objects, events, characters, story. In the rubble glisten whole only the irreducible atoms of value which do not fracture, the fundamental mimetic geometries. The inner life grows visible, traced out in the "ancient immutable spaces." In the final analysis such verbal art seems necessarily to be gesture, the manifestation of a unity: form plus emotion; distinction between object and discourse is finally illusory. If "Adam" has "meaning" it is as a gesture of experience and a shape for tomorrow.

There are several aspects of "Adam" which we may associate with a modern style. The attempt to re-create in prose the discontinuous Symbolist world—earth and cosmos, finiteness and infinity, present and future—required the creation of a double-level narrative and a corresponding double perspective. In addition to the differing perceptions of Adam and Father, the narrator's point of view is variable. But spatial and temporal discontinuities are to an extent resolved by the fact that the psychological duality is contained within Adam himself, a single character. This is a most striking aspect both of this story and of much of early Russian modernism—i.e., the movement toward integration, rather than the disintegration and alienation which are commonly associated with the idea of modern consciousness. Adam's almost complete psychological awareness is his key to the future and a pattern for the reader's own evolution. Since this kind of perception is associated with a purely intuitive grasp of the future, the reader is not permitted to identify completely with either point of view. The absence of any serious pretentions to narrative mimesis precludes an escape into the fabula, while subtle shifts in viewpoint keep the reader from establishing a "rational" position outside the text. The difficulty of the text and the search for a consistent perspective re-creates in the reader Adam's own difficulty of communication and his inability to control his environment. The humorous elements of the story and the questions addressed directly to the reader involve him further in this process.

In order to establish the cosmic "world of values" the narrative logic has often been replaced by a poetic juxtaposition of images; their accretion and especially their inherent geometries are the "objective correlatives" of Bely's vision of the absolute. Typically for Russian modernism before the Revolution, there is no concrete image of the future. Metaphors are drawn from nature, the Bible, and political events; but the image of the future itself remains shrouded in mist, just beyond the range of Bely's exquisite glass.

NOTES

1. "Adam" appeared in *Vesy* 4 (1908): 15–30. This journal has been reissued by Kraus Reprint Ltd. (Nedeln: Liechtenstein, 1968). An English translation by the author of this study was published in *Russian Literature Triquarterly* 4 (Fall 1972): 81–92. "Adam" is apparently an expansion upon the theme of a much shorter work, "We Await His Return" ("My zhdem ego vozvrashcheniya") published two years earlier in *Svobodnaya Sovest* 1 (1906): 160–63. In it the protagonist, like Adam, is a preoccupied philosopher with weak blue eyes who leaves two friends, rides away on a train, and does not return.

2. Ernst Cassirer, *The Philosophy of Symbolic Forms,* 3 vols. (New Haven: Yale University Press, 1968), 2: 24.

3. Susanne Langer, *Philosophy in a New Key* (Cambridge: Harvard University Press, 1957); *Feeling and Form* (New York, 1953); *Problems of Art* (New York: Charles Scribner's Sons, 1957); *Mind: An Essay on Human Feeling* 1 (Baltimore: Johns Hopkins Press, 1967); 2 (Baltimore: Johns Hopkins Press, 1973).

4. Langer, *Feeling and Form,* p. 376.

5. Of course to readers of *Anna Karenina,* any little man doing anything in a railroad station foretells doom!

6. For a discussion of the psychology of the *dromenon* see Jane Ellen Harrison, *Themis* (Cambridge: The University Press, 1912).

7. Cassirer, *The Philosophy of Symbolic Forms,* 3: 202.

HERBERT EAGLE

TYPOGRAPHICAL DEVICES
IN THE POETRY OF ANDREY BELY

In 1929, in the introductory chapter of his monograph *Rhythm as a Dialectic* Andrey Bely characterized the effect of typographical arrangement on verse rhythm as follows: "whether one ought to print verses in short lines or not . . . is a question not resolvable without scientifically positing the question of the relation of meter to rhythm and intonation; the division of a line is creative composition; the line is an indivisible unit; changing it, I also change the intonation" (p. 11). Two years later, in the introduction to his planned edition of poetry *Calls of Time* (*Zovy vremyon*), Bely was even more specific about the effect of typography on the intonation, and therefore on the meaning, of poetry: "One and the same complex of words, arranged in various ways, will produce various lines, a different respiration: every arrangement has its own intonation: intonation in a lyric is everything: it is like a facial expression, a gesture: intonation, gesture—change the meaning of a word. . . ." [1] Victor Zhirmunsky, writing in his theoretical work *Introduction to Metrics* (1925), had noted that the new typographical devices being used by Mayakovsky did not relate primarily to the metrical structure of the poetry, but rather served to delineate semantic and syntactic groupings.[2] This same technique was being used by Bely as early as 1903 in the collection *Gold in Azure,* although, as Bely noted later, he was not yet aware of the larger implications of the problem.

The key element of Bely's typographical innovations in verse was the use of vertical rather than horizontal linkings of words. As Bely noted in 1931: "I sometimes attempt to replace the canonical meaning—the horizontal placement of a line,—by a perpendicular chain of words arranged in intonational breaks which correspond to the accents and pauses I hear" ("Zovy," p. 94).

Bely's use of perpendicular columns of words to emphasize intonational breaks was adopted by Mayakovsky in his early verse (including "Cloud in Trousers," 1914), and such columns (*stolbiki*) have also been employed by many other Russian poets since that time. But the rhythmic and semantic effects of this device in the works of various poets have yet to be studied fully. It is in the early stage of the development of this technique in Bely's poetry that we can most easily see the possible motivation, both rhythmic and semantic, for this new typographical structure.

The poem "The Golden Fleece" ("Zolotoe runo," 1903) is written in two parts: the first in traditional stanza form; the second making use of various types of columns. Thus it provides an excellent illustration of the potentials of the new form. In the first part, we find four-line stanzas, usually with alternating rhyme scheme and with each verse comprising either two or three anapestic feet:

I

  1   Zoloteya, efir prosvetitsya,
      i v vostorge sgorit.
      A nad morem saditsya
      uskolzayushchy, solnechny shchit.

  5   I na more ot solntsa
      zolotye drozhat yazyki.
      Vsyudu otblesk chervontsa
      sredi vspleskov toski.

      Vstali grudi utyosov
10   sred trepeshushchey, solnechnoy tkani.
      Solntse selo. Rydany
      polon krik albatrosov:
      "Deti solntsa, vnov kholod besstrastya!
      Zakatilos ono—
15   zolotoe, starinnoe schaste—
      zolotoe runo!"

      Net siyanya chervontsa.
      Merknut svetochi dnya.
      No vezde vmesto solntsa
20   oslepitelny purpur ognya.
            Aprel 1903
            Moskva (*Gold in Azure*, pp. 7–8)

The regular meter and stanza form have a tendency to produce an artificial intonation, usually a regular alternation of rising and falling elements.[3] This "artificial" verse intonation tends to override the particular individual features of the syntactic structure. In the above poem (as read by most Russians) the intonational cadences will be rising at the ends of the odd-numbered lines and falling at the ends of even-numbered lines. Such a "conventional" intonation has almost become a sign of poetic language in Russian lyrics in traditional stanza forms.

In this traditional form semantic emphasis lies on the words concentrated at the ends of the metrical verses. First of all, the meter induces a longer-than-usual pause after these words; secondly, the rhyme calls attention to the words themselves; thirdly, the significant rise or fall in pitch occurs at the ends of verses. In the quoted section of "The Golden Fleece" the first three rhyme words are verbs, but all of the remaining seventeen are substantives (sixteen nouns and one pronoun). It would not be hard to recognize in this poem an allegory generally consistent with the philosophical ideas of Bely and his circle in the early years of this century. The sun (*solntse*) and the golden fleece (*zolotoe runo*) represent that divine truth which has receded from man; man is thus left with anguish (*toska*), weeping (*rydanie*) and cold passivity (*kholod besstrastya*). The only consolation is that reflection of divine truth which remains behind, here symbolized by the purple of the sunset (*purpur ognya*). Virtually all of the rhymed words (that is, the words which are semantically foregrounded) relate to the principal elements of this symbolic system. The rhymed nouns evoke either the divine ideal (*shchit, solntsa, chervontsa, tkani, schaste, runo, chervontsa, dnya, solntsa*), or the state of man in the absence of that ideal (*toski, utyosov, rydany, albatrosov, besstrastya*), or the earthly reflection of the ideal (*zolotye yazyki, ognya*). The three verb rhymes (*prosvetitsya, sgorit, saditsya*) are all closely linked semantically to the sun, the positive ideal in Bely's philosophy.

In the second part of the poem (completed half a year later) Bely again used a ternary meter, amphibrachs, with varying numbers of feet per verse:

II

1	Pozharom sklon neba obyat . . .	A
	I vot argonavty nam v rog otletany	b
	trubyat . . .	A

	Vnimayte, vnimayte . . .	c
5	Dovolno stradany	b
	Bronyu nadevayte	c
	iz solnechnoy tkani!	b
	Zovyot za soboyu	d
	starik argonavt,	A
10	vzyvaet	f
	truboy	G
	zolotoyu:	d
	"Za solntsem, za solntsem, svobodu lyubya,	E
	umchimsya v efir	H
15	goluboy! . . . "	G
	Starik argonavt prizyvaet na solnechny pir,	H
	trubya	E
	v zoloteyushchy mir.	H
	Vsyo nebo v rubinakh.	i
20	Shar solntsa pochil.	J
	Vsyo nebo v rubinakh	i
	nad nami.	k
	Na gornykh vershinakh	i
	nash Argo,	l
25	nash Argo,	l
	gotovyas letet, zolotymi krylami	k
	zabil.	J
	Zemlya otletaet . . .	m
	Vino	N
30	mirovoe	o
	pylaet	f
	pozharom	P
	opyat:	A
	to ognennym sharom	P
35	blistat	A
	vyplyvaet	f
	runo	N
	zolotoe,	o
	iskryas.	Q
40	I, bleskom obyaty,	r
	svetilo dnevnoe,	o
	chto fakelom vnov zazhzheno,	N
	nesyas,	Q
	nastigaet	f
45	nash Argo krylaty.	r
	Opjat nastigaet	f

svoyo zolotoe   o
runo . . .   N
                    Oktyabr 1903
                    Moskva (*Gold in Azure*, pp. 8–10)

There is an abundance of rhyme in the poem, but it is irregularly
patterned (cf. rhyme scheme indicated on the right). The typography is radically different from the first part, and often does not
coincide with the reader's sense of the metrical verse. Part II could
have conceivably been arranged in a manner similar to Part I; for
example:

> Pozharom sklon neba obyat . . .
> I vot argonavty nam v rog otletany trubyat . . .
> Vnimayte, vnimayte . . . dovolno stradany!
> Bronyu nadevayte iz solnechnoy tkani.
>
> . . . .
> I, bleskom obyaty, svetilo dnevnoe,
> Chto fakelom vnov zazhzheno,
> Nesyas nastigaet nash Argo krylaty.
> Opyat nastigaet svoyo zolotoe runo.

If Bely had done this, the intonation would again tend toward a
regular alternation of rises and falls, in accordance with the meter.
The unusual typographical arrangement actually chosen by Bely
calls attention to all of the rhymes which would have been line-
internal in the traditional stanza format. The short-line typography combined with the rhymes, serves to isolate and call attention
to individual words which would have otherwise been within the
metrical lines.

Yury Tynyanov, in his seminal study *The Problem of Verse Language*, noted that verse possessed a special dynamics based on the
tension between verse articulation (i.e., according to the metrical
verses) and normal intonational articulation (i.e., articulation
based on syntactico-semantic groupings). According to Tynyanov,
the unity and compactness of the verse "regroups" words into new
sets, which are perceived as unified identities, in spite of the fact
that normal syntax might group the words otherwise.[4] These new
compact sets are the verses.

As we have noted above, in the traditional metrical form the
words at the ends of verses, in general, have greater relative semantic stress due to their "foregrounded" position; this implies, of

course, that words within the verse must have relatively less semantic stress. For example, in Part I of "The Golden Fleece" the verbs
referring to the departure or disappearance of the sun are all
within the verses—and this is as it should be, since the act of
disappearance is not as important in Part I as the ideas of absence
and reflection. But what if the poet does not want the words internal
to the metrical verses to be semantically muted? What if he wants
to distribute the semantic weight more evenly than in traditional
verse form? The typographical structure of Part II of "The Golden
Fleece" represented a solution to this problem of distribution of
emphasis; it is not at all a minor adjustment, and Bely himself
pointed this out later, in analyzing the poetry of his youth from a
distance of almost three decades: "In intensifying the sonic ex-
pressiveness by internal rhymes, alliterations, etc., we first of all
annul the significance of the end rhyme: if each word rhymes with
another, then rhyme itself, as such, decreases in effectiveness . . . "
("Zovy," p. 95). For Bely the diffusion of sound play throughout
the verse rather than its concentration in the final end rhyme
reduces the semantic dominance of that final rhyme. Instead we
have a situation, as in Part II of "The Golden Fleece," where many
words in the poem rhyme with many other words. When the internal rhyme is combined with a typographical arrangement based
on intonation, then the semantico-syntactic intonation is no longer
suppressed by the "artificial" metrical intonation: "A line, held
in a metrical corset, reminds me of a unilaterally developing biceps:
the intonation in it is foreordained. A line in the structure which
I call an unbroken melody is subordinated only to the intonational
whole of the rhythm, and not, say, to a tetrametric measure . . . "
("Zovy," p. 96).

The "melody" which results from semantico-syntactic intonation
is free (in the sense of not being bound by a universal pattern
throughout the poem) but it tends to organize itself into local subpatterns. When we speak we break our utterance into relatively
small semantico-syntactic word groups, which were termed
syntagms by de Saussure.[5] Syntagms are atoms of the speaker's
perception; they are conceptual unities, indivisible segments which
together make up larger utterances. But the choice of precisely how
to break up the utterance is not completely determined by rules of
grammar and syntax. Choices are continually being made by the
speaker, and the syntagmatic segmentation which is chosen is
capable of reflecting subtle differences in meaning.

Syntagms are usually delineated by increased dynamic pressure on the last stressed syllable of the segment, by a temporal pause following the segment, and by contours of pitch.[6] A concluding cadence is used in a segment which completes a sentence (with the exception of most questions, which have rising anticadence intonation). In Russian the essential feature of the concluding cadence is sharply falling pitch on the last accented syllable of the segment or on the postictic syllable.[7]

Semicadence is the term for the pitch contour which accompanies a segment of an utterance which does not complete a statement and which will be followed immediately by something additional. Semicadences in Russian are of various types, but two basic types are most relevant to our discussion: (1) a type (resembling the anticadence) in which pitch rises gradually on the accented syllable—this type usually occurring in descriptions and monologues; (2) a type (resembling the concluding cadence) which has falling pitch and occurs in independent clauses without a high degree of tension or anticipation.[8] Of course, pitch is a difficult phonological feature to describe, since the norms can vary considerably from speaker to speaker and are also affected by emotional factors. Be that as it may, Bely's typography does foreground the intonational level of the poem's sound, creating an auxiliary rhythmic pattern which competes with the meter for dominance. Thus it actualizes the dynamic tension upon which Tynyanov built his theory of verse; it also reflects Bely's "musical" concept of poetic language: "a complex of melodic movements in the confines of one and the same visual form" (*Rhythm as a Dialectic*, p. 29).

If one marks the probable rising or falling of pitch at the end of each typographical line in Part II of "The Golden Fleece," one finds that (although there is no consistent intonational pattern) there are indeed subpatterns, musical movements if you will, which clearly echo one another:

Stanza I	*Stanza II*	*Stanza III*
1. F	8. R	16. F
2. R	9. F	17. R
3. F	10. R	18. F
4. R	11. R	
5. F	12. F	
6. R	13. R	
7. F	14. R	
	15. F	

Stanza IV	Stanza V	Stanza VI
19. F	28. F	40. R
20. F	29. R	41. R
21. R	30. R	42. F
22. F	31. R	43. R
23. R	32. R	44. R
24. R	33. F	45. F
25. R	34. R	
26. R	35. R	
27. F	36. R	Stanza VII
	37. R	46. R
	38. R	47. R
	39. F	48. F

The parallel intonational movements become more evident if we list them in the following way:

Line 1	F			
Lines 2–9	R/F	R/F	R/F	R/F
Lines 10–15	R/R/F		R/R/F	
Lines 16–18		F	R/F	
Lines 19–20		F	F	
Lines 21–22		R/F		
Lines 23–27	R/R/R/R/F			
Line 28		F		
Lines 29–33	R/R/R/R/F			
Lines 34–39	R/R/R/R/R/F			
Lines 40–48	R/R/F	R/R/F	R/R/F	

Thus, the movement in lines 2–9 is echoed again in lines 17–18 and 21–22; the movement in lines 10–15 is reflected in the poem's concluding lines 40–48; lines 16–18 and lines 19–20 closely mirror one another; lines 23–27, 29–33, and 34–39 all consist of long sequences of rising pitch capped by a single concluding cadence; line 28 recalls line 1. The intonational patterns create semantic juxtapositions paralleling the rhythmic pitch similarities in the same way that the meter creates juxtapositions based on rhythmic parallels of word accent. The interaction between two rhythmic movements, the metrical and the syntactic-intonational, has consequences for the semantic structure of the poem. Many more words are foregrounded by the combined effect of meter and intonation than would have been by meter alone.

Since we have already noted briefly the symbolic universe in which "The Golden Fleece" takes place, we can now examine the nature of the words which are given additional emphasis by the new typographical structure in Part II. Some of these words are the same nouns which were foregrounded in Part I or are nouns which serve similar functions, representing the ideal (e.g., *v efir*—line 14; *sharom*—line 34; *runo*—line 37; *zolotoe*—line 38), its reflection (e.g., *v rubinakh*—lines 20, 22; *Vino*—line 29; *pozharom*—line 32), or its absence (e.g., *stradany*—line 5). However, many of the emphasized words are verbs. Part II deals specifically with man's efforts to regain the ideals, as represented by the voyage of the argonauts and the ship Argo to recover the golden fleece, which Bely here, as before, identifies with the sun. This action, which must be taken by man to recover the ideal, is at the heart of the poem; for this reason the verbs which announce and evoke this action must not be "lost" and therefore they are foregrounded by the typographical structure (e.g., *vnimayte*—line 4; *nadevyate*—line 6; *vzyvaet*—line 10; *trubya*—line 17; *pylaet*—line 31; *vyplyvaet*—line 36; *nesyas*—line 43; *nastigaet*—line 46). A number of the emphasized nouns and adjectives also evoke this flight to the sun (e.g., *otletany*—line 2; *v efir*—line 14; *vershinakh*—line 24; *krylami*—line 26; *krylaty*—line 45). The set of emphasized words crystallizes around two "protagonists" the old argonaut (*starik argonavt*—line 9) and the ship Argus (*nash Argo*—lines 25 and 26), both of which are also foregrounded by the typographical structure.

Within the Symbolist philosophical system the role of recovery, the winged flight to ideal truth, is the domain of the poet—and both *nash Argo* and *starik argonavt* suggest that role. Furthermore, the verb *trubit* and the noun *truba* are isolated three times in the first three stanzas (lines 3, 11, and 17). We must recall here the classical image of the horn, the identification of music with poetry, as well as the crucial role of music in Symbolist philosophy. The horn also appears as the intermediary between man and the ideal in a poem by Vyacheslav Ivanov, "Alpine Horn" ("Alpiysky rog"), written two years earlier than Bely's:

Nature is a symbol—like this
   horn. She
Sounds for an echo. And the echo
   is—God.

(Priroda—simvol, kak sey
   rog. Ona
Zvuchit dlya otzvuka. I
   otzvuk—Bog.) [9]

The two parts of the poem "The Golden Fleece" combine to form a new myth based on the already existing myth of the argonauts: a myth in which certain symbols have been projected to embody (1) ideal, divine truth, (2) the emptiness of the world without this truth, (3) the reflections of the ideal upon earth, and (4) the efforts of heroic men to reach the ideal, to fly to the heights. Words representing these elements, words made concrete as symbols, are thrust before us by the new typography.

In the years 1929 to 1931 Bely returned to his youthful collection *Gold in Azure* (in which "The Golden Fleece" is included) with the aim of revising and perfecting certain of the poems for an edition of his selected poetry. Most of the revisions were quite drastic, so that readers would be inclined to regard the works as new poems on old themes. Bely, however, felt that he was only ridding the early versions of unnecessary words, liberating the potentials within the poems while preserving their essential ideas, imagery, and sounds: "in each stanza of the old text there are a couple of unnecessary words: and so: stanza by stanza, you change the ones sticking out of the structure: the poem began to look like an adaptation; but this is not so: a place was given to freeing the potential existing in me as a youth: different colors, different words, different modulations, but the meaning, the *sujet,* the light of the colors, the resonance of the shades are the same" ("Zovy," p. 93).

The revision of "The Golden Fleece" follows rather closely the directions indicated by Bely. The extra words, those with merely connective or transitional function, are eliminated. In the compressed version of the poem almost every word is deserving of special semantic emphasis, so compact is the mythical and symbolic structure:

Argonavty

```
 1   Doroga
     Dolga . . .
     I, prostyorshie strogo
     Roga
 5   Zolotye,—
               —Pod oblako—
                          —V dymy sedye
                          Trubyat—
                                    —Argonavty,—
10   Stav
     S nardami:
```

    —"Dlani
    Svoi prostirayte
    Ognyu!
15   —I—iz solnechnoy tkani
    Svoyu nadevayte
    Bronyu!"
  I dva raza—
    —Roga—
20   —Progovorili
      Strogo . . .
  Voda—
  Melk
  Almaza—
25   —I—Bleski
      Chervontsa
26 I lal,
  Nesterpimy
  Dlya glaza—
30   —Stousy,—
    Stonosy,—
    Lyot rusye
    Rosy—
      —Disk
35   Solntsa—
        —V timpannye
        Treski
        I—
        V vizg . . .
40 Argo,—
  V veter
  Natyagivaya—
    —Parus
    Bledno perlovy,
45 I—
    —Vzdragivaya
    V biryuzovy efir—
    —Kuzov
    Klonit . . .
50 Vsyo—
  Minet . . .
  Shar—
  Tonet . . .
  Zhar—
55 Stynet.
56 I nebo

```
         V rubinakh
         Nad nami;
         I—
  60     —V siny efir
           Uletaya—
                 —Uzhe
             Nad orlami—
                      —Nash Argo,
  65                  Nash Argo,—
                             —Nash
                             Argo—
         Zabil—
             —Zolotymi
  70         Krylami.        (Poetry, pp. 510–12)
```

The above graphical arrangement, in which each line consists of a single word or, at most, of two words, forces the reader to pause after virtually every substantive and verb in the poem. Although the poem is again in free amphibrachs (with some deviations), the sense of the meter is effectively dominated by the typography; the poem is not likely to be read as metrical and no artificial intonation will be induced by the meter. At the same time the usual kind of syntactico-semantic segmentation is also suppressed. The syntagms are so concise that we read them as independent units, almost as individual nominal sentences.[10] We are reminded here of Tynyanov's observations about the unity and compactness of verse series and about the dynamization of the utterance produced by the sharp dichotomy between the verse articulation as indicated by the form and the underlying prose articulation.[11] But the dominant verse structure here is actually no longer the metrical structure, but rather the very short typographical verse lines themselves. These are the compact units of the verse series; they displace the old metrical verses. In fact, the verses now first strike us visually; they define themselves before our eyes, and only then in our ears.

The importance of the visual aspects of the rhythm to Bely is reflected in the following description of Bely at work as given by his wife K. N. Bugaeva: "He used to say that when the poem was not yet written down and the eye could not scan over it line by line, as if over its own kind of musical notation, it was impossible to say anything about the poem. . . . He would patiently copy down the very same poem using various line arrangements, and then bring them to me. And he didn't read them first, rather he spread them out in front of me on the table and said: 'Look them over! Which one will *sound* best?' " [12]

In a structure in which short syntagms are isolated from one another typographically the normal prose syntax is undermined, so that the narrative is dominated instead by associations among the individual independent verses. What dominates, both visually and audibly, is the parallel series of short pulses rather than the continuum of the sentence or of the meter. The words which are emphasized in the 1929 version of "The Golden Fleece" are emblematic of the very same four elements of the myth noted in our discussion of the 1903 version. The words which indicate the brilliance and the overwhelming magnitude of the divine truth are foregrounded by their isolation on individual lines (*Voda*—line 22; *Melk*—line 23; *Almaza*—line 24; *Bleski*—line 25; *chervontsa*—line 26; *lal*—line 27; *Nesterpimy*—line 28; *Stousy*—line 30; *Stonosy*—line 31; *Solntsa*—line 35; *timpannye*—line 36; *treski*—line 37; *vizg*—line 39), as are the words which represent the emptiness of the world without this truth, (*Pod oblako*—line 6; *v dymy sedye*—line 7; *tonet*—line 53; *stynet*—line 55). The ideal is reflected upon the earth in the standard (*stav*—line 10) and in the sunset (*Ognyu*—line 14; *rusye*—line 32; *Zhar*—line 54; *V rubinakh*—line 57). The efforts of the heroes to fly to the heights are again evoked by verbs, especially imperatives and active participles (*prostyorshie strogo*—line 3; *Trubyat*—line 8; *prostirayte*—line 13; *nadevayte*—line 16; *progovorili*—line 20; *natyagivaya*—line 42; *Vzdragivaya*—line 46; *Uletaya*—line 61; *Zabil*—line 68). Other isolated elements reinforce the concepts of distance (*Doroga*—line 1; *Dolga*—line 2) and height (*efir*—line 60; *Nad nami*—line 58), and the idea of flight through the air or water (*V veter*—line 41; *Parus*—line 43; *Uletaya*—line 61; *Nad orlami*—line 63; *Krylami*—line 70). The heroes are again made prominent in the title and in line 9 (*Argonavty*), and their vessel is evoked in line 40 (*Argo*), line 43 (*Parus*), line 48 (*Kuzov*), and lines 64–67 (*Nash Argo*). The separation of *Nash Argo* into two lines even further emphasizes the emotional importance of this seeker for truth. The connection of the Argonauts with music and poetry is brought forward in lines 4 (*Roga*) and 8 (*Trubyat*). Thus, the essential elements of the original poem and only those elements are retained by Bely in the 1929 version. The place of the normal narrative connections is taken by visual chains of words.

In *Argonavty,* the rhythm based on longitudinal series of short syntagmatic pulses reflects the emblematic quality of the poem. The work approaches being a motto for the poetic circle of Bely's youth. With its emphasis on visual juxtapositions rather than metrical or syntactic connections, it becomes less of a story and more of an icon. Thus, in treating the theme of the Argonauts, Bely moves from reliance on traditional form in Part I of "The Golden Fleece," to the use of intonational parallels to create additional foregrounding in Part II, and finally to a greater reliance on concrete visual relationships in the 1929 version. Bely's own evolution in the use of typography in verse thus mirrors and in some aspects anticipates developments in this century, as traditional forms have given way to the intonational rhythms of free verse and the visual-aural effects of concrete poetry.

NOTES

1. Andrey Bely, "Zovy vremyon," *Novy Zhurnal,* no. 102 (1971): 95. Henceforth cited in the text as "Zovy." Neither the introduction nor the planned 1931 edition of *Zovy vremyon* was published in the Soviet Union.

2. Viktor Zhirmunsky, *Vvedenie v metriku* Voprosy poetiki VI (Leningrad: Academia, 1925), p. 225.

3. This regular pattern is easily verified in readings of traditional verse by native Russians. The rising and falling can even become an actual melodic marker of verse language, as in the declamatory style of Iosif Brodsky.

4. Yury Tynyanov, *Problema stikhotvornogo yazyka: stati* (Moscow: Sovetsky pisatel, 1965), pp. 53–57, 67–68.

5. Ferdinand de Saussure, *Course in General Linguistics* (New York: Philosophical Library, 1959), p. 125.

6. V. Vinogradov, "Ponyatie sintagmy v sintaksise russkogo yazyka," *Voprosy sintaksisa sovremennogo russkogo yazyka* (Moscow: Gos. uchebno-ped. izdat. Ministerstva Prosveshcheniya RSFSR, 1950): 210–11.

7. Elena Bryzgunova, *Prakticheskaya fonetika i intonatsiya russkogo yazyka* (Moscow: Izdat. Moskovskogo Universiteta, 1963), pp. 193–94.

8. Ibid., pp. 223–36.

9. Vyacheslav Ivanov, *Kormchiya zvezdy: Kniga liriki* (St. Petersburg, 1903; Ann Arbor, Mich.: University Microfilms, 1967), pp. 178–79.

10. When this poem is read out loud, the reader is unsure of the subsequent metrical rhythm, as well as of the syntax of the sentence which

is developing. This results in a tendency to treat each line as an independent unit and to give it level or falling intonation. This was verified in a number of trials with different readers.

11. Tynyanov, *Problema stikhotvornogo yazyka,* pp. 67–68.

12. Klavdiya Bugaeva, "Stixi. ob Andree Belom," *Novy Zhurnal,* no. 102 (1971): 107–8.

GERALD JANECEK

RHYTHM IN PROSE:
THE SPECIAL CASE OF BELY

The thorny question of the rhythmic principle underlying standard well-written prose has recently tended to find an answer in colonometry, an idea first put forth by Boris Tomashevsky.[1] However, the colonometric theory largely postdates Bely's activities and in fact was enunciated partly as a reaction to Bely's views on rhythm, which follow a direction that is close to traditional metrics. The subject of this study is the nature of those views and the practice of Bely's artistic prose linked to those theories.

Bely's attitude is clearly stated in his article "On Artistic Prose."[2] There he said: "Between poetry and artistic prose there is no boundary; . . . measure has characterized good prose; and in the best prosaists this measure approaches a definite measure, called meter; internal measuredness ('rhythm' or 'concord') characterizes good prose" (p. 49).

To substantiate this view, Bely compares artistic prose to the ancient Greek hexameter of the Homeric type, which was "in essence rhythmized prose," and in its dactylo-trochaic form was used for conveying past events in a "majestically slow fluency" (p. 51). What he admires is the ability of hexameter to be rhythmic and plastic at the same time and therefore both natural and elevated. This is in contrast to the more modern, ossified metric schemes. The limitations of traditional metrics resulted, in Bely's view, in the reappearance of the ancient hexameter in the new rhythmic prose: "The concept of rhythmic prose is born in us, as in the form of poetic meters which have become complicated, are theoretically not permissible, are partly implemented already, but are not taken into consideration by the narrow framework of our metric scheme" (p. 51). In the realm of poetry he has in mind the appearance of free verse, which approaches a synthesis between poetry and prose from the side of poetry rather than from the side of prose. In essence, Bely argues, it is only the prohibition against mixing dactyls and trochees or anapests and iambs that separates the two media, and this prohibition is artificial.

Bely then proceeds to illustrate the presence of these principles of rhythmic organization in a number of examples from Pushkin and Gogol. The basic idea is to scan the passage of prose as you would a poem, placing line divisions at logical pausing places and identifying the passage as either dactylo-trochaic or anapesto-iambic, depending on whether the majority of lines begin with either stressed or unstressed syllables. Thus

$$\cup \quad \text{,l} \; \cup \; \text{,l} \; \cup \quad \text{,l} \quad \cup \; \cup \quad \text{, l} \cup \cup \text{, l} \cup \cup$$
Pismo tvoyo menya chrezvychayno uteshilo (p. 52)

is anapesto-iambic with two extra end syllables and the line

$$\text{, } \; \cup \text{l , } \cup \quad \cup \; \text{l } \quad \text{, } \quad \cup \; \cup \text{l, } \qquad \cup \text{l ,}$$
Svezhy veter chut - chut naveval s Dnepra (p. 53)

is dactylo-trochaic. Obviously not all passages of well-written prose fit Bely's theories neatly, and he is forced to make a variety of accommodations. Bely resorts to omitting stresses or adding stresses to syllables, and filling in initial "missing" syllables (he terms this a pause "obuslovlennaya pustym promezhutkom," p. 52) or ignoring extra initial syllables (terming them an anacrusis). The following example given by Bely illustrates three such accommodations: the extra initial syllable, the lack of stress on *tvoí* and the extra stress on *pred-polozheniya:*

$$\cup \; \text{l } \; \cup \quad \text{,l } \cup \cup \text{ , l } \cup \; \cup \quad \text{, l } \cup \cup \text{ ,l } \cup \; \cup$$
Kak smeshny tvoi vechnyya predpolozheniya. (p. 52)

It might be pointed out, however, that with such accommodations permitted, virtually every passage of any prose at all can be made to fit into a dactylo-trochaic or anapesto-iambic pattern.

The only situation Bely does not condone is what he calls a *tolchok* or *ukhab,* that is, two stresses in a row not separated by an unstressed syllable. From Bely's point of view, the problem with a *tolchok* is that it reverses the rhythm. This is allegedly bad when it occurs without reason or artistic purpose. On the other hand, when used for a specific effect—e.g., to create a desired pause or emphasis—such *tolchki* are not only permitted but contribute to the whole rhythmic structure.

Later in his life, no doubt under the influence of the adverse criticism of theoreticians like Tomashevsky, Bely removed most of the arbitrary elements from his analytical methods, specifically rejecting some of his previous ideas.[3] In *Gogol's Craft* he puts the word boundary in position as the decisive pattern formant, thus "defining each word as an indivisible prose foot" (p. 219) and eliminating the need for extra stresses to approximate a hexametric pattern. Any interstress interval is permitted and all traditional metric feet can come into play, the question being one of predominance rather than exclusiveness. This liberalization of view led to an appreciation of the great complexity of the rhythmic situation in a writer such as Gogol. As Bely notes, "the ear notices a vague melody here not reducible to any meter; yet it is nevertheless organized somehow" (p. 222).

A scansionlike approach, based on Bely's later one, with word boundary as the main determining factor and the arbitrary factors removed, provides a convenient tool for viewing some of the characteristic features of Bely's metrically inclined prose. Such a methodology is not unlike that used in part by other investigators, but it is not meant to be a complete system for analyzing all the rhythmic features of artistic prose.[4] An outline of this methodology follows.

In Russian the syllable is rhythmically categorized on the basis of whether it does or does not carry a stress. The existence of an intermediate category between "full-stress" and "unstress" has been recognized.[5] This intermediate category, called "half-stress" (*pobochnoe udarenie*), presents a problem for analysis because it is not entirely defined as to membership.[6] One may avoid this difficulty to some extent by operating bimodally (stressed/unstressed), provided a rationale for consistently dealing with half-stressed syllables is given. The rationale I have used is that a half-stressed syllable is treated as unstressed unless such other factors as semantic emphasis, stress juxtaposition, word order, or punctuation provide a reason for considering it stressed.

Once all the syllables of a given text have been assigned to either the stressed or unstressed category one can arrive at the percentage frequency of each type of interstress interval.

The next step is to establish the word boundaries. Here we are not interested in typographical word units but in rhythmic ones—namely, all the syllables organized under a single main stress. Decisions for enclitics and proclitics are clear-cut. Only pronouns cause any difficulty and then only in the relatively infrequent situation where the pronoun is isolated or placed in an abnormal position, in which case it is given a full stress because the environment gives the pronoun more than normal emphasis. In situations where the pronoun is not emphasized, it is included in the word-unit to which it is most closely bound syntactically or semantically. Cases not belonging to either of these groups will ordinarily be few and must be studied individually. Once word boundaries have been established, each word can then be assigned to a category according to the number of syllables and place of stress in the word. Once all words have been placed in their proper pattern groups, one can compute the number and percent frequency of each individual pattern, and the number and percent frequency of each group of patterns of the same number of syllables, i.e., two-syllable patterns, three-syllable patterns, etc. The results can then be compared in percentage form with averages for artistic prose or for other types of prose.[7]

Because the usual guidepost for establishing a meter, the verse line, is absent, the only factor possibly equivalent to a line is the sentence or clause. Therefore, the beginning and ending patterns of sentences are more important than the intermediate ones. But the meter-establishing opening pattern of a sentence is soon obliterated by the usual variety of patterns within the sentence and by the sentence's length. Nevertheless, opening and closing patterns, whether or not continued in the sentence, create a certain rhythmic effect when several sentences in a row begin or end with the same pattern, and this occurrence should be noted.

If one's purpose is to ferret out quasi-metrical rhythms, these are likely to be evidenced by higher-than-normal frequency of a given interstress interval, word pattern group, or individual word pattern. In prose, even when it is rhythmically very regular, there is frequently little support for distinguishing between iamb and trochee, or dactyl, amphibrach, and anapest; meters are usually reduced to being either binary or ternary.

TABLE 1
(Results in percent)

Inter-stress Intervals	Artistic Prose[8]	First[9]	Second[10]	Third[11]	Fourth[12]	Silver Dove[13]	Petersburg (1916)[14]	Petersburg (1922)[15]	Kotik Letaev[16]	Baptized China-man[17]	Moscow[18]	Masks[19]
1. 0	6	5	5	5	9	11	7	7	3	8	7	7
2. 1	33	19	28	18	22	26	18	16	15	9	8	5
3. 2	36	46	33	38	51	36	48	52	53	78	81	80
4. 3	16	20	22	28	11	17	13	11	13	1	0	0
5. 4	7	7	9	7	5	7	13	14	15	1	1	1
6. 5	2	1	2	3	0	2	1	1	1	3	2	6
Word Patterns												
7. ´	7	4	6	4	7	6	6	7	5	9	11	6
8. ˘´	16	17	15	15	16	16	14	11	18	19	22	18
9. ´˘	17	14	18	13	16	20	10	13	7	14	10	11
10. ˘´˘	6	7	5	6	9	9	10	9	11	11	6	14
11. ˘˘´	17	21	15	16	18	14	14	14	10	13	15	17
12. ´˘˘	8	9	8	6	10	9	11	10	7	7	7	3
13. ˘˘˘´	1	1	0	1	1	2	1	0	0	0	0	0
14. ˘´˘˘	6	6	8	8	8	7	7	9	11	9	14	12
15. ˘˘´˘	10	16	9	11	10	9	16	14	13	9	6	9
16. ˘˘´˘	2	3	1	2	1	1	1	1	1	1	0	0

To be perfectly thorough in our compilation of statistics would be a monumental task involving the scansion and analysis of all of Bely's major prose works. Some day, no doubt with the help of computers and a sizable staff, this may be done; but meanwhile this study will have to limit itself to rather small, representative samples. Excerpts of 200–300 words which seem typical for the works in which they occur have been chosen and the outlined methodology has been applied to them. The works in question include each of the four *Symphonies, The Silver Dove, Petersburg* (1916), *Petersburg* (1922), *Kotik Letaev, The Baptized Chinaman, Moscow,* and *Masks.*

The data have been pared down to the most vital information: the interstress intervals of 0–5, and the word patterns of 1–4 syllables. The excluded data would have importance only if the samples were larger. Frequency-of-occurrence results have been omitted in favor of percentage results, since the latter figures yield the significant information. Table 1 shows in percentages the resultant interval and word pattern data for the major prose arranged in chronological order.

In the overall view, the most dramatic results are to be seen in the interval data (rows 1–6). The figures for ternary patterning (row 3) show a striking rise from left to right—that is, they go from figures for the early works that are nearly normal or only somewhat above normal, to very high percentages in the later novels. Bely's prose becomes in fact more and more ternary in its rhythm, until in the last novels it is almost purely ternary. To compensate for the high ternary values, the binary intervals (rows 2 and 4) are markedly reduced in number as compared to their normal frequency.

The word pattern data (rows 7–16) are much less striking, though nonetheless interesting for comparison with the interval data. The general picture is one of not much deviation from the normal frequency figures. Most results are within several percentage points of the norms, and only one figure is as much as 10 percent from the norm (row 9 for *Kotik Letaev*). The pattern group data (not given) show similar results. Further analysis requires more detailed inspection of the text and data of each individual sample.

The four *Symphonies* can be grouped together as a ground-breaking series of initial experiments in poetic prose. But each is in its own way unique and distinct from the others, as is reflected in the results of our rhythmic data. The excerpts from the *First Symphony* show a fairly strong ternary tendency (a high value for row 3 with a corresponding low value in row 2), but the *Second* and *Third Symphonies* do not. They are, in fact, quite close to normal prose rhythmically, except for a shift, more pronounced in the *Third* than in the *Second,* from the one-syllable interval (row 2) to the three-syllable interval (row 4). This is the equivalent of the substitution of a pyrrhic foot in a binary meter and, while it lightens the movement, it does not essentially change the basic rhythmic profile. The *Fourth Symphony* is, however, even more pronouncedly ternary than the *First,* with a row 3 of 51 percent (15 percent above normal) and a more marked drop in the binary intervals (rows 2 and 4).

It must be admitted, though, that these data do not adequately give the entire picture. Upon inspection of the samples, one must agree to some extent with Szilard that "in the first three *Symphonies* metrization appears only when a musical theme enters; in the remaining instances the prose is not metrized."[20] An example of this metrization from the *First Symphony* is the following passage in which the motifs of the white lily and red satin are rhythmically underlined by the metrical patterning:

> 2. I uzh ne pela ona, korolevna —
>
> belaya liliya na krasnom atlase! . . .
>
> 3. Belaya liliya! . . . (p. 53)

Often meter is combined, as it is here, with various forms of sound patterning as well. All this serves, of course, to highlight the so-called musical themes of the *Symphonies*—that is, the important verbal motifs.

Such is not always the case, however; there are passages that are metrized but not thematically important, and important motifs that are not metrized. Furthermore the meters are often not of the same type; and binary, ternary, and quaternary meters may be mixed. There are likely to be short stretches of a variety of meters. Even in the above example you have dactyls alternating with amphibrachs.

Of course, as ternary patterning becomes more predominant, as in the *Fourth Symphony,* the highlighting effect of the ternary patterns is somewhat diminished. Even so, when long passages of

regular rhythm occur, particularly in combination with sound
patterning and syntactic parallelism, the effect is very strong, as
this example from the *Fourth Symphony* shows:

Znakómaya táyna v dúshe proletála nezhdánno. Znakómye

vópli v dalí razryvális prizývno. Znakómaya táyna

dúshe proplyvála nezhdánno. (p. 7)

On the other hand, if ternary patterning becomes the norm, then a
sudden instance of binary rhythm can be striking, as in this
example:

Vsyó kruzhílos pred ním blédnym víkhrem—snézhnym víkhrem. (p. 8)

As Bely has pointed out, such a *tolchok* can, if used skillfully, be
an effective device; but he has not made much of it at this early
stage.

The excerpt from *The Silver Dove*, weighted if anything on the
rhythmic side of what would be average for that novel, shows practically no deviation from normal prose in our computations. Its
palpable rhythmic interest lies not in a direction that would be
revealed by the data but in another direction. While it is a novel of
varying styles, the single stylistic feature most typical of *The Silver
Dove* is syntactic parallelism and its variant, chiasmus. Chiasti-
cally structured sentences are more frequent in *The Silver Dove*
than in all the other novels combined, while parallelism itself is
as a whole more prevalent in it than chiasmus.[21] Many of the
other stylistic features are closely related to the predominance of
parallelism, because parallelism generates a certain rhythmic
patterning and often sound repetition.

In fact, virtually all of the rhythmic patterning in *The Silver
Dove* is a direct result of syntactic parallelism and word repetition.
The rhythm is, as a result, complex and shifting. An instance of
this from the sample is:

> *zheleznuyu svoyu vystavit kryshu—*
> ne kryshu vovse:
> *zelyonuyu svoyu vystavit kiku*
> gordaya moloditsa; . . . (p. 10)

The rhythm of the portions italicized by me is exactly the same
(‿⌣‿‿⌣‿⌣‿‿⌣‿⌣‿‿) but of a complex, nonmetrical sort, and it is not
repeated elsewhere. Although rigid patterning could develop from
such repetitions, as it does in the example from the *Fourth Symphony*, Bely in *The Silver Dove* appears to be deliberately avoiding rhythmic patterning which would be independent of syntactic
parallelism and word repetition. He thus is rather conservative
and stays fairly well within the limits that Gogol maintained.

Petersburg is the one work considered which has received a
rhythmic analysis of the present sort; it appears in the classic
study by Ivanov-Razumnik.[22] In it he compares the two main redactions of the novel (1916 and 1922) and puts forward several observations, the chief of which is that Bely's revisions shifted the
rhythmic impulse from anapestic to amphibrachic. Since this is a
substantive point, I decided to check Ivanov-Razumnik's results
and methods against my own by analyzing the same passages. The
data in the table were drawn from the entire section "Kareta
proletela v tuman," in which Ivanov-Razumnik found the example
he chose to scan in the first part of his analysis. While Ivanov-
Razumnik's comparison of the two redactions leads him to note
the marked difference mentioned above, my data reveal practically
no difference between them except for the abbreviation of the text
by one-third. The reason for this variance in results is simple
enough: Ivanov-Razumnik considers the "line"-beginning as the
decisive factor, which overrides the word boundary as in verse
metrics, while I insist on the importance of the word boundary in
prose. Thus for him, the passage (with his scansion)

$$\smile \quad \smile \,\prime| \smile \quad \smile \quad\prime \quad| \smile \quad \smile \quad\prime|\smile$$
i glyadel na prospekt sterto-serym

$$\smile \quad\prime \quad| \quad\smile \quad \smile \,\prime|\smile \quad \smile \quad\prime|$$
litsom; tsirkuliroval on

$$\smile \quad\smile \,\prime| \quad\smile \qquad \smile \quad\prime|\smile$$
v beskonechnost prospektov (1916)

is anapestic but

$$\smile \quad\prime \quad\smile| \quad\smile \quad \smile \quad\prime \qquad \smile|\smile \quad\prime \,\smile|\smile$$
glyadel na prospekt; tsirkuliroval

$$\prime \qquad\smile|\smile \,\prime \quad\smile \quad\smile|\smile \quad\smile \,\prime \quad\smile$$
on v beskonechnost prospektov, (1922)

is amphibrachic.[23] The basis for this significant change is the mere
excision of the initial "i" (the removal of *sterto-serym litsom* does

not change the rhythmic pulse). One might reasonably ask whether
this was sufficient to do such violence to word boundaries as
tsir-kuliro-val and to override even a semicolon. In my opinion, it
is not. A semicolon is surely a weighty punctuation mark and in
Bely's system of punctuation it is the closest equivalent to a line-
end in verse.[24] Thus we have, at most

$$\cup\ \prime\ \ \cup|\ \ \cup\ \ \prime$$
gyadel na prospekt;
$$\cup\ \ \cup\ ,|\cup\ \cup\ \prime\ |\ \ \cup\ \ \cup\ ,|\ \cup\ \ \ \ \cup\ \ \prime\ |\cup$$
tsirkuliroval on v beskonechnost prospektov,

a short line of amphibrachs and a long one of anapests.

Ivanov-Razumnik's next step is to choose a whole page elsewhere from the 1916 redaction and compare it to the 1922 version.
He reports a shift from 58 percent anapestic feet (1–2 percent
amphibrachic) to 41 percent amphibrachic (38 percent anapestic).
As can be seen from the above example, the dropping of one syllable
would cause the conversion of a passage from pure anapest to pure
amphibrachic, so that these results are not surprising. Ivanov-
Razumnik's results with this larger sample support his result for
the shorter excerpt; similarly, our analysis of the second sample
yielded results close to those of the excerpt used for Table 1 and
these therefore have not been given.

While Ivanov-Razumnik's conclusions are, for the reasons given,
surely overstated, his approach to the question is like Bely's own
approach, as illustrated by "On Artistic Prose," which dates from
1919, close to the time when Bely was revising *Petersburg.* Bely
would concur on the importance given to line-beginnings, though
certainly not on ignoring a semicolon. So it is fairly certain that
Ivanov-Razumnik has put his finger on part of what Bely was
trying to do to the rhythm by his revisions; and it must be con-
fessed that the real differences between the two redactions are not
well revealed in my table of data. Further analysis is needed.

An inspection of line-beginnings does indeed reveal a shift from
an opening of $\cup\cup\prime$. . . to a greater number of openings of $\cup\prime$. . . .
This may or may not make the rhythm amphibrachic, but it cer-
tainly relieves the monotony of so many lines beginning in $\cup\cup\prime$.
The move from "heavy" anapests to "light" amphibrachs results
therefore in greater rhythmic variety, which, together with the
dropping of syllables and the fact that Russian stress entropy is
toward the middle of the word (compare the norms for row 11 with

rows 10 and 12), lessens the ponderousness of the style. This trend toward normal prose is reflected in Table 1 by the word pattern data (rows 7–16) in which three-fourths of the percentages changed to be closer to the norm (rows 7, 9, 10, 12, 14, 15). Noteworthy is the fact that the amphibrach pattern (row 11) remained unchanged in this sample and was not higher than normal in the 1922 edition; and the third paeon (row 15), which was abnormally high in *Petersburg* (1916), was decreased in both samples (in the table 16 percent to 14 percent; in the other sample 18 percent to 10 percent), thus also lessening the anapestic patterning. A look at row 3 will, however, discount the conclusion that the second edition is more like normal prose than the first edition: there is a marked rise in the interval of two unstressed syllables. The second edition may be "less anapestic," but it is more ternary.

Rather than concluding with Ivanov-Razumnik that Bely changed the rhythm of *Petersburg* from anapestic to amphibrachic, I would prefer to conclude that while he intensified the ternary character of the text, he worked in other ways to remove much of the monotony and ponderousness of the 1916 edition by more closely approximating the rhythmic variety of normal artistic prose. This revision seems appropriate, since the heavy style of the earlier version runs counter to the tension and rapid forward motion of the plot. The revisions of *Petersburg* which resulted in the 1922 edition came not long after the composition of *Kotik Letaev* and seem to derive from the same frame of mind in matters of rhythm, and to be the product of Bely's definitive resolution of the problem of how to handle rhythm in poetic prose. In this sense, they are the twin apices of the whole course of experimentation undertaken by Bely.

Perhaps the most significant discovery in my dissertation investigation was that the structural devices used in *Kotik Letaev,* of which rhythmic patterning is one, were composed in a total verbal edifice in which patterns of sound, rhythm, image, and theme are thoroughly and intimately linked to each other. This is true of *Kotik Letaev* more than any other of the prose works in our corpus. Many particular instances of this interrelationship are cited in the dissertation, and so to save space, I will limit myself here to one brief example taken from the data sample.

The section *"Obrazovane soznaniya"* establishes a strong anapestic tendency, leading away from a certain amount of initial ambiguity toward clear predominance of the anapest pattern in the middle and end, where long series of pure or nearly pure anapests are to be found. A progression of associations based on the sound *m*, beginning on page 19 and continuing into the next section, links *mir, mysli, mif, materik, more, mysl-kovcheg,* and finally *mat* via alliteration and homoeoteleuton ("*materikami, moryami*" and "*morey: 'Materey'* ") forming a complex of images related as much by sound as by meaning. That Bely chose to base this relationship on one of the first sounds an infant can pronounce is singularly appropriate to the age of the child in the narrative. These associative equations appear in an increasingly rhythmic garb. And the line "V nas miry—morey: *'Materey,'* " which opens the next section, is, as it were, the emergence from initial rhythmic ambiguity of the pure anapest word *matérey,* a conclusive rhythmico-sonic deduction emphatically arrived at. The semantic aspects of the deduction are supported by, indeed based on, the rhythmico-sonic aspects.

Although the data sample is somewhat more anapestic than is typical, the rhythm of *Kotik Letaev* is *not* characterized by especial regularity. Segments of uniform (or metrical) rhythm are relatively rare and brief. The overall impression is one of rhythmicality, combined with flexibility and variety, ranging from practically normal prose to fairly lengthy inserted "poems." *Kotik Letaev* avoids the monotony found in *Petersburg* (1916) by careful modulation of rhythmic components to produce a situation in which a wide variety of regular rhythmic patterns can emerge when an effect is wanted, but in which no single pattern controls the field, so to speak. The *Symphonies* are, in this respect, rather similar, the difference being that in *Kotik Letaev* Bely has worked out the rhythmic structure, from its smallest to its largest units, with a thoroughness, richness of invention, and appropriateness to the subject that are not to be found in such degree in the earlier writings.[25]

It is tempting to conclude that in the prose of *Kotik Letaev* Bely has found a modern solution to the rhythmic question of how to create a viable large work in high style (epos). Metrical verse now seems too confining, while free verse is too flaccid to support a large form. Bely's rhythmic prose is entirely adequate to the task, having the advantages of both metrical and free verse, and of rhythmically unmarked prose.

In a way the last three novels form a set because their rhythmic profiles are much the same: the interval of two unstressed syllables (row 3) shoots up 20 percent to hover in the vicinity of 80 percent, thus making the ternary impulse virtually exclusive. So the flexibility and variety of *Kotik Letaev* have gone by the board even for its sequel *The Baptized Chinaman*. It appears, due to the similarity of the last novels, that an individual discussion of each is not necessary. Commentary on *The Baptized Chinaman* will, therefore, be omitted in favor of *Moscow* with the understanding that the comments apply to both novels.

The markedly ternary patterning of *Moscow* is reflected mainly in the row 3 value of 81 percent. In fact, however, the situation is even more pronounced than this if you take into account the 2 percent of row 9, in essence a ternary pattern with a stress missing, and also note that the figures in rows 1 and 2 result from the addition of a stress into the ternary pattern, producing the series ‚‿‿‶‿‚‿‿‚ or ‚‿‿‚‿‚‶‚‿‿‚ (there is also an instance of ‚‚‿‿‚‿‚‚‿‚‚‿‚‚‿‚ ‚‿‚‚‿‿‚). With these metrically acceptable variations added to the total, only 2 percent of the text (4 cases) is not in good ternary meter, and 98 percent is. It is not hard to find sizable passages that are 100 percent ternary.

This pattern tends to produce a monotonous impression, but we should note that within the regularity of rhythmic pulse Bely does the utmost to produce variety. This is reflected in the word pattern data (rows 7–16), which show a situation not far from the norms. The three-syllable patterns are not at all predominant; in fact they are a bit below normal, and the two-syllable patterns are also normal. What this indicates is that the placement of word boundaries is made to vary as in normal artistic prose and not to be regular to any great extent. The line lengths and opening patterns are also greatly varied. The monotony of the ternary pattern is thereby relieved as much as possible in the context.

To maintain the regular pulse, several times on the average page in *Moscow* Bely resorts to a standard "poetic license" that is worth singling out—namely, the use of archaic morphological forms, which have the result of either adding or subtracting a syllable. The most frequent of such instances involve the use of the extended feminine instrumental noun and adjective ending in *–oyu;* the neuter abstract noun ending in *–ane* instead of *–anie* in all declined forms; the long verbal reflexive (past tense) *–alisya, –alasya, –alosya;* and verbal adverb *–ayasya.* Virtually all such instances have the function of maintaining the ternary rhythm when it would have been broken by use of the normal form. These archaic forms do not apparently have a stylistic function, since they freely alternate with the normal forms in equivalent stylistic contexts, rhythmic regularity being the only evident motivation for their presence. This practice occurs throughout Bely's prose, but is more common in *Moscow* than elsewhere.

One feature which distinguishes *Masks* from the other two late novels is the relative shortness of its "lines."[26] Throughout Bely's prose, line lengths tend to vary greatly, with lines of only a few syllables freely intermixed with long lines of twenty, thirty, or more syllables. In *Masks,* however, by the heavy use of line-breaking types of punctuation, Bely produces a much greater number of short lines than had been his usual practice up to this time. The result is a rather tortured, halting style, but one in which the predominant ternary rhythm is somewhat hidden by the fragmentation.

One peculiarity regarding Bely and his introduction to *Masks* deserves some comment. There he states, "My prose is not prose at all; it is a poem in verse (anapest)." While *Masks* is clearly ternary, if our sample is in any way representative, it is certainly not anapestic. The anapestic word pattern (row 12) is well *below* normal; the sum of all patterns with anapestic beginnings (rows 12 and 15, and for the pattern $\smile\smile\prime\smile\smile$, not given in Table 1) is only 15 percent, also below normal; and only 16 percent of the lines begin anapestically ($\smile\smile\prime$. . .) as compared with 47 percent amphibrach ($\smile\prime$ . . .) and 31 percent on the downbeat ($\prime$ . . .). An analysis of this sort shows that the later novels are, if anything, more dactylo-trochaic than normal.[27] Only the middle novels (*Petersburg,* 1916 and 1922, and *Kotik Letaev*) and in particular *Petersburg* (1916), lean in the direction of the anapest.

It cannot be denied, however, in reference to the later novels that despite Bely's obvious attempts to gain a maximum of variety within the framework of nearly pure ternary rhythm, the novels are marred by a seemingly inevitable rhythmic monotony that does not serve the works well. Such regularity is hypnotic at best, soporific at worst; and in any case it blunts the reader's perceptions rather than heightening them. Gone from these late novels is the ability to emphasize and highlight important words and phrases by subtle or dramatic shifts in rhythm such as are found in *Kotik Letaev.* Only *Masks,* it seems, manages to allay this loss by skillful use of punctuation and other typographical means; but this is not a real advance either, since such means were used at least as effectively in *Kotik Letaev.* The last three novels must be seen, then, as an unhappy postlude.

I suspect that part of the problem with the works after *Kotik Letaev* was that Bely the artist began to listen too much to Bely the theoretician. As his theories of prose came to be formulated more clearly, they began to influence his artistic practice. He seems to be more and more writing to illustrate his theories, rather than theorizing to explain his writings, and this is a dangerous situation for an artist.

NOTES

1. B. Tomashevsky, "Ritm prozy: 'Pikovaya dama,' " in *O stikhe* (Leningrad: Priboy, 1929), pp. 254–318. More recent contributions include M. Girshman, "Soderzhatelnost ritma prozy," *Voprosy literatury,* no. 2 (1964): 169–82; S. Bobrov, "Sintagmy, slovorazdely i litavridy," *Russkaya literatura,* no. 4 (1965): 80–101; M. M. Girshman and E. N. Orlov, "Problemy izucheniya ritma khudozhestvennoy prozy," *Russkaya literatura,* no. 2 (1972): 98–110; M. M. Girshman, "O ritme russkoy khudozhestvennoy prozy," *Slavic Poetics: Essays in Honor of Kiril Taranovsky* (Hague: Mouton, 1973), pp. 161–69.

2. A. Bely, "O khudozhestvennoy proze," *Gorn* 2–3 (1919): 49–55. Hereafter cited in the text.

3. Tomashevsky sharply criticized Bely's article, "O khudozhestvennoy proze," in "Andrey Bely i khudozhestvennaya poeziya" [*sic*], *Zhizn iskusstva,* no. 454 (May 18, 1920) and continued in no. 458–459 (May 23, 1920). In the continuation, the title was corrected to ". . . khudozhestvennaya proza."

4. See E. G. Kagarov, "O ritme russkoy prozaicheskoy rechi," *Doklady Akademii Nauk SSSR,* 1928, pp. 44–51; G. Shengeli, *Traktat o russkom stikhe: Chast pervaya, Organicheskaya metrika,* [Izd. 2–oe] (Moscow: Gos. izd., 1923), pp. 19–22.

5. For an extensive discussion of this issue in relation to versification see V. Zhirmunsky, *Vvedenie v metriku: Teoriya stikha* (Leningrad: Akademia, 1925), pp. 90–130; also see R. I. Avanesov, *Udarenie v sovremennom russkom literaturnom yazyke* (Moscow: Uchpedgiz, 1958), pp. 46–59.

6. This problem appears to await definitive elucidation and therefore any decision on the matter, mine included, is essentially arbitrary and provisional. The following comment by Nina Berberova is extremely valuable in this context: "The problem of semi-scuds (as Nabokov calls the doubtful pyrrhic) is a VERY exciting thing. In my opinion . . . it is

always connected with the individual way of reading. Every poet, great and small, has a tendency to emphasize the pyrrhics, to make his line less monotonous. . . . Boris Nikolaevich said that the more pyrrhic the better (a simplification, of course!)—and he himself spoke with such emphasis on stressed words that the pronouns, and even sometimes the not *very* important adjectives, did not get a chance to be heard" (letter to me, July 15, 1974).

7. In addition to Kondratov's results, used in Table 1 (see note 8), Kagarov, "O ritme russkoy . . . ," pp. 47, 49; and Shengeli, *Traktat o russkom* . . . , pp. 20–21, provide comparable figures.

8. Adapted from A. M. Kondratov, "Teoriya informatsii i poetika (Entropiya ritma russkoy rechi)," *Problemy Kibernetiki* 9 (1963): 281–82.

9. Pp. 17–18 ($\#$1–10); p. 23 ("1. Vstali tumany . . . 5. . . . blednogolubaya"); pp. 52–53 ("1. Eshchyo dalyokie . . . 4. . . . s toy pory); pp. 74–75 ("1. V gorodakh . . . 7. . . . tumanom satanizma).

10. Pp. 3–6 (to $\#$13).

11. Pp. 7–8 (to ". . . 'Prixodi skoree' . . .), pp. 62–63 (to ". . . o mramornye berega").

12. Pp. 7–8 ("Metel"), p. 123 (to " 'Ya uzh tayu' ").

13. Pp. 9–10 (to "svoey fate").

14. Pp. 11–12 ("Kareta proletela v tuman").

15. Pp. 25–27 ("Kareta proletela v tuman").

16. Pp. 17–19 ("Obrazovane soznaniya").

17. Pp. 42–44 ("A zavelas prosto tak . . . —'O du: dummes Kind!'").

18. Pp. 71–72 ("Eduard Eduardovich stal zamechat . . .—Vzdor!'").

19. Pp. 21–22 ("Eleonorochka").

20. Elena Szilard, "O strukture Vtoroy simfonii A. Belogo," *Studia Slavica Hungarica* 13 (1967): 319. For a further discussion on this question, but in regard to the *Fourth,* see my "Literature as Music: Symphonic Form in Andrej Belyj's *Fourth Symphony," Canadian-American Slavic Studies* 8, no. 4 (Winter 1974): 501–12.

21. Anton Hönig, *Andrej Belyjs Romane* (Munich: Wilhelm Fink Verlag, 1965), p. 21.

22. R. I. Ivanov-Razumnik, "Peterburg," in *Vershiny* (Petrograd: Kolos, 1923), pp. 105–71.

23. Ibid., pp. 118 and 120.

24. For a discussion of this point, see my "Poetic Devices in Andrej Belyj's Kotik Letaev" (Ph.D. diss., University of Michigan, 1971), pp. 23–33.

25. A considerably more detailed discussion of rhythm in *Kotik Letaev* than is possible here is available in my dissertation. The generalizations I advance on the novel are mainly the result of that extensive study rather than of the more limited investigation undertaken for many of the other works under discussion in the present essay.

26. By "lines" is meant a segment of text set off by a major pause which results from punctuation (period, semicolon, colon, double dash). See note 24.

27. This was noted also by Vadim Safonov in answer to a questionnaire on rhythm in prose, "O ritme khudozhestvennoy prozy," *Voprosy literatury,* no. 7 (1973): 114.

SAMUEL D. CIORAN

A PRISM FOR THE ABSOLUTE:
THE SYMBOLIC COLORS
OF ANDREY BELY

Poets like Bryusov and Balmont flirted capriciously with the symbolism of colors more or less as exaggerated proof of their superficial commitment to French Symbolist theories of "correspondences" and "synaesthesia," but other poets discovered a more profound and durable complex of ideas which could be expressed in colors.[1] The foremost theoretician of color correspondence in Russian Symbolism was Andrey Bely. Vladimir Solovyov may deserve our attention for his seminal influence with such color symbols as gold and azure, and Aleksandr Blok for his additional contributions of rosy pinks, violet greens, and cathartic whites; but Andrey Bely was first to verbalize the metaphysical and theological properties of colors in his theories of symbolism.

In 1903, Bely produced his manifesto of color correspondences under the expressive title of "Sacred Colors."[2] It is a typical Belyesque article, fraught with his curious and frequently distressing blend of scientific mysticism. The cross-references scurry between physics and the Bible to create an intellectually awkward synthesis, which can be aptly described by the equally awkward title of "apocalyptic optics."

The metaphysical springboard from which Bely launches himself on his soaring flight into the rarefied realms of Symbolist theorizing is the usual Symbolist one—namely, the Solovyovian question of "all-in-oneness" (*vseedinstvo*). This ultimate oneness, implied in the concept of the Absolute, is threatened by the forces of opposition; the result is a spectral struggle, in the typical jargon of Russian Symbolism, between thesis and antithesis, light and darkness, harmony and chaos, Christ and Antichrist. In order to give a sense of historical progression within time and space—of movement from some original paradisal condition of harmonious oneness, through the present stage of chaotic plurality, and onward to a future reinstatement of unity between man and the universe—Bely employs the refractive passage of a white ray through a prism as the organizing metaphor for his article.

White is the ultimate theosophical color. According to Bely it represents infinite possibility, the mirror of divine promise and plenitude, the fullness of being. Moreover, white may be seen as the color of "all-in-oneness," the ultimate color emanating from the Absolute. Just as the Absolute represents infinity or the sum total of all things, either in the perfection of their divine nature or the imperfection of their earthly nature, the color white contains all colors within itself: "The infinite can be symbolized in the infinity of colors contained in a ray of white light" (p. 115).

Predictably enough, white's alter ego, or antipode, is the color black: "If the color white is the symbol of the manifested fullness of being, then black is the symbol of nonbeing, of chaos. . . . The color black, in a phenomenal fashion, designates evil as a principle which destroys the fullness of being and infuses it with a spectral nature" (p. 115).

Anyone experienced in the manic mind of Bely can probably see immediately that his reasoning is about to lead us to the relationship between the two arch enemies and ever-present combatants of most of his fictional works, the only two genuine protagonists: *light* and *darkness*. Indeed, his pseudoscientific mind conveniently notes that colors are created out of the special relationship of darkness to light: "Light is distinguished from color by the fullness of the colors it contains. Color is light which to a variable degree is restricted by darkness. Hence the phenomenality of colors" (p. 115).

In passing through the prism of our temporally and spatially finite and conditional being, white can be refracted to produce the shade of gray. And for Bely, gray is the operative color of evil in actuality. Gray is the archetypal color of the specters, gloom, and mist that envelop us and distort our perspective of the genuine world, of the Absolute. Gray is the emblem of urban life with its modern technology and industrialization as exemplified in ashes, dust, and factory smokestacks. This color can create illusions and spectral being, according to Bely, wherein reigns a confusion between reality and nonreality. A disjointed madness ensues, a phantasmagoria which can be penetrated only with a cry of despair or a catastrophic act.

One of the first colors which arises out of the gray mists in the initial refraction of white is a yellowish-brown hue: "The first illumination which pierces the gloom is colored with a yellowish brown, forbidding layer of dust. This forbidding sheen is quite familiar to all those who are in the process of awakening and find themselves between dream and reality" (p. 117). Significantly, this primary stage of grayness is considered by Bely to be a harbinger of apocalypse, of the thickening clouds of catastrophe collecting overhead.

The ultimate color of catastrophic revelation, however, is red. The grayish and yellowish hues may be optical illusions, possessing only a spectral nature, but red is capable of assuming real being:

> In physics it is a known characteristic of a white ray of light to become colored with a red hue when passing through a dusty nontransparent medium of a determined thickness and density. Thus the impression of *red* is created by the relationship of a white source of light to a gray medium. The relativity, the transparency of the color red is in its own way a theosophical revelation. Here the enemy is revealed in the ultimate manifestation of himself which is accessible to us—in the fiery red glow of the infernal conflagration. It must be remembered that this is the ultimate state of relativity—the specter of the specter, which, nonetheless, is capable of proving to be more real than reality once it has assumed the serpent's guise. (pp. 119–20)

Departing from Bely's article for a moment, we can briefly survey the use of the colors so far discussed theoretically as they appear in the fiction. The color symbolism inherent in the contiguity of light and darkness permeated much of Bely's earlier work. In the *First Symphony* he created the archetypal struggle which he later established theoretically in "Sacred Colors"—namely, the confrontation of light and darkness. The opposition of light and darkness hardly rises above the simple level of allegory throughout this symphony. With the death of the ancient king who had brought enlightenment to his northern land and the subsequent flight of his fearful heir, Bely is quite explicit about who rules the kingdom now: "On the burdensome throne reigned Darkness/ the master of this land" (p. 32). The granddaughter of the original king, a young princess and a scarcely veiled incarnation of Bely's abiding archetype of the "Woman Clothed with the Sun," becomes the champion of light who sets forth to do battle with darkness: "The years passed. The day arrived. The princess descended from the height of her tower, fulfilling the heavenly behest. She went forth to disperse the darkness" (p. 88). In the end she does conquer darkness, once again enlightening the kingdom. The biblical parallels are unmistakable, as are the presence of Solovyov's own sophiological inspirations. In the last symphony, the *Fourth,* we encounter essentially the same *sujet* with the same opposition between light and darkness in which darkness is conquered in an apocalyptic conclusion. The allegory is just as transparent. The protagonists are Svetlova and Svetozarov, who represent the opposing spirits of light and darkness: Svetlova is the "Woman Clothed with the Sun" who destroys the servant of darkness incarnate in Svetozarov. In Bely's early mysterium-drama, "The Maw of the Night," the expectant but disillusioned Christians find themselves seemingly in the eternal grip of darkness, waiting both literally and symbolically through the long night for the dawning of the new day and the Second Coming.[3] Premonitions of salvation are reflected in the infrequent aura of pale light surrounding the prophet and the small child in the mysterium, but even the "handfuls of light" gathered and sown like flowers by the child eventually drown in the murky gloom of night.

No doubt Bely recollected the same optical laws incarnate in the grays, yellows, and reds of his theoretical article when he came to write *Petersburg*. This sunless Russian city of mists is a perfect site in which to observe the optical illusions of appearing and disappearing points of perspective, of the illusory specters of being and nonbeing. This is the city in which the color gray reigns supreme, befogging the eye and confounding the mind. Who can tell what is real or unreal? In their individual contemplation of the Absolute, who can say whose apprehension of the world is more real, that of the Kantian Nikolay Apollonovich or that of Comtean Apollon Apollononich? Who is Aleksandr Dudkin's nocturnal visitor, appearing and disappearing out of a gray spot, Shishnarfne or Enfranshish? And what of the symbolism of yellow, bearing in itself the prophecy of catastrophe? Is this not the "yellow menace," the Mongolian leitmotif of devastation incarnate in the personages of Lippanchenko, the references to the Russo-Japanese War, the eastern origins of the Ableukhovs themselves, and the Persian Shishnarfne? Just as surely as the yellowish brown spectrum of colors appeared out of the murky grays in Bely's symbolic analysis of light's refraction, both Lippanchenko and Shishnarfne, the representatives of the yellow menace, arose out of the gray mists of the Finnish port of Helsingfors, where Aleksandr Dudkin first encountered them as he began to preach his nihilistic, anarchical theories on culture and history.

The negative being symbolized by the color red, this "final stage of relativity," is achieved by Nikolay Apollonovich when he dons the red domino—this being the ultimate degree of his "madness," of his disaffection with reality. Bely had said in his article that with the color red "the enemy is revealed in the ultimate manifestation of himself which is accessible to us . . ." (p. 120). Surely this manifestation is the unmasking of Nikolay Apollonovich at the ball, where he stands revealed for the miserable, yet tragicomical figure that he is: a man who has assumed an absurd position in relation to the world around him. Of course, the fervent pathos of Bely's article is converted through the all-pervasive irony of Russian Symbolism into parody and intentional bathos in the novel. Even the appearance of the white domino at the ball, in the wake of Nikolay Apollonovich's unmasking, seems fraught with the same color symbolism. The white domino appears to be a reminder of something absolute, of the positive values which Bely had invested in this divine color. It is quite appropriate that the white domino be present at the unmasking. And again in Bely's typically self-destructive ironic mode, it is entirely appropriate that the white domino succeeds where the red domino has failed—namely, in attracting Sophia Petrovna who is, after all, the fictional incarnation of the Divine Sophia in the novel.

Bely asserted in his article that, if the power of darkness waxed strongest in the color red, then evil is on the wane with the appearance of pink or rose, wherein the dominance of white over red becomes apparent: "The color pink unites red with white. If the theosophic definition of the color red, which relates to the struggle between God and the devil, is compared with the color pink, in which the predominance of the white source of the light of human divineness is now manifestly expressed, then the subsequent stage of spiritual experience is colored in a pink hue" (p. 122). As we shall see, this shade of pink was, in Bely's estimation, proof of Aleksandr Blok's obeisance before the same ideal of the Absolute, incarnate in the Divine Feminine, and the pink or rosy glow of the promise of a new day inherent in the glow from the setting sun.

After arriving at the "pink stage" in the prism of symbolic colors, Bely inexplicably, but typically, abandons his loosely developed scheme of symbolic refraction and becomes increasingly involved in his familiar patchwork quilt of biblical quotations, philosophical references, and mystical intuitions. His colorific scheme then turns abruptly to those early mystical colors of Russian Symbolism in which azure blue, gold, crimson purple, and white predominate. As the conclusion to the article amply shows, those very colors appear to transcend the bounds of mere symbolic adornment and actually create or evoke the ideal forms themselves:

> Proceeding from symbols of colors we are in a position to erect the image of what has conquered the world. Even though this image is misty, we believe that the mist will be dispersed. Its face must be white like the snow. Its eyes like two flights through the heavens—marvelously fathomless pale blue. Like honey spilling forth—the ecstasy of the saints over heaven—is its golden, thick hair. . . . A bloody crimson are its lips, like that crimson which closed the circle of colors, like that purple which will destroy the world in a blaze; its lips are the crimson fire. . . . First the fathomlessly profound azure blue eyes will amaze us and we will stand still before them, as though before the deeps, and then the snowy shade of the brow will remind us of the cloud which envelops the azure blue. . . . Apprehending the reflections of the Eternal, we believe that truth will not abandon us, that it will abide with us. Love is with us. Through love we shall overcome. Radiance is with us. (pp. 128–29)

Apparent to any student of Vladimir Solovyov is the image of the Divine Sophia in this description, a description which in its scant, physical detail but expressive coloration reverberates throughout the works of both Andrey Bely and Aleksandr Blok. The color white, a repository of the entire spectrum of symbolic colors, is here self-explanatory in its theoretical origins. But the genuine colors of mystical perception and revelation were indeed those of gold, azure, and crimson purple to which Bely turns in the final emotional apotheosis of his article.

Gold and azure in particular typified that early romantic and naive era of Russian Symbolism when inspiration and ecstasy had not yet experienced disillusionment and despair. More than any other colors, gold and azure, together with crimson, served both iconographical and atmospheric functions in the works of Bely. For the purposes of examining the symbolic content of these colors in Russian Symbolism one need hardly look beyond Vladimir Solovyov. In the philosopher's poetry the colors of gold and azure were painstakingly reserved for evoking the revelatory mystery of the Divine Sophia's presence and for iconographically depicting the rare physical attributes of this symbol of "all-in-oneness" or Godmanhood, with her fathomless azure eyes and golden hair. In "Three Encounters" each revelation of Sophia before Solovyov was communicated precisely through these colors. Consequently, in the minds of the youthful Solovyovian trio of Andrey Bely, Aleksandr Blok, and Sergey Solovyov, these two colors were reserved exclusively for the complex of ideas surrounding the concept of Sophia in Vladimir Solovyov's works, where she functioned as the archsymbol of the unification of heaven and earth in the philosopher-poet's radiant vision of Godmanhood.

Bely especially made emphatic use of gold and azure in his early writings. In his first book of verse, *Gold in Azure,* the colors do not betray their ecstatic and metaphysical origins in Solovyov. Hearkening to Solovyov's Godmanhood, the youthful poet basks in the azure gold of Platonic reflections: "Our souls are mirrors, / which reflect gold" (p. 11). Elsewhere he repeats the same formula: "From the heights there comes to rest on us/ the reflection of azure blue" (p. 218). As suggested in the metaphor of the "golden fleece," which structures much of this first book of verse, Bely set forth on a journey to catch the reflections of other worlds in the crimson gold sunsets and azure skies of dusk and dawn. His fellow Symbolists were no less "sunstricken" and blinded in their youthful enamorment with the sun's fiery golden symbolism. The call of eternity proved irresistible in the early years of the twentieth century for such poets as Blok and Bely as they hearkened to otherworldly voices and summonses:

> In the pale blue light
> everything grew still, sparkling:
> "I am so close to you,
> my miserable children of earth,
> in this golden ambering hour. . . ." (p. 19)

Bely's *Third Symphony* proved to be particularly rich in this color symbolism. The paradisal condition of the child is directly mirrored in the symbolism of gold and azure: "The child awoke. He lay on his back. It seemed to him that the heavenly depths, all suffused with a resounding, echoing gold, were descending to his face. . . . It seemed to him that the universe had enfolded him in its peaceful embrace" (p. 11). Like all of Bely's children, the child in the *Third Symphony* is the offspring of the Absolute, for his hair is golden and his eyes are pale blue, doubtlessly symbolizing the Platonic reflections of the universal harmony implied in these colors. His pale blue eyes are, of course, mirrors of eternity: "from the eyes [of the child] streamed azure blue rays because the child harkened to the summons which frequently emanated from Eternity" (p. 14). The child has his counterpart in the student of chemistry, Khandrikov. It is hardly a coincidence that, whereas the child's eyes reflected the fathomless blue of eternity, the author describes Khandrikov's as being "colorless" (p. 48). Moreover, the azure gold landscape of the child has its logical counterpart in the gloomy, misty, and gray Petersburg landscape of Khandrikov's despair and madness.

In later years, after the death of Aleksandr Blok, Bely was quite explicit concerning the roles of azure and gold and their origin in Solovyov: "Gold and azure are the iconographical colors of Sophia; Sophia's depiction in icons is always accompanied by those colors; and in Vladimir Solovyov, as well, 'She' is suffused with a golden azure. . . . In Vladimir Solovyov 'She' descends from the heavens to earth, bearing her *gold* and *azure* here to us. . . ."[4] The unmistakable connection between these colors and Sophia led Bely to discern immediately in Blok yet another worshipper of Solovyov's vision of the Absolute inherent in Sophia. The mention of those symbolic colors in Blok's early verses sufficed for Bely to behold the poet of the Beautiful Lady as Solovyov's natural heir: "How did that visage first appear before the poet? What colors accompanied it?" asked Bely. "A radiance, gold, and azure blue were Her accompanying attributes."[5] To be sure, Bely was not mistaken by any means in the colors of Blok's early inspiration, as even a few random verses would show.[6] Blok was not, however, as firm as Bely in being unmitigatedly attracted to the vision of azure. Yet Bely chose to ignore the warning signs which were reflected in such Blok verses as the following:

> I know not whether beyond the distant boundary
> Azure happiness does exist . . .
> Now I hearken to a foreign
> And ever-waxing passion.[7]

In their correspondence Bely and Blok often seem to be at cross-purposes. Bely simply could not conceive of the fact that Blok was abandoning the struggle for the apocalyptic vision incarnate in the gold azure symbolism Bely so passionately embraced. Even the harsh political events of 1905 and the catastrophic Russo-Japanese War could not induce Bely to put aside, even temporarily, his inspirational colors. Instead he clung all the more passionately to them, perhaps sensing in their radiant symbolism that which was eternal and immutable amid the transitory and fickle events of time and space. Early in February of 1905, Bely wrote to Blok:

> Yesterday she plunged from her soaring course into the azure sea of the vernal ether; her hair, tousled by the wind, was strewn on high. Thousands of radiant golden strands stretched across the horizon. Each strand more incandescent than fire, a melodious and glittering hair that melted the freezing icicles. And everything was asparkle with a celestial gold. . . . Dearest, dearest, the world is apt to despise us because we are bound to be not of this world, but of "gold, roses, azure, snow and crimson purple." The azure golden, snowy crimson roses of Eternity.[8]

Throughout their long and turbulent relationship, Blok and Bely conducted ideological duels that were more often than not mirrored in their symbolic use of colors. From the very first Blok had shared Bely's apprehension of the Absolute in the infinity of possibility encompassed in the color white, but with an important difference which is apparent from an early letter he wrote to Bely: "My questions are like a bottomless pit because I am fated to experience the Babylonian harlot and only to 'live in white' but not create white."[9] Obviously Blok was shying away from any concept of art as theurgy, that is, an art which is capable of the creative act of transformation. Receding into passive experience, into a purely intuitional apprehension of ideal forms, Blok wishes to escape the active involvement eventually demanded by Bely in the Symbolist commune which would bring about this great feat. Bely became morbidly sensitive to the changes in color schemata practiced by Blok. In fact, in his later memoirs Bely even typified the various stages in Blok's journey from light to darkness in the colors which he discovered in the latter's poetry. Thus the early Blok, who in Bely's estimation was still faithful to the gold and azure vision of the Divine Sophia, was characterized by a rosy or pinkish golden hue which came from Blok's constant vigilance before sunsets: "the visage of the youthful Blok was a rosy golden hue from the conflagration of the flaming sunset."[10] But just as many colors were contained potentially in the color white, so many shades of color, with corresponding shades of meaning, were contained in Blok. Bely sensed Blok's betrayal of the sophiological ideal when Blok abandoned the "rosy golden air" of early Symbolism and became fascinated with the color spectrum of violets, mauves, and yellowish blacks contained in the collection *Unexpected Joy* and the long poem "The Nocturnal Violet."[11] Even two decades later, when recalling Blok's disaffection with the common ideal, Bely reintroduced the optical concepts of his article "Sacred Colors" in order to reveal the opposing Symbolist positions of himself and Blok. What is remarkable in Bely's color characteristics here is that the colors assume what is practically an incantational or talismanic function. They do not simply suggest the presence of certain ideals or characterize those ideals. The colors appear to form part of a religious ritual which is capable of invoking, of summoning forth, the spirit of either Christ or Antichrist. As will become apparent from the following excerpt, this is precisely the theurgic function of those colors:

> The union of three colors (whiteness, azure, crimson), in my opinion, depicted a mystical triangle of colors—the Visage of Christ; I was preaching that the apprehension of Christ was in three colors; an apprehension in azure, crimson and whiteness; azure and crimson together, or a whiteness and crimson, or a whiteness and azure, these are all temptations, a heresy; and a *dark lilac* was a mixture of colors . . . and out of this arose in that hue [i.e., dark lilac] which had captivated A. A.—the mightiest seduction which alienated one from the Visage of Christ; while A. A. was softly but excitedly explaining his apprehension of this dark lilac color, I felt uneasy: it was as though someone had just placed a stove full of coals in the room; I felt the heat; it was the heat of Lucifer . . . ; aesthetically [Blok] had abandoned the three sacred colors (azure, crimson, and whiteness), mixing them with darkness; and this mixture produced a dark lilac shade, violet, the smell of Satan.[12]

Twenty years later Bely may have altered somewhat his original choice of sacred colors, but the principle of light versus darkness obviously still applied. Clearly, for Bely the contrast in colors between himself and Blok was sufficient proof of their iconographical opposition: Bely stood for Christ and light; Blok, for Antichrist and darkness.

There is little difficulty in seeing that Andrey Bely went far beyond the claims of correspondences and synaesthesia made for colors by the French Symbolists. Out of colors he was able to create a convenient Symbolist codebook for deciphering the struggle between light and darkness and the state of that struggle according to the predominance of specific colors. However, these colors were not simply a system of informative signals, additional meaningful signs in his arsenal of symbols. They became, in Bely's manipulation, practically theurgic and creative. This appears most clearly in Bely's despair over Blok's abandoning of the sacred colors which Bely had postulated in his article. It was as though Bely sincerely believed that a devout and unswerving allegiance to the sacred colors would, like the mystery of religious communion, create the divine mystery of genuine transformation. It must be said, however, that Bely never carried his analysis of the refraction of light back to the ultimate color of white. He was able to refract the white light of infinity, of all-in-oneness, into its separate parts, to identify the optical struggle between light and darkness with succeeding stages of grays, yellows, reds, and pinks. Yet when the time came, his mystical science of symbolism could not divine the final step whereby the colors could be reunited within the ray of white light representing the final goal of Symbolism, the achievement of the Absolute.

NOTES

1. See Valery Bryusov, "Sonet k forme," in *Izbrannye proizvedeniya* 1 (Moscow–Leningrad, 1926), p. 17; Konstantin Balmont, "Fioletovy," in *Polnoe sobranie stikhov* 5 (*Liturgiya krasoty*), 2d ed. (Moscow, 1911), p. 88. There are some twenty-one poems contained in this "color-cycle" which falls within Balmont's larger verse cycle entitled "Chernaya oprava."

2. "Svyashchennye tsveta" was written in 1903, and is quoted as it first appeared in Bely's collection *Arabesques* (Moscow, 1911), pp. 115–29. Hereafter cited in the text.

3. "Past nochi: otryvok misterii." *Zolotoe runo,* no. 2 (1906): 62–71.

4. Andrey Bely, "Vospominaniya o A. A. Bloke," *Epopeya,* no. 2 (1922): 115.

5. Ibid., no. 2 (1922): 114.

6. Aleksandr Blok, "Priznak istinnogo chuda . . . ," in *Sobranie sochineny v 8-i tomakh* (Moscow-Leningrad: GIKhL, 1960–63), 1: 116; "Kto-to shepchet i smeyotsya . . . ," ibid., 1: 89; "Prozrachnye, neve-domye teni . . . ," ibid., 1: 107.

7. "Ya bremya pokhotil, kak tat . . . ," ibid., 1: 131.

8. V. N. Orlov, ed., *Aleksandr Blok i Andrey Bely. Perepiska* (Moscow: Izd. Gos. lit. muzeya, 1940), p. 123.

9. Ibid., p. 4.

10. Bely, "Vospominaniya . . . ," no. 2 (1922): 213.

11. *Nechayannaya radost, Vtoroy sbornik stikhov* (Moscow, 1907). And "Nochnaya fialka" (1906). The poem first appeared in the collection *Nechayannaya radost* (1907).

12. Bely, "Vospominaniya . . . ," no. 2 (1922): 279–80.

~~~~~~~~~~~~~~~~~

A MEMOIR AND A COMMENT:
THE "CIRCLE" OF *PETERSBURG*

Long ago I made an observation: Russians (especially old men) like to use old envelopes. Rozanov in *Secluded* (*Uedinyonnoe*) and *Fallen Leaves* (*Opavshie listya*), after writing down a thought, puts in parentheses: "Written on an old envelope." Merezhkovsky would be searching for an address. "Look for an old envelope," Zinaida Nikolaevna would say.

Khodasevich had in his possession two envelopes which he cherished. One was old, gray, large, and addressed to him when he was living at the House of Arts (Moika 59, Apt. 30a) in 1921. Bely came to visit him in May or June (before my time) and Khodasevich was not at home. Boris Nikolaevich waited, found this old envelope on Khodasevich's desk, and wrote on it twenty or twenty-five lines of the First Part of "The First Encounter": "Zhil borodaty, grubovaty/ Bogov belogolovy roy" (where at first *belogolovy* was *lysogolovy*). The second envelope was yellow. In January 1923, in Saarow, Germany, as I have written in my autobiography, *The Italics are Mine* (*Kursiv moy*), Boris Nikolaevich used to read to us in the evening hours what he had written during the day. This work was *The Beginning of the Century*, which at that time did not yet have a title. One time Khodasevich, puzzled by a certain inconsistency of structure in the memoirs, asked him: "What would the line, the main pattern of these volumes be? Would it be a straight line, an ordinary chronological scheme? Or a curved line, or a broken one? Or a spiral? Or two lines intertwined?" (Khodasevich was always tremendously conscious of the structure of a work—a poem, a novel, a critical article. He could even talk at length about the "architectonics" of the Gospels. The Symbolists, of course, as well as my own generation, never used the word "structure" or "structural" in these years. We all spoke about "architectonics." Webster, as a matter of fact, explains architectonics as "a system of structures.") Boris Nikolaevich answered: "It is a line. And *Petersburg,* no matter what Berdyaev said, is a circle. Not a cube, but a wheel." He snatched an old envelope from a table and on it he drew a circle, and immediately another one. And he started to talk about them. (Both envelopes were destroyed in 1942 when the apartment in Boulogne was ransacked by the Germans. I vaguely remember that Smolensky was shown both of them. And perhaps Nabokov.)

Calling the drawings sometimes circles and sometimes wheels, Boris Nikolaevich went through a short "introduction"—from ancient mythology to modern symbolization, from pagan to Christian imagery, and to Dr. Steiner's Anthroposophy. But before going on to some Anthroposophical implications and Steiner's concepts, he commented, with a sly smile, on the strong Russian tradition of coaches in literature: Pushkin's post chaise, Turgenev's cabriolet, Chichikov's carriage, Rostov's coach of 1812, Ableukhov's brougham—"*A travers les ages*"—he liked this expression. Then Boris Nikolaevich fantasized about the beauty of the wheel. (This reminds me of Coleridge's marveling about the same object in *Miscellanies Aesthetic and Literary:* "An old coach wheel lies in the coachmaker's yard. . . . There is beauty in that wheel. See how the rays proceed from the center to the circumference, and how many different images are distinctly comprehended at one glance, as forming one whole, and each part in some harmonious relation to each and all.")

Here are a few of Steiner's ideas about the circle which Bely mentioned:

It is the basis of the Universe.

The whole cosmogony is a circle.

The circle is perfection of the inner unity of man.

The square symbolizes the lowest state of man. The octagon is the intermediate stage.

The wheel rotates around the sun, which is a wheel in itself and a spiritual illumination.

The center of a circle is, of course, immobile—the Aristotelian "unmoved mover."

A spider—an obsessive image in mythic thinking—sits in the center:
   God, as a spider, in the middle of his web.
All this gives us a figure in two parts: periphery and center.
And the rose-window of the Gothic cathedral,
And the rose—the mystical flower,
And the lotus, in the East.

Besides these Steinerian concepts, Bely commented on some Indian rituals:

The Dakota, the Shawnee, the Algonquin, and the California Indians apparently have "circular time." Life-birth-death is a circle (he said). In a cabin, Indians are sitting in a circle. In the center is the seer, the bard, the savior (*myself,* of course, he said). He knows everything. He tells his mysteries to the initiated. The Dakota Indians say: The year is a circle around the world. And also: the Cosmos and cosmic time are designated by a circle. The World is round. The year is round. The skies are round. Life is round. The listeners will sit in a circle for seven days and seven nights.

(Afterwards Khodasevich said to me, "You and I will agree to sit, with him in the middle, for seven days, but not seven nights! Shall we tell him this?")

The two circles (or wheels) which Bely drew were divided into seven sections. The first circle might be discussed as the signifier for the second one, which could be regarded as the signified for the first one. In discussing the meaning of Bely's drawings, and keeping in mind Bely's full knowledge of the mystical implications of the figures, I would like to say two things. First, we do not expect consistency from Bely; in his writings one can find other images of the cosmos, such as the musical scale. Consistency is not one of the main features of Bely's thinking, although he was, with all his whimsicality and even "irresponsibility," far more consistent than, for instance, Blok or Tolstoy. Second, the two figures he drew were not the result of elaborate thinking. This was an improvisation, maybe even a tongue-in-cheek gesture. He never went back to these matters (as far as I know). They were images of his mind, no more; but no less, either. And they should be accepted as such.

The first wheel, clockwise, has seven themes that in our time we would call Empire, Oedipus, Sex, Revolution, Mystery, the Yellow

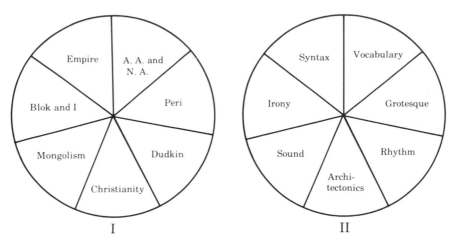

I   II

Danger, and Love-Hate. Since the wheel is supposed to be turning, these themes become a blend of myths, personal idiosyncrasies, real happenings, cosmic events, historical occurrences, nonsensical fantasies, and much more. The second wheel supports the first one and is supported by it, and in the narrowest sense permeates it at every moment of time. In any future analysis of these figures, one should keep in mind this latter point. All the levels of stratification of *Petersburg* could thus be integrated. I would even venture to suggest that, Bely's ratiocinations being more often than not methodically unsound or muddled, we should not take this explanation too seriously and should stick to the drawings themselves. He certainly had no terminology, as nobody in those years had any, in Russia, France, or elsewhere. He knew no *signans-signatum* division; no words expressing levels of stratification, no synchronic and diachronic organization, in discussing a work. (By synchronic I mean Bely's work in connection with the work of Joyce, Kafka, T. S. Eliot, etc.; and by diachronic I mean his work related with Gogol, Dostoevsky, and minor writers whom he read and from whom he learned something, such as Boborykin, Morskoy, and others, whose dialogues set in the Petersburg pubs around Sennaya strikingly resemble certain pages in *Petersburg*.)

Analysis would probably have to concentrate on the novel's structural complexity and attempt to reveal it. Each level would then yield its own substance and the multitude of its correlative functions. And *in their linguistic aspect,* the abundant meanings would relate to the plot, the characters, and the metaphysical values as well.

Bely knew the works of William James, though not those of Henry James. But this is what Henry James said about his own novel *The Awkward Age:* (He drew on a paper a figure of a circle consisting of a number of small rounds disposed at equal distance about a central object.) "The central object was my situation, my subject in itself, to which the thing will owe its title, and the small rounds represent lamps . . . the function of each of which would be to light with all due intensity one of its aspects."

At this point I would like to touch upon the extremely interesting subject of Bely's reading. We will never know what books he had in his personal library, as we know about Pushkin, Stendhal, or Henry James. For many years I have thought of sketching a tentative list, an approximate draft of his readings between 1899 and 1923. I will try to do it now, possibly giving only the direction of his interests, or making a cautious guess based more on what he said than on what he wrote.

The Germans were at the center of his young and adult readings. He certainly knew the mystics, the poets (mainly Romantics), the philosophers—of East and West. He read the books of Blavatsky and Steiner (all his output: the volumes open to laymen and those open only to the initiated). With absolute assurance I would say that Boris Nikolaevich knew every line of Goethe and Nietzsche, since familiarity with the works of both was a condition *sine qua non* for a Steinerian. But he certainly did not know either Frazer or the great anthropologists of our century. In 1923 he could not have read Freud's book on dreams, nor any other book of Freud for that matter, although Professor Georges Nivat tells me that in 1915 in Dornach there was a symposium on Freud in which Steiner explained the complete worthlessness of the author of the *Interpretation of Dreams*. This does not mean that Bely read Freud. He did know his name—this is what we may deduce from Professor Nivat's valuable remark.

As only a makeshift attempt, my list of Bely's readings would be broken down as follows. Works that Bely knew, having read them: Goethe, Nietzsche, Hegel, Stirner, Schopenhauer, Spengler, Otto Weininger, Krafft-Ebing, Edward Carpenter, Kant, Neo-Kantians, Windelband, Hermann Cohen, Wundt, Steiner. *Der Ring des Nibelungen* (he loved Wagner not only for himself, but also for the Saga), Schiller, Novalis, Kleist, Tieck; Swedenborg, Boehme, Dante (he knew him better than Homer, which was unusual in Russia at this time), Ruskin (translated into Russian in 1856 and 1890), the *Memoirs* of Casanova (very much in fashion); French Symbolists, Stefan George, Strindberg. Works that Bely might have read: Carlyle, Croce (the article on Goethe was translated in 1919), the early work of Cassirer, William Blake (because of Balmont), Baudoin-de-Courtenay, and Shcherba (but not de Saussure). Works which Bely did not read either because they were not published before 1923 or for some other reason: Frazer, Jung, Freud, Yeats, Santayana, T. S. Eliot, Pound, Apollinaire, Valery. (Bely knew neither Italian nor English.)

Could Bely have known Pico della Mirandola's "On Human Dignity," and God's words to Man from that work: "I have placed you in the *center* of the world so you can behold comfortably *around* you what is in it"? He knew Campanella, he lectured on him, but then Campanella lived 100 years after Pico. Whether Bely's readings went back to Pico must remain unknown.

THE TIME BOMB

The writer is a mythmaker, says Bely. The point from which the myth originates is mysterious and sacred and must remain hidden from the reader. Through words—their structure, their special usage, and their sound—the writer teases the reader, plays a game with him. "Thus every novel is a game of hide-and-seek with the reader, while structure and sentences have only one goal: to direct the eye of the reader away from the sacred point: the birth of the myth" (*Notes of an Eccentric*, p. 63). According to Bely, a writer who does not possess a mysterious point is not a writer, since his work can have only a surface meaning. By contrast, a novel by a genuine writer has many meanings and never reveals its mysterious center.

Bely's warning notwithstanding, every reader—and especially the literary critic—looks beyond the verbal structure and the games the author plays. But since a Symbolist work has no "certain meaning," one can offer only suggestions and speculations which, though plausible, may be substantially different from the mysterious core which inspired the work. Since Bely's technique is to use verbal virtuosity to hide the mystery from the reader, it is perhaps best to approach his work by trying to discover the rules of his verbal games. It is even possible that in doing so one might stumble upon the "sacred point."

The best way to read Bely's works, especially *Petersburg*, is to read them aloud. When read aloud the sounds of letters, syllables, and words acquire an importance that often goes beyond their obvious meanings. Bely claimed that the name Apollon was chosen by him because of the "pl" sound, suggesting explosion; and Nikolay, because of the "kl" sound, suggesting asphyxiation. Such a statement seems bizarre at first. However, as one reads the text and finds other sounds that turn into words, it becomes evident that we are really discovering one of the rules of Bely's verbal game. Indeed, in *Petersburg* Bely uses that technique in several ways. He starts with disconnected sounds or syllables, letting them clump into words. The sound "y" for instance, which he does not like and which he calls *tatarshchina*, becomes *mylo, tyl*, etc.; *pravo* turns into *provokatsiya;* and so on.

Another method of playing with sound and meaning can be demonstrated by the syllable *shish*. As a word *shish* is rather vulgar (meaning fig, *fico*). *Pokazat shish* is much more vulgar than "to show a long nose." *U nego net ni shisha* is a vulgar way of saying "he hasn't got a thing, or a penny." *Shish* alone is not used in the novel, but the Russian ear detects it even when it is part of another word, especially since these words are quite unusual and seldom used. We have *shishkovidnaya zheleza* ("pineal gland") and *shishak* ("spiked helmet" from Lithuanian). Finally the syllable becomes part of the name of a character, Shishnarfne, and then a magical word, *enfranshish*, the same name spelled backwards.

But the most interesting and consistent technique is used in *Petersburg* in connection with the time bomb. Here the process is somewhat different. Instead of sounds being clumped into words, scattered words used with a variety of meanings are eventually crystallized into one final phrase: *sardinnitsa uzhasnogo soderzhaniya,* the sardine can which explodes at the end of the last chapter.

The first chapter starts on page 3 and already on the next page time and timing are hinted at.[1] On page 5 Apollon Apollonovich is said to manage huge mechanisms (apparently of state). Then there is mention of an "explosion of mental forces." The cranium is also mentioned. In Russian the word for cranium is *cherep*, one word; but Bely calls it *cherepnaya korobka*, since he needs the word *korobka*, meaning box. However, this early in the game the words *mechanism, box*, and *explosion* do not as yet suggest the horror of a time bomb explosion. But as the narrative continues these words and others, close in meaning and used in unexpected combinations, are repeated several times; and gradually the reader becomes aware of a mounting tension through this reiteration of a certain group of words.

The novel has eight chapters. In the first four—half of the book—
I counted over forty entries connected with the time bomb, or hint-
ing at it, though no mention is made in these four chapters of the
word *sardinnitsa.*

We have the hoarse ticking of the clock, the mysterious bundle
with some undisclosed and apparently fragile content, spherical
objects, eyes popping out, hearts painfully enlarged. Then for the
first time the phrase "of horrible content" (*uzhasnogo soderzhaniya*)
appears. However, the formula does not refer to a bomb or a box; it
is just a "fragment" of dialogue, *obryvok uzhasnogo soderzhaniya*
(p. 22). The last word—*content*—is repeated again, but used in a
different word combination. It is now the "frightening content of a
whisper" (p. 38). By the same token the word *horrible* is elsewhere
used with the word *offer—uzhasnoe predlozhenie* (p. 83). The
phrases *terroristichesky akt* ("terrorist act") and *podpisyval kazn*
("signed the execution order") (pp. 126 and 129), though used in an
abstract sense following a paragraph concerning a future "world
explosion" (p. 124)—obviously meaning revolution—leave little
doubt in the reader's mind what direction the novel is taking.

Then something new is introduced, not a word yet, but the root
sard in *sardonichesky smekh* ("sardonic laughter") (p. 139). It is a
hint, but the reader hardly notices it during a first reading. Not
until the second part of the novel will the root *sard* be developed,
but a clue to the direction of future events has been planted. The
tempo of events increases and with the phrase *pismo uzhasnogo
soderzhaniya* (p. 147) the theme of the time bomb reaches a new
intensity signified by the "letter of horrible content" which Sofya
Petrovna is about to hand to Nikolay Apollonovich.

As we continue to look for the expanding verbal shape of the
bomb image, we find the following in chapter 4 in the section entitled *Nu a esli* . . . ("Well, and if . . . "). Sofya Petrovna has
just handed Nikolay Apollonovich the fateful letter, containing the
command to fulfill his promise. She still hopes that the whole thing
is a hoax, but then she asks herself, "Suppose it were true, suppose
Nikolay Apollonovich did hide in his desk objects of horrible content?" (p. 186). In this silent monologue the verbal formula has
almost achieved its final form. On the following page Sofya's
stream of consciousness continues and finally the word *bomb*
(*bomba*) is spelled out. But Sofya obviously does not know in what
shape the explosive object is presented. To her "bomb" means the
traditional round missile fired from an old-fashioned cannon.

Therefore she sees it as "something round, something that could not be touched" (p. 187). Nikolay Apollonovich reads the letter, which tells him the terrible truth about the bundle hidden in his desk. He knows now that it contains the material *v vide bomby* ("in the form of a bomb").

Finally, the title of chapter 5 spells out the complete formula of the time bomb: *sardinnitsa uzhasnogo soderzhaniya*. This information, however, is given only to the reader. Nikolay Apollonovich does not yet know what kind of explosive material is hidden in the drawer. While engaged in nervous speculation about the real meaning of the letter handed to him, the distraught Nikolay is followed on his way home by the secret agent Morkovin, who drags him into a cheap restaurant. All through the restaurant scene Nikolay still ignores the shape of what he is going to find in his desk. In the meantime the word *sardinnitsa* begins to be built up during the painful conversation with Morkovin. The emphasis is on disgust and nausea provoked by the sight of sardines.

"No, no sardines," says Morkovin to the waiter, "they swim in slime" (p. 231). And again by Morkovin: "You made a spot with sardine oil" (p. 232). Finally, Nikolay gets home, opens the fateful bundle and sees the sardine can. Almost a whole page is devoted to this dramatic moment (p. 262). Nikolay tries to believe that the can is an ordinary sardine can, but at the bottom of the page he is forced to admit that it is not. *Net-net-net! Ne sardinnitsa, a sardinnitsa uzhasnogo soderzhaniya!* Now the verbal form of the bomb is complete and is known to Nikolay. The rest of the novel presents a constantly increasing crescendo with repetition of the phrase and of separate words of that phrase in a variety of meanings, in several instances more than once on the same page. From that page to the end of the novel there are again over forty entries, the last one at the very end of chapter 8: "It exploded: he understood everything!" (p. 478).

Bely's choice of a sardine can as a time bomb remains puzzling. Neither the relentless buildup of the verbal formula of the bomb nor the fantastic previews of imaginary explosions in the second part of the novel creates a feeling of imminent disaster; rather both devices arouse the suspicion that some farcical denouement, and not tragedy, lies ahead. The question still remains: why a sardine can? Several quick answers can obviously be given: it is an imported product, foreign, not Russian; its shape is neither circular nor rectangular, since the corners are rounded; it has to be opened with a key. But Bely's constant preoccupation with words allows one to speculate that in creating the image of a bomb in the shape of a sardine can, he could have been attracted by the word *sardine* itself. The root *sard* forms a number of words with a variety of meanings, all of them pointing to themes which are explicit or implicit in the novel.

Sardinia, the island, gave its name to the fish. But the island might have been of interest to Bely in connection with Theosophical theories concerning prehistoric cultures, since it is one of the earliest inhabited places in the Mediterranean area and many traces of prehistoric man have been found there. Moreover, and this perhaps attracted Bely most of all, the *risus sardonicus* known to the Romans was produced by a poisonous grass found on the island of Sardinia. This pathological sardonic laughter (or rather grimace, facial distortion) was the symptom of the madness caused by the plant. All modern usages of the adjective sardonic derive from that laughter. Sardis, capital of ancient Lydia, may not be derived from the same root, but it contains the same sounds. Sardis had been the cultural center of Asia Minor in the seventh and sixth centuries B.C. Later, an early seat of Christianity, Sardis was the site of one of the Seven Churches in Asia (Rev. 3:1). Since in the novel Bely mentions the Church of Philadelphia, also one of the Seven Churches, one could suppose that Sardis too was on Bely's mind. Finally, a similarity exists between the root *sard* and the root in the Russian word *serdtse* ("heart"). This may allude to the enlarged hearts of father and son. Moreover, in cabalistic and Hermetic terms the heart is the center of man; thus we may have an allusion to the central role played by the sardine can in the structure and the hidden ideas of the novel.

Although the symbol of the bomb destined to explode seems to be very different from the piercing symbol of the unicorn which appears on Ableukhov's crest, both symbols are quite similar in function. While the round (or rather rounded) object acts by expanding violently to tear apart its own walls and the house wall from inside, the piercing object, through the impact of its thrust, tears the wall (or armor, or skin) from the outside. Both symbols connote death and destruction and, by implication, rebirth.

Bely might have developed the association of the two symbols on the basis of a familiar sight in his native Moscow. Bordering on the south of the former Senate Square were the imposing Kremlin Barracks. In front of the main facade stood twenty old-fashioned cannons. Especially noticeable were (and still are) two huge cannons: one called *Tsar pushka* ("Tzar cannon"); and the other, *Edinorog* ("unicorn").[2] Though I have not found a reference to either of the two cannons in any of Bely's works, this source for the two symbolic images in his novel is quite plausible. From one he took only its missile, the bomb; while the other became its own name, the unicorn, a realized metaphor.

These two ideas—of explosion and tearing apart on one hand and of breaking through by piercing, cutting, goring, on the other— seem to symbolize the kind of violence without which no progression toward Steiner's "higher existence" is possible. These ideas are closely connected with the Ableukhovs, especially with Nikolay Apollonovich, and it seems quite credible that they constitute the main occult tenets embodied by Bely in his novel.

NOTES

1. All pages refer to the 1916 edition, reprinted by Bradda Books in 1967.

2. Karl Baedeker, *Russia with Teheran, Port Arthur and Peking* (New York: Charles Scribner's Sons, 1914), p. 295.

JOHN D. ELSWORTH

BELY'S *MOSCOW* NOVELS

In the introduction to his recent translation of *The Silver Dove* G. Reavey declares that *Kotik Letaev* has no thematic connection with Bely's earlier novels.[1] I believe that is mistaken. On the contrary, all Bely's novels are concerned with a single fundamental theme: the crisis of European culture and the possibility of overcoming it. The symptoms of the crisis are the disruption of man's inner life and the conflicting functions of his rational and non-rational activities, his lack of an integral awareness of the external world, and the dislocation of interhuman relations. The root cause to which he attributes these symptoms is the dominance of analytical thought and the consequent viewing of the world in terms of functional, mechanical dependences. The only solution is to be found in a transformation of man's approach to the world, a change in his way of understanding his own cognitive processes—ultimately an act of self-transcendence. It is with this act that the novels are concerned.

The way in which this act is conceived and represented varies substantially in the course of Bely's career. Since the world men inhabit is the product of their way of thinking, Bely's novels come to embody in their structure a relationship between inner experience and outer world. If we take the word plot to denote a series of events in the material world which are connected by material causes, then I believe it is possible to trace Bely's development as a novelist in terms of the relative importance of plot in his novels. There is a more or less straight line of development from *The Silver Dove* to *The Baptized Chinaman*, in the course of which plot consistently decreases in importance, while each novel's motivation is increasingly carried by the imagery that represents inner experience. In *The Baptized Chinaman* the external events follow causally not from each other, but from the inner development of the hero, which is expressed in the imagery. In the sense defined above, the novel does not have a plot, as the episodic events in the material world are given as reflections of the stages of spiritual growth in the hero.

As regards the act of self-transcendence, there is then a gradation from that of Daryalsky, who performs a real physical act and dies a real physical death, to that of Nikolay Letaev, who symbolically reconciles in himself the conflicting forces represented by his parents. The novels display an increasing interiorization of meaningful experience, and a decreasing willingness to measure that experience against the real world. There is a concomitant stylistic development in these novels, as Bely endeavors to make the language perform the function he held it ought to perform, that is, renewing man's perception of the world. Without their stylistic achievements, which are designed to convey to the reader the spiritual growth that the hero is described as attaining, *Kotik Letaev* and *The Baptized Chinaman* would merely be parables.

My purpose in this paper is to try to define briefly the position of Bely's last novels—*The Moscow Eccentric* and *Moscow in Jeopardy* (which comprise volume one of *Moscow*), and *Masks* (which is volume two)—in terms of these three factors: theme, the role of plot, and stylistic peculiarities.

Bely tried to make it appear that the theme of his *Moscow* novels was the decay of bourgeois culture in prerevolutionary Russia (*Moscow*, 1:8). But despite his flirtation with Marxist vocabulary and his lengthy satirical depictions of the cultural scene in prerevolutionary Moscow, it is clear that the theme is much broader and that the crisis he is concerned with is not susceptible to political solution. The pervasive imagery of barbarism, prehistory, and defunct or mythical civilizations, which is the predominant device for expressing the present state of the world and the need for further evolution, can be explained only by reference to the teachings of Anthroposophy. These images represent forces that retard evolution. Every race, in Steiner's theory, has an allotted task to perform in the spiritual evolution of mankind. Some, however, have succumbed to the temptations of destructive cosmic spirits and have failed to fulfill their functions; and so they remain at a lower stage

and retard further evolution.[2] This idea appeared in Bely's published work at least as early as some of his newspaper articles of
1916 and is abundantly evident in *One of the Mansions of the
Realm of Shadows* (1924).[3] In Bely's hands this theory is carefully
distinguished from biological theories of racial supremacy.[4] In 1916
he spoke of cubism and futurism as steps towards barbarism.[5] And
in the *Moscow* novels it is clear that the imagery stands as an interpretation of the spiritual meaning of the culture he is depicting.

The form of thought to which this state of affairs is ultimately
attributable is embodied in the novel's hero, Professor Korobkin.
His mathematical genius has produced a discovery with implications which he failed to perceive. It has a practical application that
would give its possessor unassailable military supremacy. The professor's analytical thought could destroy the world. There are those
who wish to possess his discovery. It is only in this limited sense
that the external action of the novel is caused by the professor's
thought: given that impulse it develops by its own momentum. The
inner action concerns the professor's realization of the true state of
affairs intimated in the imagery of barbarism, his understanding
that his present mode of thought is responsible for that state of
affairs, his gradual transformation of his approach to the world,
and his opportunity of facing the world afresh with his new understanding. The theme of the transformation of consciousness is reflected in various of the minor characters, and the idea that
through its achievement a new form of human community will
come about is expressed as a desire on the part of some. But its
principal expression is in the main plot of Professor Korobkin.

Korobkin's antagonist is one Eduard Mandro, ostensible busi-
nessman and actual German espionage agent, who has learned
about Korobkin's discovery and tries to obtain it. When deception
and bribery fail he turns to violence, and the climax of the first
volume comes when he ties Korobkin to a chair and burns his eye
out with a candle. Korobkin resists the torture and refuses to part
with the discovery. In the course of the scene both men go mad. For
Korobkin this episode marks the final collapse of his belief in the
rational harmony of mathematics, and the transcendence of his
former self. His torture is presented as a crucifixion.

Crucifixion is, of course, a motif that occurs in all Bely's novels.
There is an Anthroposophical explanation for its use, inasmuch as
the three stages of true cognition, or initiation, by which Steiner
would replace analytical thought, are seen as recapitulations of

Christ's birth, crucifixion, and resurrection.[6] The motif was used in both *Kotik Letaev* and *The Baptized Chinaman*, where the child's spiritual development was a painless anticipation of crucifixion in this sense. Only for Daryalsky among Bely's earlier heroes did crucifixion have a literal meaning of physical suffering. But for one thing he died partly because he was simply unable to escape—his affirmation of suffering was at best half-hearted—and for another, he was not resurrected. Korobkin's crucifixion denotes not merely suffering and not merely insight, but both, and their necessary connection; moreover, it is the result of a voluntary decision on his part. Furthermore, in volume two, *Masks*, he is resurrected. Korobkin differs from all of Bely's earlier heroes in one crucial sense: the insight he achieves is ethical in nature. It results from an ethical decision made in a world of real ethical alternatives. And in the second volume that insight is tested in action.

At the beginning of *Masks* Korobkin is suffering from amnesia. His recuperation consists in the gradual recollection and reinterpretation of his past life, the content of volume one. When he has recovered, he is faced with the question of revenge, which is the linking theme of the various strands of action in volume two. Mandro has escaped from the prison hospital and is living under a pseudonym masquerading as a French journalist. His true identity has been guessed by a group of Russian counterintelligence agents, but they cannot act against him until his identity is positively confirmed. The confirmation is to come from his daughter, whom he raped in the first volume and who is now married to a former friend of Korobkin's, a wanted revolutionary; she is therefore also living under a pseudonym. The agents cannot take Mandro out of his hotel to be identified because he is protected by some British agents, and any such action would cause friction between the allies. Professor Korobkin also guesses the identity of Mandro. He does not hold the torture against him, considering that they are both victims of the general state of the world, and that if Abel should rise and kill Cain the whole process will only be repeated indefinitely. He plans to take Mandro to his daughter to be reconciled with her, and since there is nothing to stop him from taking Mandro out of the hotel, he does so. But the consequences of his action are the contrary of his intentions. Although the reconciliation of father and daughter does take place, both are unmasked in the process. Mandro is kidnapped and murdered; his daughter and her husband are exposed and their house is attacked. In the course of the attack a stock of explosives is ignited and the house with all its occupants is blown up.

One of the things the professor has to remember is his discovery. At first its whereabouts are unknown; then it transpires that Kierko (or Titelev), the revolutionary, has it in his possession. He has not told the party he has it, and he plans to withhold it from them unless he can persuade the professor that he has a moral duty to make it available to them. That is to say, he undertakes to persuade Korobkin of the rightness of the revolutionary morality of expedience, the Marxist class morality that Bely, in an article of 1910, had declared to be a denial of all ethics (*Arabesques,* p. 184). Korobkin is unmoved. He rejects the idea of changing the world by violence and destroys his discovery.

By selecting only the main strands of plot in these novels I may have made their plot structure sound more successful than in fact it is. Various faults can be found—for instance, with the motivation of the subplots. There are various characters who suddenly disappear after careful introductions. In general, Bely perhaps was not very good at constructing plots. Nonetheless, the presence of this plot in Bely's work at this time seems to me an important development. Objective reality is accorded an autonomy it has never before possessed. To approach the world with right thoughts is no longer enough; Korobkin's change of mind changes nothing in the external world. But even his action results only in the destruction of the man he was trying to save. Korobkin reaches a viewpoint very similar to Zosima's belief in the responsibility of each for all, but his action is as disastrous as Myshkin's. Mochulsky's and Stepun's conception of the older Bely as a Communist, and of these last novels as a studied betrayal of all that he formerly valued, could hardly be further from the truth.[7]

From the point of view of style the first volume of *Moscow* marks no real advance on *The Baptized Chinaman.* Khodasevich found that the "complex and delicate devices" of the earlier novel had been debased in *Moscow* (*dovedeny do lubka*).[8] And it does lack almost completely the lightness that was so typical of *The Baptized Chinaman. Masks,* however, marks a new stage in Bely's prose and deserves far more attention than I shall give it now. I merely want to make brief mention of one or two features of the language of *Masks.* It is an essential article of Bely's thinking, both in his theory of Symbolism and in his later Anthroposophical writing, that true reality results from the fusion of object and thought.

It can only be expressed in language, and it is therefore language that actually makes the world real. A language of concepts and abstractions, however, in referring men only to past acts of cognition, renders the world unreal (*Symbolism,* pp. 429–48). One of Bely's principal concerns throughout his creative writing was the avoidance of abstraction. In *Masks* he found some new ways of doing this.

It is here that he first developed a new vocabulary of color. The origin of his observations in his collections of stones and leaves is probably well enough known.[9] He had written several years before, in his Sicilian travel notes, that the real colors of nature were infinite gradations, while the notion of color (*kraska*) was a mere abstraction.[10] In *Masks* he attempted to find verbal formulations for the real color gradations of nature. In the introduction he wrote of: "the author's right to color the content of his heroes with objects of their daily life" (*Masks,* p. 11), referring particularly to his use of colors as musical leitmotifs. Since they are conceived as a means of rendering the inner experience of the characters and must therefore carry implicit reference to some system of equivalence between color and experience, these colors certainly retain a symbolic function. At the same time, however, by their appeal to unprejudiced perception, the new words for color shades refer the reader directly to nature instead of to its reflection in previous thought systems.

In the same passage of the introduction Bely speaks of the importance in the novel of the characters' gestures: "the main content of the heroes' spiritual life is given not in words, but in gestures" (*Masks,* p. 11). He conceived of gesture as the expression of that which lies below verbal formulation, without which the words themselves may be misleading. One of the means he employs for the rendering of gestures is a particular type of neologism, a substantival neologism derived from the root of a verb, often with a prefix attached. Some such words are not original neologisms, but preexisting popular forms recorded in Dal's dictionary. Words of this class occur much more frequently in *Masks* than in Bely's earlier novels.[11] Examples are such words as *porkh* (from *porkhat*), *torch* (from *torchat*), *bod* (from *bodat*) (*Masks,* pp. 201, 206, and 242). The expression of gesture through nouns, instead of verbs, of course removes something of the temporal quality of the action, giving the gesture itself a certain existence independent of the performer.

The device is perhaps comparable to Fernand Léger's practice of putting the color slightly to one side of the object in his paintings.

Lastly I want to mention one particular sentence in *Masks* which, it seems to me, provides a good illustration of the basic concern underlying Bely's linguistic innovations: *"—i—ser: skryla rot razodranstvom platka . . . "* ("—and—the grayness: hid his mouth with the tatteredness of a cloth . . . ") (*Masks*, p. 27). What Bely is describing here is a man wearing a torn gray cloth over his mouth; the sentence might be rewritten into standard Russian as: *razodranny sery platok skryl rot . . .* (the tattered gray cloth hid his mouth . . .). This would be the logical sentence resulting from the assimilation and interpretation of all the phenomena observed. Bely, however, presents the phenomena not in this already interpreted order, but in the order of perception, as though they were being perceived for the first time. The first impression is the color gray; the second is the position of this color, where the mouth should be; the third is the quality of the object bearing the color; and only finally is the object identified. The sentence reenacts the process of perception instead of referring the reader to the established concepts derived from past perceptions.

As I see it, these stylistic features have in common the characteristic of revitalizing the immediate, unprejudiced perception of nature. In this way they parallel the inner action of the novel, the professor's gradual abandonment of analytical thought. At the same time they reveal a concern with nature itself which has not been much in evidence in Bely's earlier work. Nature is accorded an autonomy that was unthinkable in the period, say, of *Notes of an Eccentric,* when the outbreak of the world war was attributed to the development of the author's Ego. It seems that Bely came in his later years close to a Goethean conception of art as the perfecting of nature.[12] This is consistent with his view of the function of language and with his hostility towards abstract art, such as cubism. And obviously it is consistent with the reappearance of plot in the novels.

The fact that the plot of these novels is none too well achieved cannot be sidestepped. Nor is it claimed that the innovations described are entirely successful. The widely held view that the *Moscow* novels are Bely's weakest achievement in the genre may well have to stand. Nevertheless, I am arguing that these novels represent a separate, third stage in Bely's development, and not a retrogression. Given the stylistic developments of *Masks* and their consonance with the novel's plot, it is impossible to think of the novel as a whole as some kind of return to the traditions of the nineteenth-century novel. Weak though they may be, the *Moscow* novels will need to be studied with greater and more sympathetic attention than hitherto, if Bely's work after his return to Russia in 1923 is to receive adequate consideration.

NOTES

1. Andrey Bely, *The Silver Dove,* trans. G. Reavey (New York: Grove Press, 1974), p. xiii.

2. R. Steiner, *An Outline of Occult Science* (London: R. Steiner Publishing Co., 1939), passim.

3. See particularly: A. Bely, "Mertvye goroda," *Birzhevye vedomosti,* no. 15745 (17 August 1916): 2; A. Bely, *Odna iz obiteley tsarstva teney* (Leningrad: Gos. izd., 1924), pp. 39–64.

4. Andrey Bely, 'Die Anthroposophie und Russland,' *Die Drei,* 4. Heft. (July 1922): 320–21; A. Bely, *Putevye zametki. Sitsiliya. Tunis* (Moscow, Berlin: Gelikon, 1922), p. 297.

5. Andrey Bely, "Mertvye goroda," p. 2.

6. A. Bely, *O smysle poznaniya* (Pb.: Epokha, 1922), p. 73. This work leans heavily upon Steiner's *Philosophie der Freiheit.*

7. K. Mochulsky, *Andrey Bely* (Paris: YMCA, 1955), p. 265; F. Stepun, *Mystische Weltschau* (Munich: Hanser, 1964), p. 351.

8. V. F. Khodasevich, "Andrey Bely. *Kreshcheny kitaets,*" *Sovremennye zapiski,* no. 32 (1927): 455.

9. A. Bely et al., *Kak my pishem* (Leningrad: Izd. pisateley, 1930), p. 14; K. N. Bugaeva, *Memoirs of A. Bely,* ch. 3, "Rabota nad *Maskami.* 'Tematika,' 'Mozaika,' " typescript, p. 7.

10. A. Bely, *Putevye zametki. Sitsiliya. Tunis,* pp. 147–49.

11. Their frequency can be checked against the lists in: L. Hindley, *Die Neologismen Andrej Belyjs* (Munich: Fink, 1966), pp. 24ff.

12. Bely attributes to Goethe the opinion that "poetry is the mature fruit of nature"; *Putevye zametki. Sitsiliya. Tunis,* p. 132. I have not succeeded in tracing the source of this quotation, but Goethe certainly speaks of art as "the light of nature" and "the most worthy interpreter of nature"; *Goethes Werke* (Weimar: Hermann Böhlaus Nachfolger, 1887–1919), vol. 37 (1896), p. 87; Goethe, *Maximen und Reflexionen* (Stuttgart: Alfred Kroner, 1943), p. 86. I am grateful for Professor B. A. Rowley's help in finding these quotations.

PART II

BELY AND HIS MILIEU

ROBERT P. HUGHES

~~~~~~~~~~~~~~~~

BELY'S MUSICAL AESTHETICS

The musical scale enforms
For me the universe—
From urban deformation
To the formless mysteries of Erebus,
And to the light of human forms
In multi-formities of the sky
(trans. by G. Janecek)

Mne muzykalny zvukoryad
Otobrazhaet mirozdane—
Ot bezobrazy gorodskikh
Do tayn bezobrazy Ereba,
Do sveta obrazov lyudskikh
Mnogoobraziyami neba . . .
"The First Encounter"
(Poetry, *p. 426*)

This brief study is an attempt to elucidate in Bely's earliest theoretical writings the philosophical and aesthetic bases for some of the content and certain formal techniques of his literary work.[1] More particularly, it deals with the impact of the philosophy and aesthetic system of Schopenhauer on the young Bely, with specific attention to his notions about the preeminence of music as an art form. Even a characteristic outburst "against music" by Bely was predicated on the assumption that it is the ultimate art. These ideas were later modified, but they nevertheless remained fundamental to his thought.

Any reader of Andrey Bely is soon made aware of the overwhelming importance of music for him, in his private and public life, in his personal and professional activities.[2] Music is present in almost everything he ever wrote—be it memoir, literary and aesthetic theory, criticism, fiction, or poetry. It was no exaggeration on his part to say, in 1921, that for him "the musical scale enforms [or: depicts] for me the universe." Indeed one might wonder, then, why Bely's genius did not express itself in music. (It seems he had the technical wherewithal.) Some speculation on this point will be forthcoming.

A source of Bely's fascination and absorption with the art of music, in an abstract and philosophical sense, was his reading of Schopenhauer's *World as Will and Representation* in Afanasy Fet's translation (*Mir kak volya i predstavlenie*, 1881).[3] Bely also, of course, found a similar exalted view of the position of music among the arts in Nietzsche's *Birth of Tragedy out of the Spirit of Music*, which itself owed a good deal to Schopenhauer.

Schopenhauer considered art the most perfect form of cognition, a means of perception that could grasp the actual form or image of the world in its essence. (One is prompted to consider in this light Bely's play with the root word *obraz* in the passage from "The First Encounter.") This cognition, which relies on intuition, Schopenhauer juxtaposed to a "lower" rationalistic, scientific cognition, which relies on the intellect. To be clear, Schopenhauer's aesthetics, including the positioning of music at the summit of his hierarchy of the arts, must be seen in the context of his metaphysics. It is in the first two books of his principal work that his view of the metaphysical structure of the world is set forth. Schopenhauer saw the world as subjective. For the individual, the world can be posited only in relation to his own consciousness: being, then, is dependent on perception. But the world revealed in ordinary acts of perception is only a phenomenon, only the idea or image or representation of it. The world is more than image, representation, or idea; it is the externalization or objectification of something prior to matter and consciousness, the ultimate reality which is spoken of as the cosmic force, impulse, desire, striving, blind universal instinct—the true thing-in-itself, that is, the Will.

Schopenhauer's aesthetics are developed in the third book of his magnum opus. The basic presupposition of his aesthetic theory is that art is an escape from the workings of the Will, an interlude of peace. In artistic contemplation, man is oblivious of his own selfhood because he becomes the mirror of the object of perception. Even though, however, art releases the individual from the bondage of life, the release is only temporary, for art ultimately is not perfect.

The capacity to apprehend the Idea, to penetrate to the Ideal world, constitutes genius; genius, for Schopenhauer, implies becoming a pure subject of knowledge. But a genius is doomed to suffer madness. The true artist is, of course, a genius; consequently, he is a madman. The notion agrees with the theories and the behavior of Bely. He surely could subscribe, as did Fet, incidentally, to the proposition that madness was the mark of the true poet and that poetic inspiration was a matter of intuition and irrationality.

Schopenhauer arranges the arts in a hierarchy. Their value is determined on the basis of the grades of objectification of the Will which they manifest and express. The arts reproduce the Ideas, the recurrent universals: they are architecture, sculpture, painting, poetry (i.e., literature), and music. The art of arts for Schopenhauer is music. It is neither like architecture, which attempts to express the Ideas by showing them directly manifesting themselves in natural materials, nor like painting, sculpture, and even poetry, which exhibit particular things in another medium. Actually, music is not concerned with expressing the Ideas at all. It is *the* nonconceptual art. Music is the direct expression of the Will: it does not represent, it does not contemplate—it is the Will become audible. Therefore it is the inmost metaphysical reality of the cosmos, which "proclaims in melody its essential being."

Music is the language of emotion, as words are the language of reason. But, importantly, music has no direct relation to feelings and passions, for it expresses the inner nature rather than the phenomenon itself. Music "does not therefore express this or that particular joy, this or that sorrow, or pain, or horror, or delight, or merriment, or peace of mind; but joy, sorrow, pain, horror, delight, merriment, peace of mind *themselves,* to a certain extent in the abstract, their essential nature, without accessories, and therefore without their motives. Yet we completely understand them in this extracted quintessence." [4]

Schopenhauer emphasizes the lack of specific content in music. It is for this reason that music is a consolation: it allows, to a far greater extent than any other art (which can only represent the Ideas in another medium), the recipient to become a creator, to invest the feeling-pattern of music with the content of his own mood, of his own being. Universal joy becomes a specific joy, so also with sorrow; and thus the line between being and music is obliterated. Music more perfectly consummates and clarifies and organizes experience than does any other art.

These, then, were among the stimulating ideas that Bely the gymnasium student was discussing in the highly charged yet homely atmosphere of the Solovyov apartment, his home away from home from the mid-nineties until the death of both Mikhail and Olga Solovyov in January 1903. Publically, Bely's views were aired at the meetings of the Argonauts (devoted primarily to the religious and mystical ideas of Vladimir Solovyov) and other philosophical discussion circles in Moscow.[5]

Sometime in 1902, Bely read two reports on his aesthetic ideas to the Trubeckoy Philosophical Circle; it was a résumé of these two papers that he published as his essay "The Forms of Art" in *Mir Iskusstva* toward the end of the year.[6] Bely accepts—and elaborates—the hierarchy of the forms of art established by Schopenhauer. As in both Hegel and Schopenhauer, the two categories of time and space are essential. The three spatial forms, in ascending order of perfection: architecture, sculpture, and painting. The two temporal forms: poetry and music.

Two determinants of this specific hierarchy emerge in Bely's argument: the quality and the quantity of raw material; and the potential of one art form for influencing another art form, which is possible only between those standing next to each other in the hierarchy. Thus we have what might be called statuesque painting, poetic painting, picturesque poetry, etc. We need not pause on the specific materials of the spatial arts, except perhaps to note the operation of the principle, as it were, of economy of means: the colored paints and the two-dimensional nature of a painting are more economical or "laconic" (the word Bely uses) than the three dimensions and the bulkier and more numerous materials of sculpture and architecture.

Next we "ascend" to the temporal arts: poetry, which can be rendered by a one-dimensional line on a page or be a human utterance of a sound; and, ultimately, music, which Bely views as pure movement, as rhythm (the most natural and economic material possible). Some years later, in recalling his early article, Bely summarized its contents in the following terms: "The basic idea of the article: Art forms are arranged in a temporal gradation from the inertia of spatial forms to the active dynamism of the musical world. The evolution of the world of arts is from architecture to symphonic music. In a temporal order, music historically takes shape later and, in a formal order, it is the most perfect art. In abolishing the material of the arts, it is the figured-bass of all the arts and the primary kernel of the art of the future, which is in the creative activity of human relationships, in the mystery of life." [7]

Bely followed very closely the hierarchy of the arts proposed by Schopenhauer; also implicit in the article is the whole metaphysical outlook of the philosopher. For Schopenhauer the Ideas can in some sense be directly perceived (i.e., manifested in art), whereas the Will cannot be, although an inner knowledge of it is possible. The inner side of man, his instincts and his passions (i.e., his will), finds its most profound and complete expression in music; and we feel that it embodies something profoundly true about ourselves and the world. Man experiences, and the composer reveals, the essence of the world in a language which his reason does not understand. Schopenhauer's, and Bely's, conception of music is closely bound up with the view of each individual as a microcosm carrying the kernel of the whole of existence.

Most interesting and important—vis-à-vis both Bely's art in particular and modern literary art in general—is Bely's focus on Schopenhauer's assertion that our individual human consciousness has as its form not space, but only time. The constant change in the world around us—the old Heraclitean flux—is perceived as a series of continuous instantaneous photographs by our senses. It is for this reason that reality cannot be rendered complete by a spatial art, but only by a temporal one. What places Bely squarely in the modern world is his attempt to render in his art the flux, the constant changes in time, that constitutes the individual self-consciousness. And this he does, of course, by employing the techniques of music, the temporal art par excellence. Connected with this is the necessity of rendering causality in a work of art that depicts the real world (which is what all art is, according to Bely). This again is impossible for the purely spatial arts; and only in those arts which move in time can this be represented—above all, again, in music.

However, the ultimate justification for poetry, in Bely's view, is its potential for depicting changes in and among spatial forms; i.e., it represents forms and their causal movement. Poetry is the "nodal" form of art, as it links time and space. It is the bridge which extends between the spatial and the temporal arts. The direct rendering of one or another aspect of reality is the realm of the spatial forms. In poetry we meet with an indirect rendering of reality. In the most typical forms of music apparent reality disappears.

Beginning with the lower forms of art and ending with music, we are present at a slow but certain weakening of the images of reality.

In architecture, sculpture, and painting these images play an important role. In music they are absent. As it approaches music, the work
of art becomes deeper and broader.

. . . every form of art has as its starting point reality and as its
concluding one, music, as pure movement. Or, to express it in Kantian terms, every art goes deeper into the "noumenal." Or, according
to Schopenhauer, every art leads us to the pure contemplation of
the universal Will. Or, speaking Nietzsche's language, every form
of art is defined by the degree of the manifestation in it of the spirit
of music. Or, according to Spencer, every art is directed to the future. Or, finally, [Hanslick] "The realm of music in actual fact is
not of this world." (*Symbolism*, pp. 165–66)

This passage, repeated with variations twice in the course of
Bely's essay, is a revealing one: it suggests that even though music
is the art form nearest perfection, there is a danger clear and present in it. Notwithstanding its profundity, music is in touch with
reality only in a most tenuous way; movement alone cannot render
reality. Poetry, on the margin between the spatial and the temporal
arts, is the single art form that can suggest both the images of
reality and their interrelationships and movement in time. There
can be little doubt that the motivation for Bely's choice of poetry
over music lies in these considerations.

Not unlike Pushkin's Salieri, confronted with the pure music of
Mozart, Bely feels compelled to fend off the seductive siren of music.
Perhaps the most striking evidence we have is his abandoning of
the forms of his prose symphonies, after publishing four of them
between 1902 and 1908. Further proof is available in his theoretical
and polemical articles published in the same period. In his 1903
article "On Theurgy" Bely gave warning of the dual nature of
music, the possibility of its becoming "demonic magic." [8] His little
notice "Against Music" and the ensuing polemical exchange with
his friend Emily Metner in 1907 are similarly motivated.[9]

Bely's clearest summary statement—and let it serve as conclusion, therefore—on the relationship among the arts, and particularly that between poetry and music, is to be found in an article of
1906, "The Principle of Form in Aesthetics." [10]

Reality is divided among the existing forms of art. There is no
form in art that encompasses all reality. In studying the means of embodying artistic creative activity, we have to do above all with differ-
entiation. Some forms of art more perfectly render the elements of the

spatial; others, the elements of the temporal. Sculpture and architecture have to do with three-dimensional spatial depiction.

Architecture depicts the correlation of masses; sculpture, the correlation of forms. Painting is abstracted from three-dimensional spatial depiction. Its province is the plane. Thanks to this abstracting, painting gains in the richness of depiction. It puts foremost emphasis on color. Music has to do with reality itself, abstracted from the visible. It depicts the changing of experiences, without trying to find for them the corresponding form of the visible. Time is the most essential formal element of music. It advances the meaning of rhythm to the fore. Poetry combines the formal conditions of temporal and spatial forms of art *through the medium* [*posredstvom*] of the word: the *word depicts medially* [*posredstvenno*]; this is poetry's weakness. But the word depicts not only the *form* of the image, but also the *changing* of images. This is poetry's strength. Poetry is medial, but the diapason of the sphere of its depicting is broad; poetry converts spatial features into temporal features; and conversely.

[In music] the temporal is expressed in rhythm. The spatial is not rendered. Space is expressed in music through the medium of vague analogies. Pitch and intensity of tone are analogous to the density of and the distance [in space between] masses. The quality of a tone is analogous to color. These analogies give no ground for any kind of essential conclusions. In music there is ideal space before us. Consequently, also the images evoked by music are ideal. If art is symbolic, then the task of its images is to combine the ideal and the eternal in the elements of what is finite. But the images evoked by music are perfect: that is why music, being a temporal form, influences the spatial forms of art also. That is why the spirit of music is possible in forms of art that are nonmusical in essence. It is there rendered potentially. Music therefore is the latent energy of creative activity; the fewer the formal means expended on the embodying of this energy, the more perfect the form of the image. Time is the form of internal feeling. And it is for this reason that music, as a purely temporal form, expresses symbols that seem to us especially profound. Music intensifies anything it touches: music is the soul of all the arts. That is why in it there are clearly projected the basic demands which we must make on art. A symbol is the joining of experience with the form of an image. But such a joining, if it is possible, is accessible through the medium of the form of inner feeling, i.e., time. That is why any true symbol is involuntarily musical—i.e., it involuntarily idealizes empirical reality, to a greater or lesser degree abstracted from the actual conditions of space.

In poetry the element of the temporal, pure rhythm, so to speak, is overgrown with images. Thus is born the Apollonian vision out of the depths of the soul. Only music reveals to us that the visible is a veil thrown over the abyss. Poetry scrutinizes the visible musically, as a veil above the unuttered secret of the soul. Such a scrutiny is a musical scrutiny. Music is the skeleton of poetry. If music is the common trunk of creative activity, then poetry is its leafy crown. The images of poetry, as growths upon a rhythm free of images, restrict rhythmical freedom, so to speak; they burden it with the visible. A musical theme then becomes a myth. If poetry burdens music with images, also then conversely: thanks to poetry, music permeates the visible. In poetry we have to do with images and their changing. As a result there is a significant complicating of the formal elements of art. This complicating is expressed in the medium of the images. The medium of depiction facilitates the substituting of the images of a poetic myth by the causal basis of their linking. If the myth, so to speak, is a growth upon the rhythm, then the complicating and the breaking-down of the myth leads to the growth on it of elements that have no direct relationship to art. Myth as it were is parasitic on a free musical theme; tendentiousness [then becomes parasitic] on the myth. All this removes the elements of pure art from its primary, musical basis. Such a removal complicates the formal elements of art. The music of creative activity now becomes a distant background, the form of the images exclusively moves to the fore. Only sometimes is the motherland of poetry (the musical element) revealed in its forms. (*Symbolism*, pp. 177–80; italics are Bely's)

NOTES

1. The focus here is on the material published between 1902 and 1908. Note that this is the fourth (the first literary) of the "seven-year periods" into which Bely divided his life and work. See his memoirs and, recently and significantly, Georges Nivat's publication of Bely's autobiographical letter to Ivanov-Razumnik in *Cahiers du monde russe et soviétique* 15, nos. 1–2 (Janvier-Juin 1974): 45–82.

2. See, for example, Simon Karlinsky, "Symphonic Structure in Andrej Belyj's 'Pervoe svidanie,' " *California Slavic Studies* 6 (1971): 61–70.

3. Fet, who had returned to literature in the 1880s and 1890s with his *Vechernie ogni* and who was taken up by the modernists for the melodiousness of his verse, was a favorite poet of Bely's in his early years. (Perhaps only Vladimir Solovyov is quoted more frequently in his initial epistolary exchange with Aleksandr Blok.) Fet thus plays an important if somewhat indirect role in the shaping of the aesthetics

of the young Bely, both through his translation of Schopenhauer and by the example of his suggestive, musical lyric poetry.

4. Arthur Schopenhauer, *Selections*, ed. DeWitt H. Parker (New York: Charles Scribner's Sons, 1956), p. 182.

5. See, among others, Vladimir Orlov, "Istoriya odnoy 'druzhby-vrazhdy,'" in *Puti i sudby* (Leningrad: Sovetsky pisatel, 1971), especially pp. 532–36.

6. Andrey Bely, "Formy iskusstva," *Mir Iskusstva,* no. 12 (1902): 343–61. As evidence of Bely's fascination with *real* music, see his "Pevitsa," a lavish tribute to the singer Mariya Olenina d'Algeym in the previous issue of *Mir Iskusstva,* no. 11, 302–4. The theoretical essay was republished in a somewhat revised version, with copious commentary, in *Symbolism,* pp. 149–74; commentary, pp. 507–23.

7. Andrey Bely, "Vospominaniya ob A. A. Bloke," *Zapiski Mechtatelej,* no. 6 (1922): 17.

8. Andrey Bely, "O teurgii," *Novy Put,* no. 9 (1903): 100–123.

9. Boris Bugaev, "Protiv muzyki," *Vesy,* no. 3 (1907): 57–60; Volfing [Emily Metner], "Boris Bugaev protiv muzyki," *Zolotoe Runo,* no. 5 (1907): 56–62; Boris Bugaev, "Pismo v redaktsiyu (po povodu stati Volfinga v *Zolotom Rune:* 'Boris Bugaev protiv muzyki,'" *Pereval,* no. 10 (1907): 58–60. I am grateful to Thomas Beyer for drawing my attention to this exchange.

10. Andrey Bely, "Printsip formy v estetike," *Zolotoe Runo,* nos. 11–12 (1906): 88–96. The article was reprinted in *Symbolism,* pp. 175–94; commentary, pp. 524–35.

GEORGE KALBOUSS

ANDREY BELY AND THE MODERNIST
MOVEMENT IN RUSSIAN DRAMA

As was the case with many of his fellow Russian Symbolist poets, Andrey Bely was very much interested in the development of a new Russian theater. During the period 1900–1910, Bely participated in many of the debates among Russian intellectuals regarding the creation of such a theater—debates which centered upon the theory of drama, the meaning of art, and the forms that new plays should take. Bely's contributions to these debates are primarily in the area of drama theory, rather than through the creation of plays. Unlike other Symbolists, such as Sologub and Blok, who wrote a relatively large number of plays, Bely published only two dramatic sketches between 1900 and 1906.[1] It was only in 1925 that Bely wrote a full-length play that received production: a dramatization of *Petersburg* entitled *Gibel Senatora* (Mochulsky, p. 259).

Bely's theoretical works are valuable on two accounts: first, they present the ideas of a significant literary figure of the Russian Symbolist movement on the theater; and second, they reflect an ambivalence toward the drama that is typical of Russian Symbolist literature—namely, a lack of consistency in supporting either a drama that is overtly symbolic and uses the imagery of Symbolist poetry, or one that is overtly realistic, yet in which symbols underscore various significant moments in the drama. In this essay I will endeavor to address myself to this ambivalence in Bely's writings on the theater and to comment upon how they reflect and parallel some trends within Russian Symbolism during the years 1900 to 1910.

Konstantin Mochulsky, in his critical biography of Bely, mentions more than once that Bely was an avid theatergoer, and that by the age of eighteen he had already written his first dramatic piece, the poetic mystery play, *Prishedshy*, most likely inspired by Maeterlinck and Adam (p. 23). In the early 1900s, Bely's search for a transfigurative force in art led him to seek the creation of a new *misteriya* (mystery play) which, through its symbolism, mythological imagery, and structure which fused the arts, would create a religious experience for its audience and reveal a world hidden within the real one. Bely, of course, was not alone in this search; many other Symbolists, inspired by Nietzsche's *Birth of Tragedy*, were also searching for ways to revive mystery plays at this time. In 1906, however, with the disillusionment of the revolution, the Japanese war, and disagreements among the Symbolists, Bely abandoned the idea of reviving the mystery play and instead began to advocate the writing of drama in the manner of his favorite playwright, Henrik Ibsen, whose plays revealed to Bely a vision of the future through a symbolism which did not rely on mythological language or any strong attempt to fuse the arts.

Bely and the other Symbolists were frequent visitors to the theater. Mochulsky briefly relates that Bely lectured on Przybyszewski's *Vechnaya skazka* at Komissarzhevskaya's theater and that, after the lecture, the great actress proposed to Bely that the two of them consider the creation of a special theatrical university which would, in turn, create a "theatrical man" (pp. 140–41). Unfortunately, little is known about this proposal; perhaps it is related to some of the ideas that Komissarzhevskaya's director, Nikolay Evreinov, was developing at that time.

Drama and theater are discussed in Bely's views on the aesthetics of art; these views stand closer in his writings to the philosophical aspects of aesthetics than to their practical applications in the theater. To Bely, drama represents a complicated form of creative expression which captures the interplay of various forms of art, ranging from the purely formal, such as music, to the more content-ridden, such as poetry, prose, and the visual arts. Besides being a "link" genre in which these various forms of art interact, drama is connected to religious experience through its Dionysian beginnings and is thereby endowed with a power to enlarge art from an aesthetic to a religious-philosophical experience. The existence of the realistic or naturalistic drama in the nineteenth century stands as an aberration in the historical development of drama, preventing the religious drama from continuing in its legitimate role as a form of religious expression in a given culture. Bely hoped that if the new drama did return to its historical role, a new, religious theater could be created, providing a unique, transfiguring experience to the spectator that was unavailable in the realistic theater of the time.

In his writings from 1900 to 1906, Bely strongly advocated the idea that drama should again be the *misteriya*. Bely was not alone within Symbolism in advocating this idea at this time; a number of articles were written together with Bely's discussing Dionysian mystery plays and their possible meaning to the development of modern drama.[2] Several of the Symbolists, notably V. Ivanov, I. Annensky, K. Balmont, and Z. Gippius attempted to write such plays; indeed over twenty-five original mystery plays were written between 1890 and 1910, most of them between 1900 and 1906.[3] Moreover, several theaters attempted to resurrect mystery plays of various periods in apparently faithful productions. Bely was no doubt familiar with the attempt of the Moscow "Literaturno-khudozhestvenny kruzhok" to stage Polotsky's *O tsare Navukho-donosore, o teltse zlatom i o tryokh otrokakh v peshchi* in 1903.[4]

Yet, while Symbolist literature clearly identifies the ancient Dionysian mystery as the model for the *misteriya* of the future, each critical work on the mystery posts its own ideas regarding exactly how it should look. In some writings, *misteriya* means a return to a rather accurate re-creation of the liturgical drama of the middle ages and of the Dionysian rituals. In other cases, the drama should contain the spirit of the mystery play; this is the position that Bely takes: "The seeds of future drama and opera are found in the the dithyrambs honoring Dionysus. Today, drama draws closer and closer to music (Ibsen, Maeterlinck and others) while opera is becoming musical drama."[5]

Agreement is generally reached in the notion that mystery plays intertwine the natural and the supernatural and that the presentation is somehow involved with a fusion of the arts, particularly of words with music. Yet, as we shall see, the term *music* does not necessarily relate to singing and musical instruments. Unfortunately, literary history has only noted satires on the mystery, such as the play-within-a-play in the *Seagull* and Mayakovsky's *Mysteriya-buff.*

In one of his first articles on aesthetics, "Formy iskusstva," quoted in the above paragraph, Bely presents some ideas that drama is the medium which connects music with the spoken word. As a transitional form of art, drama is able to combine aesthetically the continua of time, in which music exists, and space, in which one finds action and the visual arts. The promise of modern drama, which casts aside the conventions of nineteenth-century realism and naturalism, is to recapture drama's religious origins. In modern dramas Bely finds the "musical" together with the realistic. However, Bely's use of the term *musical* is abstract—that is, music is an art which is pure form. The "musical" occurs at special moments in a drama; the master of creating such moments is Ibsen. Ibsen's dramas are symbolic because they contain various levels; the intersection of those levels creates these moments of "music":

> When we immerse ourselves in Ibsen's symbolic mood-dramas, we are overwhelmed by the dualities, and sometimes even triplicities of their meaning. Allegory occasionally emerges within the ordinary drama, yet the allegory does not exhaust the drama's depths. The background upon which the dramatic and allegorical action develops is the "mood" [*nastroennost*] of these dramas, i.e., their *musicality* [italics mine], imagelessness, "bottomlessness." . . . This simultaneous presence of dramatic effects with musicality, the unification of these two elements inevitably leads to symbolism.[6]

Thus, the "symbolic" in the drama occurs when an art form of one type is unified, perhaps momentarily, with that of another; the emerging relationship creates an endless number of possibilities of understanding. Merezhkovsky, in his Symbolist "manifesto" "On the Reasons for the Decline, etc. . . ." written ten years earlier, cites an example of Ibsen underscoring a moment of truth in a drama by having a servant carry in a lighted lamp.[7] Merezhkovsky, of course, is paying attention to a dramatic device common to virtually all dramas of all times and he probably endows it with greater "symbolic" significance than it deserves. Bely, on the other hand, truly admires Ibsen's ability to create numerous levels in his works, from the purely contextual to the most highly abstract and symbolic. If a symbol is to be an image with "n" number of possible meanings, then Bely sees in Ibsen's plays "n" number of levels, and therefore they are true works of symbolism.

Nevertheless, Bely has moved away slightly from the Nietzschean idea of "fusion of the arts" in which the traditional forms of art are united on the stage in a musical drama. "Music" is that part of a drama which, in its formlessness, sets a mood and communicates the existence of something greater than what is on the stage. He continues:

> In the future, according to Solovyov, Merezhkovsky and others, we must return to a religious understanding of reality. The musical qualities of contemporary dramas, their symbolism—do they not indicate that drama is striving to become a mystery play? Drama emerged out of the mystery play. It is destined to return to it. If drama approaches a mystery play, returns to it, then it will inevitably descend from the stage and spread into life. Do we not have in this a hint regarding the transformation of life into a mystery play? Are they not preparing in life to perform some world-wide mystery? [8]

Music, then, is very close to symbolism. In his review of the Moscow Art Theater's presentation of Chekhov's *Ivanov,* Bely criticizes the theater for not infusing music into the presentation. Obviously, Bely is not referring to guitars and pianos—the theater was famous for injecting actual music into its productions—but rather to the fact that the theater lacked the kind of "music" that Bely defined as the result of several art forms interacting on the stage at the same time. Bely even adds that this lack of "music" is so prevalent in the Art Theater that the theater would be incapable of endowing a Maeterlinck play with any symbolism.[9]

In "Apocalypse in Russian Poetry," Bely suggests that the mystery play should incarnate the vision of Solovyov's "Eternal Feminine": "The image of the Feminine incarnate must become the focus of the mystery play, embodying the all-unified beginning of mankind. The Feminine, as revealed to Solovyov, must descend from the sky ánd immerse us in the Sun of life, in the mystery play." [10]

This is perhaps the most specific Bely is regarding a possible cast of characters in the mystery play. Unfortunately, he is rarely more specific, and his terminology is much more strongly metaphorical than it is technical. His comments, however, do demonstrate how he sees the symbol expressed on the stage—namely, as that point when several of the arts converge on a particular moment in the drama, or when they illustrate a certain abstract understanding. Bely's understanding of the symbol in the drama, at this point in his writings, shows that he is clearly avoiding some of the more traditional understandings of symbolic drama, such as allegory, or verse drama; instead he is searching for ways that drama could express the Symbolist vision of the universe, both through time-bound images and moments of music.

Mochulsky states that the end of 1905 also represents the end of Bely's "mystery" period. Bely, of course, was again not alone in abandoning some of the earlier ideas and theories of Symbolism; after the many disappointments of 1905, many of the Symbolists interested in the drama began to look to other forms than the mystery play as possible outlets for their creativity. As the writing of mystery plays diminished, two different kinds of dramas began to appear more frequently: the short, satirical, and device-conscious "fantasy-play" (my term) such as Blok wrote (*Balaganchik, Neznakomka*); and the longer, "realistic" drama, in the manner of Ibsen, in which the symbolic was found beneath the layers of reality. Bely chose the second type of drama, which I term the "contemporary-symbolic" play.[11]

Bely's rejection of the mystery play is closely related to a change in his attitude regarding the function of a symbol in the drama and, indeed, with the very definition of the symbol. In the articles mentioned above, Bely refers to the "symbolic" as occurring when the stage expresses the "musical," in other words, in the intersection of various interacting art forms. After 1906, Bely comes up with a new idea of the symbol, suggesting that it is an image presenting a vision of the future, a way of expressing that which is to come without knowing exactly what it will be. Again, Bely finds this kind of symbol in Ibsen. Ibsen's dramas of the *Master Builder* type, which present dynamic visionaries as their main heroes, provide momentary glimpses into the future world. Bely again advocates that art reach out beyond limits of the stage, but not to create a religious experience as before; now he hopes that drama should present a prophecy of the future. The drama remains a "link" genre; but instead of a unifying of the arts, it now unifies the future with the present.

In his post-1905 articles on Ibsen, Bely advocates the idea that the future hero will change drama because Ibsen's characters somehow decide to act: "Ibsen's heroes always go off into the mountains. This means that they strive for the sun. Dostoevsky's heroes speak of the sun-drenched city as if they had actually been there, yet they remain in their rooms." [12] Future drama is ultimately optimistic; the action of Ibsen's dramas promises that man will ultimately conquer the fates. In "Theater and Contemporary Drama,"

Bely writes: "When Ibsen shows us his [characters], he speaks about what he knows: there will come a day when the dead awaken. But how this will happen, Ibsen does not know." [13]

Along with Bely's new understanding of the symbol in drama, he also rejects his former ideas regarding the mystery play. Certainly the mystery play, envisaged in the way Bely had, had to have been created out of a readily understood image-system, or mythology. Perhaps by 1906 Bely understood only too well that neither he nor any other poet could create a new mythology which would be readily understood by masses of people. It was over ten years later that Vladimir Mayakovsky succeeded in doing this, but by using the image-system of Marxism and in a humorous way. Bely, of course, was serious in his former undertaking.

Bely's writings after 1906 reflect the idea that without a new mythology, the mystery play will always remain an archeological or poetic oddity, and that the industrial-oriented twentieth-century audience could never become a Dionysiac chorus:

> We are supposed to convert life itself into drama. And we enter the theater-temple, we don white clothes, crown ourselves with garlands of roses, and perform a mystery play. . . . at the proper moment we take each other by the hand and begin to dance. . . . Will it be we that circle together around the sacrificial victim—all of us: a woman dressed in *Style moderne,* a stockbroker, a worker, and a member of a government council? I am convinced that our prayers will not coincide. . . . No, it is better to dance a waltz with a beautiful girl than to participate in some choral dance with an Actual Privy Councillor.[14]

Yet Bely still maintains a hope for the drama to convert the spectator, endowing drama with an extra function that poetry and prose do not have. While rejecting the mystery play and accepting the contemporary-symbolic drama, Bely really continues to look for a special philosophical and visionary quality in drama.

Bely also bitterly rejects the types of plays Blok had begun to write. Blok, too, rejects the idea of the mystery play, but he chooses to satirize it and the idea that the poet is a visionary in his so-called lyric dramas. History has it that Bely's motives for attacking Blok are not purely aesthetic; that Blok had satirized Bely in *Balaganchik,* giving the prideful Bely little choice but to reject the kind of drama which Blok had begun to create. It should be noted, moreover, that Blok's *Balaganchik* represents the very first of a genre of "fantasy" plays in Russian dramatic literature in which the devices of the stage play an important part in the development of the plot and that, in this way, they are the Russian contribution to this new genre of dramas which were to become very popular in western Europe. Bely, however, sees little value in Blok's dramas: "Blok's lyrics, a drama torn up into shreds, did not pass over into drama; drama supposes a struggle or a perishing for something. There is perishing in Blok's dramas, but not for any purpose whatsoever. It is simply perishing for the sake of perishing." [15]

Contrary to Bely's hope that drama should provide a window into the future, Blok's dramas scorn the poet and anyone who has hopes and visions of a new world. Moreover, "perishing for the sake of perishing" is another way of saying "art for art's sake," or that the artist is free to do with his characters what he pleases, a principle which Bely chose to subordinate in the drama. Blok's theater presents a miniature world out of which there is no exit; Bely looks to the theater to provide new exits for man's aspirations. Blok, as dramatic history has shown, correctly predicted that western twentieth-century drama would be mostly engaged with the theme of no exit.

Bely's "Theater and Contemporary Drama" also contains some practical ideas regarding stage presentations. Bely no longer advocates that stage barriers be dropped. In reflecting upon Ibsen, Bely states that he cannot imagine anything more ludicrous than a presentation of *Enemy of the People* in which Stockmann gives a speech and the audience is forced to imagine that it is a crowd of Norwegian townspeople listening to him.

Acting, at this point in Bely's understanding, is meant to communicate the fact that the symbol expresses a vision of the future. Each character, to Bely, is both a person in the present and a person in the process of becoming. Acting, therefore, must be engaged in capturing that moment between being (in the present) and becoming (in the future). An actor who can succeed in conveying this aspect of the character will contribute to making actual the symbolic dimensions of a play. Bely thus continues to assert the need for capturing the moment when interactions take place; while formerly it was an interaction between two different art forms, now it is between two aspects of time.

In the same article, Bely also makes a small prophecy regarding "democratic theater." Having abandoned the idea that a religious theater will enrapture the masses, Bely predicts that the new medium of the cinema will succeed in the same goal. Perhaps his prediction about the cinema is one of his most perceptive prophecies on the theater of the twentieth century. "Theater and Contemporary Drama" represents Bely's most significant contribution to the literature of Russian Symbolist theory of the drama. After 1910 the Russian Symbolist movement loses much of its strength and is replaced by various other poetic schools. Its legacy in drama, however, remains strong throughout the teens, particularly in the presentations of original fantasy-satires written for the intimate theaters of Meyerhold, Evreinov, Tairov, and others. Bely, however, did not contribute much to these theaters.

If one can find a common theme in Bely's writings on the drama, it is that the drama has a special, prophetic role in society. In both his pre- and post-1906 periods of writing, Bely strives to impose nonartistic goals on the drama: the mystery play must implant a religious appreciation of the world into the spectator; the contemporary-symbolic drama must present a vision of the future. Both types of drama are meant to inspire man to create a new world, to change the spectator from a passive onlooker into an active participant in the creation of life. Everywhere in his writings, moreover, we see the shadow of Ibsen, who provided models for the kinds of dramas Bely hoped his Russian colleagues would write.

NOTES

1. Sologub wrote eighteen plays; Blok, seven. Some of the other playwriting Symbolists were Gippius, three; Merezhkovsky, six; Minsky, nine; Annensky, four; Balmont, one. A. Bely, "Prishedshy" *Severnye tsvety,* 1903, pp. 2–25; "Past nochi," *Zolotoe runo,* 1906, no. 1, pp. 62–71.

2. Between 1900 and 1906, thirteen articles appeared in various journals on the Dionysiac mystery. V. Ivanov, "Ellinskaya religiya stradayushchego boga," *Novyg Put,* nos. 1, 2, 3, 5, 8, 9 (1904) is probably the most famous.

3. Z. Gippius, *Svyataya krov, (Severnye tsvety,* 1901); I. Annensky, *Melanippa-filosof* (St. Petersburg, 1901); *Tsar Iksion* (St. Petersburg, 1902); K. Balmont, *Tri rastsveta, (Severnye tsvety,* 1905); V. Bryusov, *Zemlya, (Severnye tsvety,* 1905); V. Ivanov, *Tantal, (Severnye tsvety,* 1905).

4. N. E., "Voskreshennaya starina," *Teatr i iskusstvo,* no. 3 (1903): 65–66.

5. A. Bely, "Formy iskusstva," *Mir iskusstva,* no. 12 (1902): 346–48. Also *Symbolism,* p. 155.

6. "Formy iskusstva," p. 360. Also *Symbolism,* p. 172.

7. D. Merezhkovsky, *Polnoe sobranie sochineny,* 18 (St. Petersburg: Sytin, 1914), p. 248. A fuller discussion of mystery plays as well as the other kinds of plays generated by the Symbolists may be found in my essay, "From Mystery to Fantasy: An Attempt to Categorize the Plays of the Russian Symbolists," *Canadian-American Slavic Studies,* no. 4 (Winter 1974): 488–500.

8. "Formy iskusstva," p. 361. Also *Symbolism,* pp. 172–73.

9. A. Bely, "Ivanov na stsene," *Vesy,* no. 11 (1904): 29–31.

10. A. Bely, "Apokalipsis v russkoy poezii," *Vesy,* no. 4 (1905): 24. Also *Lug zelyony* (1910), pp. 241–42. "Ideal" women do indeed descend from the sky in two Symbolist plays, Sologub's *Zalozhniki zhizhni* and Blok's *Neznakomka.*

11. The three terms I develop in "From Mystery to Fantasy . . . " are "mystery play," "contemporary-symbolic play," and "fantasy-play."

12. A. Bely, "Ibsen i Dostoevsky," *Vesy,* no. 12 (1905): 53. Also, *Arabesques,* p. 98.

13. A. Bely, "Teatr i sovremennaya drama," in *Teatr, kniga o novom teatre* (St. Petersburg, 1908), p. 283. Also *Arabesques,* p. 36.

14. "Teatr i sovremennaya . . . ," p. 274; *Arabesques,* pp. 27–28.

15. A. Bely, "Oblomok mirov," *Vesy,* no. 5 (1908): 65–68. Also *Arabesques,* p. 465.

STANLEY J. RABINOWITZ

BELY AND SOLOGUB: TOWARD
THE HISTORY OF A FRIENDSHIP

Students of Russian Symbolism are well aware that Andrey Bely's personal and professional relationship with Fyodor Sologub (1863 – 1927) has received almost no attention either in the Soviet Union or the West. We know a fair amount regarding Bely's links to figures such as Bryusov, Gippius, Merezhkovsky, Blok, and Vyacheslav Ivanov, yet precious little has been written about his association with and critical evaluation of Sologub, to whom he wrote as early as 1908, "I can relate to only two or three names in literature (and you are one of them)." [1] It should be noted at the outset that Bely's twenty-two-year acquaintance with Sologub was, with the exception of their final meeting, never particularly strong or intense. They were of different generations, they lived in different cities, and, as Bely attests in *The Beginning of the Century*, Sologub was usually indifferent towards Bely's literary efforts.[2] Yet toward the end of their relationship, about a year and a half before Sologub's death, the two appeared closer than ever before when, together with Ivanov-Razumnik, they spent a pleasant summer in Tsarskoe Selo, just outside of Sologub's native Leningrad. Certainly Bely's tone when describing this final period with Sologub in *The Beginning of the Century* is warm and nostalgic, particularly when compared to his description of the difficulties encountered in the early years of their acquaintance.

Of even greater interest is the professional aspect of the Bely-Sologub relationship, for it is quite clear that Sologub's writings left an indelible impression upon Bely's literary consciousness. Despite the numerous ups and downs of Bely's personal ties with

Sologub, his admiration for him as an artist and literary craftsman remained unchanged for thirty years. In a letter written six weeks after Sologub's death, Bely reminisced about and summed up Sologub's role in his life; he admitted to Ivanov-Razumnik that "[Sologub] *very, very* much influenced me; and in a real, writer's sense, Sologub was more a teacher of my prose than 'master' Bryusov was of my poetry." [3] By using all available published, and some heretofore unpublished, material, we shall discuss the personal and professional aspects of the Bely-Sologub link and review how both developed and strengthened between 1905 and 1927. [4]

Bely's account of his first social call on Sologub, while visiting Petersburg in the winter of 1905, captures the feeling of tension which initially existed between the two men. Indeed, in their pedigrees, outward appearances, and temperaments the two could hardly have been further apart. Bely—the child of a prominent professor of mathematics and a cultured woman of rare beauty—was vibrant, garrulous, and attractive; he enjoyed the excitement of Rozanov's and Merezhkovsky's gatherings and he had come to see Sologub not because he felt any particular desire for genuine social intercourse, but rather because he was struck by a sense of guilt over not paying his respects to the elder writer, as was expected. Sologub—the son of a tailor and a laundry woman—was morose, aloof, and intimidating; he looked two decades older than his forty-three years and from his evenings "where time stood still, where Rozanov and the Merezhkovskys literally were erased from (my) memory, as from a blackboard," people gladly escaped (*The Beginning of the Century*, p. 442). A sense of distance continually pervaded the Bely-Sologub relationship, especially in literary matters where Bely always considered himself a young and deferential pupil, while Sologub was the experienced and venerated master. To be sure, the need to acknowledge Sologub as teacher appears in practically everything Bely wrote about or to him. For example, despite his lack of enthusiasm for Sologub's collection of verse, *Zmiy*, Bely was quick to stress in his 1907 review of the book that "we should like to begin our note about *Zmiy* with a grateful and deep bow to our respected teacher." [5] The undeniably authoritarian aspect which permeated the personal relations between the men, particularly at their incipient stage, appeared to take the form of a confrontation between obedient schoolchild and strict school inspector, a position which, incidentally, Sologub held until

1907. Certainly it is no accident that Bely several times uses the word "menacing" (*ugrozhayushchy*) when recounting his early visits to Sologub; nor is it insignificant that his description of their first meeting emphasizes the 'educational' aspect of Sologub's character—in a most negative fashion:

> And I shuddered when I stepped onto the premises of the school, where [Sologub] lived and where he gave lessons, passing the empty classrooms; blackboards and desks could be seen there. . . . He made me feel [as if he were saying] "Better draw Pythagoras's pants* and don't fool around." . . . That is how teacher Teternikov,† his smile concealed in his moustache, scoffed at me, making out of a writer a school boy. . . . Just sit there and pant for a while (he seemed to say)! "You get an F Bugaev!" . . . In appearance, this schoolteacher, who had become a writer, recalled a Buddhist priest . . . [and] it appeared as if you had fallen into his strong paws.
>
> (*The Beginning of the Century*, pp. 442–43)

Bely himself best characterizes the initial phase of his relationship with Sologub when he maintains that "personal contact was very easy with V. Ivanov, but with Sologub personal contact seemed practically impossible" (ibid., p. 442).

This early reaction notwithstanding, Bely was to espouse a wholly different attitude toward Sologub some three years later, when he wrote, warmly and sincerely, that "in a worldly sense we know each other little; it is valuable and joyful for me to think that there is between us a possibility for a mutual drawing together." [6] Highly significant is the fact that it was precisely between his first uninspired meetings with Sologub in 1905–1906 and his above-quoted statement, written in 1909, that Bely plunged into serious study of Sologub's works and wrote several reviews and one article about them. In fact, Bely's increased affection for Sologub as a person as well as his desire to strengthen their personal contact seems to have depended largely on his growing respect for Sologub as an artist. For example, a conversation with Sologub in 1909 about

---

*"Pythagoras's pants" is a humorous allusion to Pythagoras's theorem which, because it deals with a triangle, recalls the shape of a pair of trousers. Sologub himself was a mathematics teacher who published a textbook on geometry.

†Teternikov was Sologub's real name which he used in all official capacities as well as in his correspondence. The name Sologub was used exclusively as a *nom de plume*.

literature produced this friendly response: "Our talk impressed me enormously, my dear Fyodor Kuzmich; I have a great need to see you and speak with you." [7] To suggest that in later years their relationship was significantly closer or consistently smooth would be a mistake; however, it does appear that with further exposure to Sologub's works, Bely's attitude toward him as a man did seem to mellow.

Bely's interest in Sologub's writing, as he reports in *At the Boundary of Two Centuries*, dates from his school days, when, at age sixteen, he "discovered" Sologub along with Dostoevsky, Pushkin, Turgenev, Ibsen, and others. By 1896, *Severny vestnik* had already published Sologub's first story, "Shadows," as well as his first novel, *Bad Dreams*. Several other stories appeared in 1896, and the first volume of Sologub's verse was also available. In 1906, Bely writes in his memoirs, "Blok's poetry and Sologub's prose attracted me. . . . for a long time I penetrated the dry, staid, dimly lusterless style of his early stories, lapidary, distant, and foreign to me in world-view, but I extracted much, analyzing his mastery" (*The Beginning of the Century*, p. 442). And finally, in 1908, claiming that "two-thirds of all contemporary literature is charlatanism," Bely could admit to Sologub that "I have become accustomed to consider myself your fervent worshipper." [8]

Bely's statement that, "being a truly ardent admirer of Sologub's prose, I am far less a devotee of his poetry, but here he is [still] a head taller than many geniuses who have recently been making a lot of noise," demonstrates his specific area of preference concerning Sologub's writing, although this predilection did not prevent him from studying Sologub's versification.[9] In his article "A Comparative Morphology of the Rhythm of Russian Lyricists in Iambic Dimeter" (1909), Bely makes some important discoveries about Sologub's relation to Fet, Baratynsky and Lermontov; and considering Sologub's admitted respect for the latter ("a genuinely great poet and a truly great man"), Bely's findings about the poetic ties between the two would seem to carry particular weight.[10] Yet Bely's primary interest in Sologub was as a prose writer, and if anything, it was Sologub's narrative fiction which played a part in Bely's own literary development. Bely's initial public pronouncement on Sologub, published in *Kriticheskoe obozrenie* of 1907, reflects his unequivocal admiration for the writer's craftsmanship in prose: "Fyodor Sologub is one of the greatest stylists of our time." [11]

Bely characterizes the style of the ten stories published under the title *Rotting Masks* as resplendent and finished, marked by a combination of simplicity and sophistication, elegance and severity; yet only in his second review of Sologub, a piece on the collection of eleven stories entitled *A Book of Enchantments*, does Bely define the term "style" and elucidate Sologub's particular strength in this area. With its careful attention to the importance of sound texture, rhythm and instrumentation in a literary work, Bely's evaluation of *A Book of Enchantments* exemplifies some of the experimental methods which he was applying in literary criticism at that time.

Bely finds in Sologub's writing a unique combination of *stil*, which he defines as "the unconscious expression in words of the rhythm of the soul," and *slog*—"the realization of *stil*," or the conscious instrumentation of rhythm. As the great perceiver and orchestrator of the music of the soul, Sologub is for Bely a perfect mixture of an "elemental artist," such as Dostoevsky, who feels the spiritual rhythm of language, and a "jeweller," such as Turgenev, who meticulously chooses the most suitable words for the verbal expression of that rhythm: "Here in one artist the elements of the unconscious are combined with the elements of the conscious; a contradiction between *stil* and *slog* is absent in Sologub; his *slog* is his *stil;* his *stil* is his *slog*." [12] As an example of the harmony which is responsible for Sologub's "artistic perfection," Bely cites a sentence from the story "She Who Changed Water into Wine," where he observes that the arrangement of words imitates the rhythm of movement of the maiden-heroine, and that "this rhythm—the rhythm of a chorale or a funeral march—is the very meaning of the story—the chorale of death or the funeral march of life." The sentence from Sologub reads: "Deva shla za nimi, i pela, i vosklitsala, i plyasala, i, zabegaya pered uchitelem, padala litsom na zemlyu, i tselovala uchitelyu nogi, i opyat plyasala, i smeyalas', i plakala." Insofar as Sologub employs the melody and musicality of words to transmit ideas, Bely finds in him a kindred spirit. As a fellow Symbolist, Bely could only praise Sologub's practice of conveying meaning with the aid of what he deemed to be the irrational and emotional medium of music. The enchantment and charms implied by the title of Sologub's collection reflect a level of reality which is higher and more beautiful than our empirical, physical life; that this sphere should be described in a sonorous, cadenced prose conforms well with Bely's own aesthetic principles. In fact, Bely must be seen as the first to observe in Sologub's prose the frequently profound connectedness between form and content, the correlation between Sologub's "higher realms" and the lyrical, rhythmically organized language which is used to describe them.

With its reference to Gogol's influence on significant portions of Sologub's prose, Bely's 1909 review prefigures by twenty-five years his chapter in *Gogol's Craft* (pp. 291–94), where the stylistic ties between the two are established in substantial detail. Indeed, knowing Bely's enormous admiration for Gogol, we can say that he must have been paying Sologub the greatest compliment he could when he wrote to him in 1908 that "I see among writers only Gogol whom I would give clear preference over you." [13] Yet even at this time, Bely notes (as he would later) a markedly Pushkinian quality to Sologub's prose, observing that the latter's sentences tend to be polished, terse and delicate, whereas the smaller internal semantic clusters are rich in melodiousness which "always accompanies the thought." Thus, even where metaphors, similes or elegant epithets are lacking, there is still none of the almost sterile exactitude of Pushkin's prose. On the contrary, Bely finds an "elusive enchantment" in the simplicity of Sologub's *slog*. This is why, in *Gogol's Craft,* Bely could evaluate Sologub's writing as a highly successful fusion of the Pushkinian and Gogolian stylistic antipodes, falling happily between Bryusov's essentially Pushkinian tendencies, exemplified by *The Flaming Angel,* and his own predominantly Gogolian stamp. As he wrote about *The Petty Demon:* "Sologub's *The Petty Demon* reproduces Gogol's stylistic traits, revealing them with the restraint of Pushkin's prose; Sologub's Gogolism has the tendency to recolor itself in Pushkinism" (*Gogol's Craft,* p. 291).

Bely's appreciation for Sologub's prose fiction, particularly the pieces mentioned above as well as other stories such as "The Sting of Death" and "Miss Liza" and the novel *The Created Legend,* must ultimately be attributed to the sense of stylistic balance which it conveys. While Bely is happy that "the sounds of Gogol flare up in Sologub's prose" (*Gogol's Craft,* p. 294), he is similarly pleased that the music is controlled, that the *roy* and the *stroy,* to use terminology found in Bely's own *Kotik Letaev,* are in equal proportion to one another. To a man who himself was torn between differing approaches toward perceiving reality—the rational and scien-

tific versus the intuitive and mystic—Sologub's blending of the
elemental and complex with the simple and transparent had obvious appeal.

Bely's evaluation of Sologub's writing is not confined exclusively
to questions of style; in the article "The Dalai Lama from Sapozhok," philosophical interpretations predominate, although the
piece must be considered unsuccessful, if for no other reason than
Bely's comic and frequently mocking tone deeply offended the
author to whom the remarks were directed.[14] But in all fairness to
the customarily hypersensitive Sologub, it must be noted that
Bely's argument as such, which the former called "very clever but
totally arbitrary," does appear to lack much of the rigor and ac-
curacy of his previous statements on the writer's works.[15] His insistence both upon treating Sologub's fiction as one large tapestry
rather than as autonomous pieces viewed in their proper chronological context and upon seeing this tapestry as a steady progression toward Nirvana and death, may be original; but it is ultimately too schematic and general to be regarded as a wholly accurate statement on Sologub. Bely's claim that "all of Sologub's
work systematically develops and deepens his fundamental idea—
the approaching of death," not only fails to acknowledge other
equally important Sologubian concerns, such as the importance
of man's creative will; but also implies a consistency of thought and
sameness of tone and mood which are not always present in
Sologub's writing.[16] As the critic Johannes Holthusen rightly
argues in a reference to Bely's mistaken assumptions, repeated
again in *Gogol's Craft,* "In Belyjs Satz steckt ein gewisser Wahr-
heitsgehalt, aber es heist doch Sologub einseitig auf seine Rolle als
'Sänger des Todes' festlegen, wenn man nicht seine Wendung zur
Utopie, zu einem Traum vom 'anderen Leben,' die sich schon vor
1905 abzeichnet, mit berücksichtigt." [17]

The immediate aftermath of Bely's article signals a low point in
the writers' relationship, and Professor Maslenikov's observation
that "at one time or another in his career, Bely was at odds with
practically every one of his literary friends," holds true in the
present case as well.[18] Sologub was infuriated by the unscholarly
and frivolous style of Bely's piece. Several times the author is
chatteringly referred to as "Fyodor Kuzmich"; he is called a witch
and is compared to a flea whose witchcraft is no more than a flea-
bite; and at one point Bely even derogatorily hints at the wart on

Sologub's nose. Such flippantly hostile criticism of Sologub was frequent during his time, yet from fellow writers he came to expect —and not unreasonably so—greater respect and seriousness. Bely's apologies to Sologub were profuse, and only recently his letter to Sologub regarding the incident was published.[19] Here Bely is sincerely repentant, and once again, the disciple-teacher stance is fully evident, with Bely insisting: ". . . scold me, convict me—I shall always be able to listen to you as a teacher. . . . I may be an insignificant poet and literary critic—but that's not the point: in this matter, I look at you as a dear teacher." [20] Bely's description of his motives for writing "The Dalai Lama from Sapozhok" reveals the great power which Sologub's style had on him, for the origin of the piece seems to have sprung from Bely's need consciously to counteract an alien philosophy which, by the sheer force of its expression, was holding him in its sway:

> In your works alongside an enormous talent there is a special note which gives an unanalyzable charm to [them]: it is an understatement to say that you infect the reader with a certain experience: you hypnotize him, and thus your world-view penetrates the reader like contraband; I have experienced this "witchcraft" several times. Your position as a writer is exceedingly clear: one has to struggle with you. I at least have struggled with the "sorcery" of your words, but I, as a writer, pray to "other gods," not yours.[21]

And in defending his methodology of approach to Sologub, Bely sheds light on his concept of himself as a literary critic by openly confessing the reasons for the tendentious position from which he operates: "If I had been only a critic, if I hadn't my own 'sacred things' for which I were ready to give up my life, then I would have merely established your place in literature; but as a warrior, I am obliged to lay bare my sword and defend my own [philosophy]." [22]

Such excuses left Sologub largely unmoved, and it was only Bryusov's personal mediation that prevented the two writers from severing their ties with *Vesy* (where Bely's article had appeared), as Sologub had threatened and Bely had volunteered. Sologub's anger notwithstanding, no permanent rift between the two came about; in fact, although occasional squabbles continued, all evidence indicates that Bely and Sologub became even closer after the events of 1908. Bely's insistence in that year that, "after all, we are acquainted and in the bottom of my heart I have become accustomed to respect you profoundly," was an accurate assessment of his present and future sentiments for Sologub.[23] And it was this esteem which guaranteed a lasting friendship between the two.

Despite a different philosophy of life, Bely regarded Sologub as a co-member of a small group of writers who had a special calling. And when he assured him that "I feel that the time is coming when there must arise a unity among those who possess the high banner of service," Bely's belief in the need to consolidate and draw closer as fellow artists with a common mission is implicit.[24] Certainly this spirit of "comrade-writer" predominates in a keynote address which Bely delivered at a jubilee dinner for Sologub in January 1924. Having recently returned to Russia after his second two-year stay in western Europe in six years, he made a special journey from Moscow to Leningrad in order to deliver the speech. This heretofore unpublished document represents the culmination of Bely's admiration for Sologub as a person and a writer. Stressing that Sologub's writing was instrumental in forming the literary tastes and aesthetic sensitivities of his entire generation, Bely remarks that "Tolstoy, Pushkin, Lermontov, Dostoevsky, Turgenev, Gogol, Fyodor Sologub were, are, and always will be our teachers." [25] Equally important to Bely was Sologub's dedication and seriousness as an artist—a paragon of the professional writer who is fiercely devoted to teaching and enriching his audience. So careful to distinguish between his feelings for Sologub the writer and Sologub the man in the early years of their relationship, Bely now appreciates him as both: "You are close to us not as an artist only, but also as a dear, necessary man in the highest sense of the word— 'chelo-veka.' "

Bely's regard for Sologub as a friend and distinguished man of letters assumed particularly large proportions at this time undoubtedly because he deeply perceived that both were remnants of a fast-disappearing generation. In this context, one recalls K. Mochulsky's contention that "at the end of the twenties, the former Symbolist felt himself lonely, unrecognized, and surrounded by enemies" (Mochulsky, p. 265). Thus, the tone of Bely's speech is at times less festive than nostalgic, and in a sense his words represent a kind of swan song. To be sure, of the literary giants of Russia's Silver Age, Bely and Sologub were among the few remaining, and the latter certainly served as a visible reminder of Bely's own exciting past. Balmont, Ivanov, the Merezhkovskys, Remizov— to name a few—had emigrated; Blok and Rozanov were already dead; and, significantly, Bely felt the need to open his remarks about Sologub by mentioning that "we have gathered to honor you and those other Russian artists *who are not present.*" Undeniably, Bely's final contact with Sologub in 1926 represents the high point of their relationship, and his account of his last meeting with Sologub constitutes one of the warmest and most touching scenes recounted in *The Beginning of the Century:* the two men sitting together, the elder smiling in a way in which he never had during their long acquaintance, while Bely, upon request, was reading him his poetry, and, in the process, "remembering, remembering without end my youth" (p. 449).

Future investigation may very well demonstrate that Sologub had a direct and significant influence on Bely's fiction. Certainly, when Bely insists that " 'The Sting of Death,' *Rotting Masks, The Petty Demon, Little Fairytales,* were really my necessary books: I *traveled* in them, I *lived* in them, and didn't only read [them]," we have every right to assume that the "teacher's" attitude toward the function of language in prose rubbed off on the "pupil," particularly since the titles which Bely names all commonly reflect a remarkable stylistic and verbal performance.[26] Along these lines, a comparison of the two greatest novels of the Symbolist period, *The Petty Demon* (published in 1905) and *Petersburg* (published in 1913–14), is quite likely to reveal the authors' similar use of language as an actual theme in the works and also their shared concern with the purely auditory quality of words, which occasionally displaces the predominantly visual level of their books. Indeed, it is this prominent role of sound which not only connects Bely with Sologub, but also ties both of them to Gogol. Whatever the extent of Sologub's direct influence on Bely, there is little doubt that, indirectly, his works, with the considerable amount of creative imagination and craft which they reflect, played a role in Bely's development as an artist. For Sologub's meticulousness as a craftsman, his respect for the writer's serious calling, his attempt to create legends and myths, his frequent artistic boldness and originality—all of this was crucial in heightening the consciousness of the man who continually grew to respect and esteem him.

NOTES

1. Bely to F. K. Sologub, 30 April 1908, in *Ezhegodnik rukopisnogo otdela Pushkinskogo Doma* (Leningrad, 1972), p. 132.

2. In *The Beginning of the Century* Bely describes the Sologub of 1905 as "vzirayushchy i ravnodushno i sukho na nashi dela, kak na bloshkin trepukh" (p. 442), yet several years later this indifference was to end. We know that in 1912 Sologub, along with Blok and Ivanov, vigorously supported Bely in his efforts to have *Petersburg* published in *Russkaya mysl;* Sologub even went so far as to arrange a dinner to encourage support for Bely in this venture. For an account of these events, see *Literaturnoe nasledstvo,* 27–28 (Moscow, 1937), p. 600. In this same volume (p. 636), an unpublished letter from Bely to Sologub (dated Switzerland, 1916) is reported to contain a request that Sologub help Bely set up his literary affairs upon his return to Russia. This document is interesting not only because it shows Sologub's decreasing "indifference" to Bely's literary activity but also because it proves that despite different opinions about Russia's involvement in World War I (Sologub was vigorously nationalistic during the war, while Bely was considerably less so), their personal relations remained friendly.

3. A. Bely to R. V. Ivanov-Razumnik, 8 February, 1928, in *Ezhegodnik rukopisnogo otdela Pushkinskogo Doma* (Leningrad, 1972), p. 131. This is quoted by S. S. Grechishkin and A. V. Lavrov in some brief introductory remarks to their publication of two previously unpublished letters of Bely to Sologub (see note 19). The remainder of this long letter, which I have had occasion to read, does not deal with Sologub. A good friend of both Bely and Sologub, Ivanov-Razumnik seems to have served as an intermediary between the two, and may very well have been largely responsible for their drawing closer together in the later years of their relationship. Immediately after attending Sologub's funeral on 7 December 1927, Ivanov-Razumnik wrote Bely a long letter describing Sologub's intense suffering during the last months of his life and recounting the details of his final days. In a despondent tone which reflects his realization of the continual passing of two generations of Russian writers, Ivanov-Razumnik ponders, "Dva goda tomu nazad provyol poslednie chasy v Volfile Esenin, pered otpravkoy tela v Moskvu, teper provyol noch Sologub . . . Poklonilsya ya Fyodoru Kuzmichu i ot Vas—potseloval ego —prostilsya navsegda. Kto-to trety budet provodit noch v zale byvshey Volfily? [Volnaya Filosofskaya Assotsiatsiya, see Note 32, S.R.]" In conjunction with a memorial dinner to be held in honor of the late Sologub, Bely wrote three letters to Ivanov-Razumnik (the organizer of the event), dated 25 December 1927, 7 February 1928, and 8 February 1928. Grechishkin and Lavrov quote the latter two letters, but they have never been published in their entirety. For their location in the Soviet Union, see Grechishkin's and Lavrov's note.

4. In their account, "Literaturnoe nasledstvo Andreya Belogo" (published in *Literaturnoe nasledstvo,* 27–28, Moscow, 1937), K. Bugaeva and A. Petrovsky mention the existence of seven letters of Bely to Sologub written between 1905 and 1917. Only two are briefly summarized: the

first of 1908, which has been subsequently reprinted in full and from
which I have already quoted (see note 1); the second (Switzerland, 1916),
which I have also quoted (see note 2), but which has never been published. Bely wrote two reviews of Sologub's short stories and one review
of his verse. In addition, there exists one full-length article on Sologub's
prose, entitled "Dalay-lama iz Sapozhka" and a brief etude on Gogol and
Sologub in his *Gogol's Craft*. In volume two of his memoirs, *The Beginning of the Century*, Bely includes a chapter on Sologub. Besides these
published pieces, I have drawn upon an unpublished speech which Bely
made in Sologub's honor in January 1924, for which see note 25. Sologub's
letters to Bely have never appeared in print, and in his published writings, he mentions Bely only once in an article "Iskusstvo nashikh dney,"
Russkaya mysl, no. 12 (1915): 57, where he quotes Bely's definition of
symbolism.

    5. A. Bely, review of: F. Sologub, *Stikhi. Kniga shestaya*. "Zmiy" (St.
Petersburg, 1907), *Pereval*, no. 8–9 (1907): 100–101.

    6. A. Bely to F. K. Sologub, 5 July 1909, in *Ezhegodnik rukopisnogo
otdela Pushkinskogo Doma* (Leningrad, 1972), p. 136. This is the second
(and last) of the seven letters to Sologub mentioned in note 4 which has
been published in full.

    7. Ibid., p. 135.

    8. A. Bely to F. K. Sologub, 30 April 1908, in ibid., p. 132.

    9. A. Bely, review of: F. Sologub, "Zmiy," in *Pereval*, p. 101. Despite
these early reservations about Sologub's poetry, Bely was later more
favorably disposed toward the latter's verse. The collection *Plamenny
krug* (1908) was Bely's favorite, and in his 1924 address to Sologub, he
refers to his poetry as "elevated and wise."

    10. Bely, *Symbolism*, pp. 331–95; F. Sologub, "O gryadushchem khame
Merezhkovskogo," *Zolotoe runo*, no. 4 (1906): 103.

    11. A. Bely, review of: F. Sologub, *Istlevayushchie lichiny. Kniga
rasskazov* (Moscow, 1907), *Kriticheskoe obozrenie*, no. 3 (1907): 27.

    12. A. Bely, review of: F. Sologub, *Kniga ocharovany. Kniga rasskazov*
(St. Petersburg, 1909), *Vesy*, no. 5 (1909): 82.

    13. A. Bely to F. K. Sologub, in *Ezhegodnik rukopisnogo* . . . , p. 133.

    14. A. Bely, "Dalay-lama iz Sapozhka," *Vesy*, no. 3 (1908). All quota-
tions are from the reprinted version in *Lug zelyony* (Moscow, 1910).

    15. F. Sologub to A. Bely, 1 May 1908. Quoted by Grechishkin and
Lavrov in *Ezhegodnik rukopisnogo* . . . , p. 135.

    16. Review of: F. Sologub, *Istlevayushchie lichiny*, p. 28.

    17. Johannes Holthusen, *Fedor Sologubs Roman-Trilogie: Tvorimaja
Legenda* (The Hague: Mouton, 1960), p. 17.

    18. O. Maslenikov, *The Frenzied Poets* (Berkeley: University of Cal-
ifornia Press, 1952), p. 99.

    19. In *Ezhegodnik rukopisnogo* . . . S. S. Grechishkin and A. V. Lavrov
of Pushkinsky Dom in Leningrad have written a brief introduction and

extensive commentary to two of Bely's letters to Sologub. The first (30 April 1908) consists solely of Bely's apology to Sologub over the issue of the "Dalay-lama" article and is highly conciliatory. The second letter (5 July 1909) is a description of Bely's current stay in the country at Sergey Solovyov's estate, Dedovo, outside Moscow.

20. A. Bely to F. K. Sologub, in *Ezhegodnik rukopisnogo . . .* , p. 133.

21. Ibid., pp. 132–33.

22. Ibid., p. 133.

23. Ibid., p. 133.

24. A. Bely to F. K. Sologub, 5 July 1909, ibid., p. 136.

25. The text of Bely's speech to Sologub, which exists in two parts, is housed in the manuscript division of TsGALI (Moscow). The first and longer part is an address on behalf of the Free Philosophical Association (Volfila), which Bely himself helped found in 1919. (It was closed in 1924.) Sologub is praised for individually expressing and embodying the searchings and torments of the "collective." Insofar as artists unite "separate consciousnesses into new collectives," insofar as they "bring us closer to the truth of the future, showing its unclear contours in forms and images of a 'created legend,' " Bely sees Sologub as an expert in his profession. In the second part of his speech, Bely makes reference to specific works by Sologub, emphasizing their importance for an entire generation of writers. The first two passages quoted from Bely's speech are from the second part; the third passage which I have cited is from part one. Bely mentions this occasion, as well as Sologub's reaction to it, in *The Beginning of the Century,* pp. 447–48.

26. A. Bely to R. V. Ivanov-Razumnik, 8 February 1928, in *Ezhegodnik rukopisnogo . . .* , p. 131.

ARTHUR LEVIN

ANDREY BELY, M. O. GERSHENZON, AND *VEKHI:* A REJOINDER TO N. VALENTINOV

In his memoir account *Two Years with the Symbolists* (1969), the former Menshevik, N. Valentinov (N. V. Volsky), testifies to the extraordinary intellectual influence exerted on Bely by the Russian-Jewish man of letters, M. O. Gershenzon, at the time of the appearance in March 1909 of *Vekhi* (*Signposts*), which Gershenzon edited.[1] According to Valentinov, under Gershenzon's influence Bely turned away from socialism and was deradicalized. From a supporter he became a militant opponent of revolution, and this change was reflected in his subsequent writings. I have undertaken in this article to refute this charge by Valentinov and to determine the true nature of Gershenzon's influence on Bely.

Valentinov met Gershenzon only once. In December 1908, while in Moscow, Valentinov dropped in on Bely, whom he had known since 1905 mainly as a fellow revolution-inclined intellectual, and Gershenzon happened to be there. Valentinov claims that when Bely introduced him to Gershenzon as a former underground revolutionist, Gershenzon unleashed a tirade against the political maximalism of the Russian intelligentsia, allegedly going so far as to condemn the 1905 revolution, and he insulted Valentinov personally.[2] Valentinov retorted that Gershenzon's reproaches would be better addressed to Bely inasmuch as since 1907 he, Valentinov, had opposed further revolutionary action, believing that the gains already made should first be consolidated; whereas Bely only recently had been praising Nechaev and arguing that a new revolutionary upsurge needed to occur so that the "lemonade" revolution of 1905 could become a real revolution. Valentinov then asked Bely to confirm the veracity of his remarks, but the latter maintained silence. When several such requests elicited no response, Valentinov understood that Bely had fallen under Gershenzon's sway and angrily departed.

On the basis of his impressions of this meeting and Gershenzon's essay, "Creative Self-Consciousness," which appeared soon afterwards in *Vekhi,* Valentinov concludes that Gershenzon's political ideas were then so right-wing as to border on "black-hundredism." Gershenzon's extreme antirevolutionism allegedly already colored Bely's *The Silver Dove* and was reechoed in Bely's ecstatic review of *Vekhi* printed in *Vesy* in May 1909—a review, Valentinov observes, which Bely conveniently failed to mention in his memoirs, written in the Soviet Union in 1933.[3] Nor, according to Valentinov, did Gershenzon soon afterwards renounce the views he expounded in *Vekhi,* as Bely claimed in trying to cover up for a friend and for himself. Indeed, these reactionary ideas had a long-lasting influence on Bely, being particularly evident in *Petersburg.*[4] And Valentinov dismisses out of hand Bely's assertions that it was the Mensheviks —i.e., Valentinov—who were for a "lemonade" revolution, whereas after 1905 he, Bely, continued to seek a true revolution (and the same can be said of Gershenzon, whose influence then on Bely, both Valentinov and Bely agree, was great).[5]

Given the tendentiousness of Bely's memoirs (correctly noted by Valentinov), Gershenzon's confusedly worded essay in *Vekhi,* and also, as we hope to show, Valentinov's own gross misunderstandings, it is not a simple matter to determine Gershenzon's actual sociopolitical views at the time when Bely was under Gershenzon's influence. To ascertain these views requires, first of all, an understanding of Gershenzon's *Vekhi* article, which, owing to its vagueness, exaggerations, and contradictions, must be placed in the context of relevant statements by Gershenzon that predate 1905.

As clear a political statement as Gershenzon ever made is found in the 1903 open exchange of letters with P. B. Struve, published in the first book-length anthology entitled *Liberation.*[6] Here Gershenzon took Struve and the constitutionalist movement to task for concentrating on political matters to the neglect of other social and moral evils. He declared that the liberal intelligentsia was hypocritical in demanding political rights from the government while not renouncing its own economic privileges vis-à-vis the mass of peasants and workers. Though admitting that political reforms were badly needed, Gershenzon argued from the vantage point of utopian socialism, a la Herzen-Ogaryov and Tolstoy, and declared that it was of much more vital importance to bring about society's spiritual transformation. "Revolutionize the consciousness of individuals: Here is the shortest path to a real, not simply a superficial social revolution." [7]

Later, writing during the peak of the events of 1905, Gershenzon was enthralled more by the revolution from below than by the liberal, political movement: "In our revolution, which has only begun, there is something that is amazing the entire world . . . it is amazed that the active element of the revolution, as represented by our workers and peasants, is exhibiting a greater sense of social justice than it has in any revolution hitherto. *Socialism as an active expression of the masses*—here is the phenomenon which for the first time on such a scale Russia is displaying to the Western world, that world which created the ideology and tactics of struggle for the social ideal." [8] With the onset of reaction in 1907, Gershenzon still more insistently stressed the theme that the intelligentsia's preoccupation with politics to the neglect of its psychic health was rendering even its political efforts ineffective. In one essay he said, "There is no society more permeated by the idea of the good, more capable of moral feats, than Russian educated society, but also nowhere in the West is there a greater abyss between people's moral consciousness and their everyday life than with us." [9] And in another essay he judged, " 'Politics' is a great, sacred endeavor. . . . But it is terrible when politics becomes everything . . . because then the personality remains simply unformed." [10]

Gershenzon believed that man is spiritually linked to the cosmos.[11] Cosmic reason could not be fully comprehended in human terms, yet it had to be perceived and accepted if man were not to torment himself by futile attempts at explaining and controlling cosmic fate. Only cosmic awareness (or self-consciousness) and hence acceptance of the world could produce a state of spiritual harmony in an individual, enabling him to function effectively in society. "I see two questions tormenting mankind: the meaning of existence and social justice. They must be resolved separately . . . because they belong to different spheres, the first to the metaphysical, the second to the material. The first is resolved by the agonies of the individual soul, the second by the development of technology and production, the spread of knowledge and humanitarian ideas, legislative initiative, *et al.* Yet between them there is an undeniable bond which resides in the common soil from which everything springs—the human psyche." [12]

Convinced that religious (i.e., cosmic) awareness was the basis of moral action, Gershenzon was aggrieved by the Russian intelligentsia's unconcern for spiritual matters, which also caused it to be isolated from the spiritual-minded Russian people. A consequence of this isolation was the nation's failure to win a decisive victory over the autocracy in 1905. "Separated by an abyss from the people, the intelligentsia can be neither healthy nor strong enough for victories; in order to unite with the people it must return to common soil with them, to the soil of religious and metaphysical thought. . . ." [13]

If the foregoing be an accurate summary of Gershenzon's apolitical "political" views during the decade prior to *Vekhi*,[14] then the essay "Creative Self-Consciousness" reveals that in *Vekhi* he simply reiterated his earlier statements concerning the need for cosmic awareness, the spiritual gap between the Russian people and the intelligentsia (whom Gershenzon equated with all of Russian educated society regardless of political affiliation), and the intelligentsia's self-defeating obsession with politics.[15] The implication of Gershenzon's essay was that in 1905 the intelligentsia simply had not been prepared spiritually for the socialist revolution supported by the masses. Still, looking to the future, Gershenzon was not pessimistic. Encouraging signs were to be seen. In western Europe the middle classes were being won over to socialism.[16] And in Russia the events of 1905, besides weakening autocratic rule, had provided the shock that had made the intelligentsia more aware of its shortcomings. Indicative of this were its present interest in modernist art, religion, and even sexual problems. Paradoxically, this shift of attention away from politics to more introspective matters was opening up the possibility of a real social transformation. Moreover, a positive legacy of the intelligentsia's past absorption with politics was that, accustomed to seeing the object of life in social service, its ideal remained suprapersonal.

It should now be sufficiently clear that Valentinov's characterization of Gershenzon's essay in *Vekhi* as akin to "black-hundredism" is ludicrous. Equally so is his implication that Bely's review of *Vekhi*, which especially acclaimed Gershenzon's article, was likewise ideologically counterrevolutionary. What Bely's review did express was dismay over the initial response to *Vekhi* in the Russian press. This was not so much because *Vekhi* had been received hostilely but because the issues it had raised were not being conscientiously debated.[17] Instead, literary warfare had been declared, in effect demonstrating the claims advanced in *Vekhi* that the intelligentsia subordinated everything to politics, was deaf to cultural values, was self-satisfied, and urgently needed to reexamine its philosophical premises. And like Gershenzon, Bely labeled the intelligentsia a "spiritual bourgeoisie." [18]

Interestingly enough, one of *Vekhi*'s earliest reviewers and detractors was N. Valentinov, a fact which for some reason he forgot to mention in *Two Years with the Symbolists*.[19] His review, unfortunately, is as distorted as his later memoirs. It sees *Vekhi*, following in the wake of *Problems of Idealism*,[20] as a landmark in the thinking of a segment of the bourgeois intelligentsia evolving from Marxism to idealism to Octobrism (an analysis very similar to Lenin's). [21] Much more strained was Valentinov's imputing to Gershenzon the idea that the intelligentsia ought to live egotistically in the manner of the Western bourgeoisie. The latter's remarks, though not well phrased, lend no credence to such a farcical interpretation.[22] Finally, Valentinov, who, like Lenin, had concerned himself sufficiently with philosophy to write books in that field, concludes that "idealist metaphysics always serves as an embellishment for bourgeois rule and institutions." [23]

In his preface to the English edition of Valentinov's uncomplimentary reminiscences of Lenin, the well-known sovietologist, Leonard Schapiro, speaks of Valentinov's "intellectual integrity." Schapiro says, "He [Valentinov] never evaded the facts which did not fit in with his ideas or beliefs." And as regards Valentinov's rather remarkable reconstructions of conversations with Lenin held half a century earlier, Valentinov himself proudly stated that they benefited "from a surge of 'old-age' memory." [24] Unfortunately, we cannot corroborate the presence of such qualities in Valentinov's account of Bely, Gershenzon, and *Vekhi*. Here his memory, apparently, was not too good. As already noted, he failed to mention his review of *Vekhi*—although it comprised three separate articles in the newspaper *Kievan Thought* and then was reprinted in *In Defense of the Intelligentsia* (Moscow, 1909), one of several collective works that appeared in response to *Vekhi*. No less surprising— some would say astonishing—is Valentinov's failure to recall that both he and Bely had contributed to another anthology evoked by *Vekhi*, *Where Are We Going?* (Moscow, 1910).

The latter book, which appeared after a year's heated debate among Russian intellectuals over the issues raised in *Vekhi*, comprises some forty replies to the query posed by the book's title. The respective responses by Valentinov and Bely are illuminating. Valentinov's brief and pedestrian comment addresses itself primarily to the political level. It chides pessimists who feel that nothing has really changed since the turn of the century. There have been "enormous changes," but now a long period of small deeds awaits Russia. Defending gradualism, Valentinov considers that the intelligentsia must undergo reeducation and "amputate from itself a number of elements of its ideological and psychological baggage, including its old idealism. . . ." [25] Different in spirit and theme is Bely's "The Present and Future of Russian Literature." Here Bely enthusiastically repeats in short compass his eschatological views on art that he was propounding elsewhere.[26] Rejecting both narrow aestheticism and professionalism ("art for art's sake") as well as shallow tendentiousness which degrades art by turning it into a vehicle for party propaganda, Bely affirms that art has a great purpose. Praising nineteenth-century Russian literature for its purposefulness in seeking the meaning of life and in maintaining strong ties to the people, Bely boldly declares that in future art will be the "religion of life," the "means of re-creating life." [27]

Without proceeding further, we can see that Valentinov's memoir description of Bely, Gershenzon, and *Vekhi,* and his 1909 review of *Vekhi* are equally marked by distortion and intellectual shallowness. We can only speculate as to the causes of such incomprehension. No doubt Valentinov was piqued by the behavior of Bely and Gershenzon at their meeting. Perhaps, too, owing to a very superficial reading, he was misled by the ambiguities in "Creative Self-Consciousness." (To be sure, he makes no distinction between Gershenzon's and the other *Vekhi* essays, despite the fact that their differences were given publicity in P. B. Struve's *Patriotica*—see note 15.) Valentinov appears ignorant of the general tenor of Gershenzon's or, for that matter, Bely's major theoretical writings (*Symbolism,* for example) from that period. If we had to hazard a guess at the chief cause of Valentinov's misunderstandings, however, we would attribute them to ideological "blinders." Insensitive to spiritual concerns, Valentinov was unable to fathom artistic temperaments such as Gershenzon's and Bely's, let alone render accurate judgment on their highly personal and finely nuanced ideas. In his preface to *Two Years with the Symbolists,* Gleb Struve noted that when this work was originally published serially in *Novy Zhurnal,* the then editor, Michael Karpovich, refused to include the section on Aleksandr Blok because of its obvious misrepresentations. While agreeing with Karpovich that Valentinov wrote "onesidedly" about Blok, Struve concluded: "This does not diminish the memoir value of the story of his [Valentinov's] relationships with Andrey Bely, Ellis and Gershenzon." [28] Based on my research presented here, I believe that Professor Struve has been too generous in his assessment of Valentinov.

In conclusion, I would like briefly to clarify the nature of Gershenzon's influence on Bely at the time of *Vekhi.* First of all, even at that early period in their relationship intellectual stimulus did not by any means flow in one direction. As Bely stated, Gershenzon was, for him, "least of all a teacher." Indeed, in my judgment, Bely's was much the more creative mind. Gershenzon's great talent was chiefly as a biographer who discerned and dramatically retold the spiritual odysseys of inspired seekers of a better world. His imagination was fired, in particular, by poets of genius from Petrarch to Pushkin. Gershenzon believed that these poets, while absorbed with their own feelings and seemingly indifferent to the world about them, were, thanks to their gift of artistic intuition, the persons best able to discover insights into man's nature and, hence, into the cosmic meaning of life. They therefore served as agents in the ultimate transformation of the world. In Gershenzon's eyes, Bely was another great poet-seer contributing to man's "creative self-consciousness," a primary condition for the establishment of a new, revolutionized, and just society. These views, of course, were very similar to Bely's conception of the theurgical role of the artist, i.e., to Bely's own self-definition. Such similarity, incidentally, I would attribute mainly to common sources, especially to German idealist philosophy and fellow Russian champions of Symbolism, as, for example, D. S. Merezhkovsky. Still, it should be emphasized, as Bely does in his memoirs, that thanks to the concordance of their views and the warmth of their friendship Gershenzon, as the older and more established writer, fortified Bely's faith in himself.

Bely and Gershenzon were then both writing about the eschatological nature and purpose of art (*tvorchestvo*), and I surmise that in molding their ideas they reinforced each other. In his foremost theoretical work from this period, *Symbolism,* Bely stressed that art was fundamentally concerned with philosophy, religion, and ethical problems. It was art, because of its superiority over cognitive knowledge both in expressing and appealing to the subconscious depths of the human psyche, that could transform the psyche and, hence, re-create the world (*Symbolism,* pp. 8–10). Art's ultimate meaning, moreover, was expressed not in the logicality or truthfulness of the ideas it presented but in its formal aspects of expression, form and content being integrally connected.

Echoes from Bely's *Symbolism* are clearly audible in Gershenzon's most significant work on literature at this time, his "Afterword" (1911) to his translation of Gustave Lanson's essay, "La méthode de l'histoire littéraire." [29] Whereas previously Gershenzon had considered Platonic idealism as providing the eschatological element in art (as in his study of Ogaryov's metaphysical poetry),[30] he now sees the artist's clairvoyance emanating from his mysterious gift for artistic forms. In a work of art, form and content are inextricably linked by the artist's intuition (or "vision"). Content, therefore, cannot be delineated in strictly logical terms, but needs to be perceived through images, sounds, and rhythms expressed in words.[31] The foremost task of the literary scholar, consequently, is to trace the evolution of artistic intuition insofar as it manifests itself in creative writing. If then, as Bely intimated, the artist's task is to plumb the psychic depths, according to Gershenzon the critic's role is to act as the artist's surrogate and spokesman. Or, as he put it in a later work: "Literary criticism is nothing other than the art of slow reading, i.e., the art of perceiving the artist's vision through the fascination of form." [32]

Finally, it bears noting that Bely and Gershenzon, like Russian Symbolists generally, despite their militant defense of cultural values against the demands of everyday politics, stood squarely within the dominant "civic" tradition of Russian literary criticism. The civic school of thought with its many differing branches taught that art's primary purpose was to contribute to the betterment of society and took pride in the fact that nineteenth-century Russian literature had fought heroically against social injustice. Prior to the Symbolists, however, it was generally believed that in pursuing this purpose literature, and art generally, would be subordinate to political economy and moral philosophy. These were the branches of knowledge that would uncover the truths needed for society's liberation and reconstruction. Literature's role was to disseminate such truths obtained from the social sciences, a task for which it was well suited because of the ability of creative writers to communicate with and inspire readers.

At the turn of the century, with the emergence of Russian Symbolism, which like other modernist movements rejected Realism and Naturalism as modes for creative expression, the role of art came to be reevaluated. While accepting the civic school's basic credo that art's purpose was to serve society, Symbolists elevated the function of art to the highest heights. No longer was it to be dependent on the evolution of the social sciences. As we have seen, for Symbolist writers like Bely and Gershenzon, it was artistic creation itself that could furnish the ethico-religious truths to pave the way to a new world. For Bely and Gershenzon, salvation could come via the road of art. Even the most violent political upheavals could prove to be transient, "lemonade" revolutions. But, as spiritual revolutionaries from Christ to Tolstoy had taught, the Kingdom of God is within man.

NOTES

1. On *Vekhi* see Leonard Schapiro, "The *Vekhi* Group and the Mystique of Revolution," *Slavonic and East European Review* 34 (1955): 56–76; Nikolai P. Poltoratzky, "The *Vekhi* Dispute and the Significance of *Vekhi*," *Canadian Slavonic Papers* 9, no. 1 (Spring 1967): 86–106; and Arthur Levin, "M. O. Gershenzon and *Vekhi*," *Canadian Slavic Studies* 4, no. 1 (Spring 1970): 60–73. In addition, *Vekhi* has been translated into English and edited by Marshall Shatz and Judith Zimmerman, appearing serially in *Canadian Slavic Studies* beginning with the summer 1968 issue (vol. 2, no. 2).

2. N. Valentinov, *Two Years with the Symbolists* (Stanford, Calif.: Hoover Institution, 1969), p. 206.

3. Reference is to *Between Two Revolutions.*

4. Valentinov, *Two Years with the Symbolists,* p. 214.

5. Here is Bely's statement: "Gershenzon, least of all as a teacher but rather as an elder brother, was the only person who helped me in those years [1907–09]. His house was like a hut in the icy wastes, where a brazier glowed—and here I thawed out. He buoyed up faith in myself, both by an understanding of my rage and by turning me to the thought that my mission was not what I had imagined it to be. My mission was to develop myself to the utmost as a writer. Various plans of poemas and novels had issued from me like puffs of smoke from cigarettes. Many of them had been "smoked out" in conversations with friends, but the result had been only ash. Then I told Gershenzon about the plans of my

novel *The Silver Dove*. With unselfish rapacity he took hold of me and sternly demanded the realization of these plans. And perhaps it was he who got me to make something serious out of this novel. Under his gentle but incessant pressure, I began to shut myself away from a swarm of friends. I even fled to the country where I in fact carried out my plans and wrote *The [Silver] Dove*, a work filled with power. Then I understood that a part of my anguished longing had been a longing for creative work, which had been thwarted by futile squabbles. I consider Gershenzon the godfather of my novels" (*Between Two Revolutions*, p. 297).

6. Under the title *Osvobozhdenie* there appeared, besides two anthologies, a semimonthly journal (1902–05), also edited by Peter B. Struve. This journal, which was published first in Stuttgart and then in Paris, was the chief organ of the liberal opposition to the autocracy in the years prior to the revolution of 1905.

7. N. N. [Gershenzon], "Pismo s beregov Zhenevskogo ozera" in *Osvobozhdenie* bk. 1 (Stuttgart, 1903), p. 228.

8. M. Gershenzon, "Literaturnoe obozrenie," *Nauchnoe slovo* 8–9 (1905): 178.

9. M. Gershenzon, "Posle ekzamena," *Russkie vedomosti* (31 January 1906): 5.

10. M. Gershenzon, review of Adam Lel, *Zapiski studenta 1900–03 g.g.* in *Vestnik Evropy*, 43, no. 6 (November–December 1908): 767–68.

11. Gershenzon movingly described his own spiritual awakening in 1902 in three letters to his brother Abram, which were published in *Russkaya mysl*, 28, no. 2 (February 1907): 86–96.

12. Junior [M. O. Gershenzon], "Pisma k bratu," *Russkaya mysl* 28, no. 2 (February 1907): 92.

13. M. Gershenzon, review of B. V. Dobryshin, *Zadachi sovremennoy intelligentsii* in *Vestnik Evropy* 48, no. 5 (September–October 1908): 796–97.

14. These views, moreover, were completely in line with those of his formative years, which were likewise marked by an idealistic striving to remove injustice and better the world. See Arthur Levin, "The Making of a Russian Scholar: The Apprenticeship of M. O. Gershenzon," *California Slavic Studies* 7 (1973): 99–120.

15. It was in defining the term "intelligentsia" and, hence, the object of their criticism, that Gershenzon differed most from his fellow contributors to *Vekhi*. The latter employed the term in the theretofore traditional Russian way to designate the rationalistic, radical segment of educated society. (On the use of the term, see Martin Malia, "What Is the Intelligentsia?" *Daedalus* [Summer 1960]: 441–58.) Such usage distinguished "we" from "they" and was partisan in its thrust. Gershenzon's usage, however, was more manifold and cut across all political boundaries. In all of its ramifications it applied, in effect, to the bour-

geoisie as a whole. This basic difference in definition, which, of course, reflected differing outlooks, explains why one of *Vekhi*'s contributing authors, P. B. Struve, shortly after publication sought to dissociate himself and *Vekhi* as a whole from Gershenzon's essay. Since Struve took "intelligentsia" to mean radicals, he naturally denied that the 1905 revolution had witnessed the isolation of the intelligentsia from the masses and condemned Gershenzon's views as being a kind of mystical slavophilism. (See P. B. Struve, "O. Vekhakh" in *Slovo* [25 April 1909], reprinted in Struve's *Patriotica* [St. Petersburg, 1911], pp 228–32.) Yet Gershenzon had not employed the term so narrowly. As in his previous disagreement with Struve, he was focusing his assault primarily on the bourgeoisie. Another contributor to *Vekhi*, S. L. Frank, who stood close to Struve politically, also has testified to the rift between Gershenzon and *Vekhi*'s other authors. "I once told Gershenzon that, so to say, we [the *Vekhi* majority] intended to attack one another and only because the 'Russian intelligentsia' stood in between us did we undertake jointly, but from different sides, to inflict blows upon it." (S. L. Frank, *Biografiya P. B. Struve* [New York, 1956], p. 82. For this and the many other controversies provoked by *Vekhi*, see Gisela Oberländer, "Die Vechi-Diskussion [1902–1912]," Inaugural-Dissertation, University of Cologne, 1965.) Finally, apropos of Gershenzon's and Struve's divergent views, two additional facts seem relevant here. First, Struve, in his capacity as editor of *Russkaya mysl*, rejected Bely's *Petersburg* for publication, apparently considering it a lampoon of middle class intellectuals playing at revolution. (See Oleg A. Maslenikov, *The Frenzied Poets* [Berkeley: University of California Press, 1952], p. 124.) And second, of *Vekhi*'s authors Gershenzon was the only one who did not emigrate from Soviet Russia; nor did he contribute to *Iz glubiny* (1918), the anti-Bolshevik anthology edited by P. B. Struve which was intended to be a sequel to *Vekhi* and included as contributors all of *Vekhi*'s other authors, save B. A. Kistyakovsky.

16. M. Gershenzon, "Creative Self-Consciousness," *Vekhi*, 4th ed. (Moscow, 1909), p. 88.

17. Andrey Bely, "Pravda o russkoy intelligentsii," *Vesy* 6, no. 5 (May 1909): 65.

18. Ibid., p. 66.

19. See Valentinov's review in *Kievskaya mysl* (19 and 22 April and 14 May 1909), reprinted in *V zashchitu intelligentsii* (Moscow, 1909), pp. 101–16. One can only speculate whether Bely knew of Valentinov's review when he was writing his own review condemning the initial press reaction to *Vekhi*.

20. Edited by P. I. Novgorodtsev with the aid of P. B. Struve, *Problemy idealizma* (Moscow, 1902) was a collection of essays by young intellectuals, most of them former Marxists, which provided a many-sided

critique of Marxism and materialism generally, coupled with an acceptance of spiritual values. Five of its contributors (N. A. Berdyaev, S. N. Bulgakov, Frank, Kistyakovsky, and Struve) later participated in *Vekhi*.

21. See Lenin's "O Vekhakh" in *Sochineniya,* 4th ed., vol. 16 (Leningrad, 1950). This article originally appeared in *Novy den* (13 December 1909).

22. Gershenzon, *Vekhi,* p. 88.

23. *V zashchitu intelligentsii,* p. 111, as quoted in Gisela Oberländer, "Die Vechi-Diskussion," p. 171.

24. See N. Valentinov, *Encounters with Lenin,* trans. Paul Rosta and Brian Pearce (London, New York, Toronto, 1968), pp. vi and xix.

25. N. Valentinov, *Kuda my idyom; sbornik statey i otvetov* (Moscow, 1910), pp. 18–19 and 20.

26. Primarily in his major theoretical work, *Symbolism.*

27. *Kuda my idyom,* pp. 4–5.

28. Valentinov, *Two Years with the Symbolists,* p. v.

29. M. Gershenzon, "Posleslovie" in G. Lanson, *Metod v istorii literatury,* trans. M. Gershenzon (Moscow, 1911).

30. M. Gershenzon, "Lirika N. P. Ogaryova," *Vestnik Evropy* 38, no. 9 (September 1903): 292–312.

31. Gershenzon, "Posleslovie," in *Metod v istorii literatury,* p. 65.

32. M. Gershenzon, "Videnie poeta," *Birzhevye vedomosti* (31 December 1915): 1.

BERNICE GLATZER ROSENTHAL

REVOLUTION AS APOCALYPSE:
THE CASE OF BELY

Though opposed to Marxism because he abhorred both materialism and determinism, Andrey Bely hailed the Bolshevik Revolution; he believed it was part of a greater spiritual revolution yet to come. Though the juxtaposition of Bolshevism and spiritual revolution is somewhat unusual, from an apocalyptic perspective war, revolution, and unprecedented suffering are portents of the events leading to the Second Coming of the Messiah. The Apocalypse itself, moreover, is a terrifying event involving unheard-of catastrophes in both the human and the cosmic spheres. Comets and falling stars herald the Last Days: war, revolution, plague, and famine destroy the social order, while earthquakes, volcanic eruptions, and other natural calamities destroy the physical universe.[1] These images, appearing in Bely's writings, indicate the apocalyptic orientation that led him to invest first the February Revolution, and then the October Revolution, with eschatological significance as the prelude to the "new heaven and the new earth" of Revelation. In other words, Bely's enthusiastic acceptance of both revolutions of 1917 was the product of his long-standing apocalyptic orientation, an orientation, furthermore, that reflected more Bely's personal problems than the problems of the world around him.[2] In support of this argument I will trace the development of Bely's eschatology, discuss his perceptions of war and revolution, examine the significance of his apocalyptic imagery, and advance a psychological interpretation of his apocalyptism.

Bely's apocalyptic inclinations were already visible at the turn of the century. Admirers of Vladimir Solovyov's poetry by 1899,

Bely and his closest friends were influenced by Solovyov's thought (in 1900 Solovyov had predicted the imminence of Antichrist and the end of the world). Moreover, dissatisfied with the positivist culture of the intelligentsia, the young Bely dabbled in Theosophy, mysticism, and occultism. In 1902 a common interest in religious questions drew him to the Merezhkovskys, who were then attempting to develop a new form of Christianity based on the Second Coming of Christ.[3] Apocalyptic themes appeared in Bely's work in 1898 and became more prominent after 1903.[4] Liturgical, religious, and scriptural images appear on almost every page of his *Fourth Symphony* and each part ends in a quasi-liturgical rite,[5] evidencing his otherworldly orientation. Though the images Bely employed are those of traditional Orthodoxy, the thrust of the *Symphony* is toward Resurrection.

Bely's apocalypse, at that time, was primarily a spiritual event, an internal transformation of individuals; and his social ideal, a community of artists, did not immediately involve the rest of society. But the Russo-Japanese War and the Revolution of 1905 appeared to confirm Solovyov's prophecies, particularly pan-Mongolism (the expectation of a final conflict between East and West); and Bely proclaimed, "the great mystic was right."[6] Concurrently, he began to extend his previous ideal of community to encompass the entire population. Though he did write of the cold and hunger of the people, his primary concerns remained spiritual. Nonetheless, the Revolution of 1905 gave an enduring external dimension, a social and political cast, to his apocalyptism.

Seeking alternate ideologies after the disappointing results of 1905, Bely around 1908 came under the influence of Rudolf Steiner, whose doctrine, Anthroposophy, introduced a new element, cosmic evolution, into Bely's world view. Anthroposophy establishes a close bond between spirit and matter through a process of cosmic evolution in which spiritual forces are primary. At each stage the evolution of the physical universe and of human consciousness corresponds. To Steiner, Christ's birth was the central event in cosmic evolution and the sacrifice at Golgotha introduced a new spiritual mystery into the universe. The Second Coming, Steiner believed, would not be a resurrection of Christ's physical body but of the "divine I" within man. Once humanity attains higher levels of consciousness through spiritual evolution, the etheric Christ (his living spirit) would be visible to all.[7] This would occur, Steiner predicted, in the twentieth century.

Opposed to materialism and greatly esteeming aesthetic expression, especially music and dance, Steiner's philosophy seemed to accommodate both Bely's notion of the artist as a magus who literally creates a new reality and his belief that art is a form of prophecy.[8] Adding to Steiner's attractiveness was his admiration of Solovyov, his attribution of a messianic role for Russia (Russia will solve the social problem), and his "recognition of the Mongol danger." [9] Thus Steiner's conception of cosmic evolution merged with and ultimately reinforced Bely's earlier apocalyptism. Steiner himself was quite vague on the exact mode of transition from the materialistic present to the spiritually elevated future. But since the first three periods of his scheme were terminated by volcanic cataclysm, storm, and flood, it would seem that his doctrine does not preclude terminating the fourth (the present) by further violent eruptions in both the physical universe and the human sphere.

In 1912, Bely became a disciple of Steiner and in 1914 he settled in Steiner's colony at Dornach, Switzerland. Aggravated by intensifying personal problems, the Anthroposophical tendency to dissolve the boundaries between spirit and matter caused Bely to become so solipsistic that he thought the sound of gunfire from the battlefields of World War I was the sound of his own thoughts on the destruction of Europe.[10] "The catastrophe of Europe and the explosion of my personality are one and the same event. One could say that my 'ego' is the war or conversely that the war gave birth to me" (Notes of an Eccentric, 2, p. 114). In At the Pass, a product of the Dornach period, he treated the crises of life, thought, culture, and the word as the passage to the new era.[11] Here also, Bely's perception of external events reflected his own internal crisis as he sought both psychic and social wholeness through some sort of eschatological resolution.

A spiritual critique of modern civilization constitutes a major theme of At the Pass. Bewailing the state of twentieth-century man as a "meatless skeleton swollen with blubber" and ruled by the brain and the stomach (At the Pass, 1, p. 14), Bely sought guidance in the Gospels, Thus Spake Zarathustra, and The Path of Dedication (ibid., 3, p. 13). Critical of Nietzsche for ignoring the Dionysian qualities of thought (ibid., 2, p. 51)—by which Bely meant its creative power—Bely moved closer to Richard Wagner, whom he regarded as an "authentic revolutionary in his own sphere," and more than once he proclaimed "We wait for Parsifal" (ibid., 2, pp. 116, 118–21; 1, p. 108).[12] (Nietzsche disapproved of Parsifal, particularly objecting to its Christian theme.) But the juxtaposition of the violent end of European civilization with the explosion of Bely himself suggests that the world crisis was primarily a backdrop for Bely's personal agony. One example: "Man these days is like a gun; he is loaded with a crisis. The theme of crisis is interlaced with renascence. The theme of the death of the world is connected to the theme of birth. Not accidental, therefore, are the voices that call us to spiritual heights: it is time to be reborn" (ibid., 1, p. 15). Another: "Politics will dissolve in spiritual war. . . . The forms . . . of the old society will be blown up . . . there will be wars the likes of which have never been on earth . . . I am dynamite . . . I know my fate" (ibid., 3, p. 11). In *Notes of an Eccentric,* which also reflects the Dornach period, Bely proclaimed, "I am a bomb flying to explode into pieces" (1, p. 198). Relatively conventional apocalyptic statements such as "that history—will end and that time—will not be," and "not only Christ . . . but we will all be resurrected," and "the Second Coming has begun," (*At the Pass,* 1, p. 87; *Notes of an Eccentric,* 1, pp. 77–78) also punctuate both works.

In 1916, Bely returned to Russia, where the coincidence of personal crisis and imminent revolution raised his already reactivated apocalyptism and pan-Mongolism to even greater heights (*At the Pass,* 1, pp. 85–88). In August 1917 he proclaimed "Russia! Russia! Russia! / Messiah of the Days to Come!"[13] Solovyov's *Sophia,* a theme of Bely's early work, reappeared as the apocalyptic figure, the "Woman Clothed with the Sun." Bely's long poem "Christ Is Risen" (April 1918), generally considered his hymn to the Revolution, illustrates his unique eschatology. Russia is the "Woman Clothed with the Sun," the "God-Carrier" (Messiah of the nations), and the "Conqueror of the Serpent."[14] To Anthroposophists, the serpent represents the lower forms of knowledge through which humanity must pass; they believe that knowledge without spirituality (i.e., pure science) will lead people astray. The statement "an atmosphere of radiance lowering on each of us / Burning through the suffering of the century" (*Poetry,* p. 402; see also p. 386), is an allusion to the cosmic ether of Anthroposophy and to the after-images of departed spirits, most notably Christ's, becoming visible as Steiner had predicted. There are references to Nazareth cutting through the heavens (ibid., pp. 386, 388) and to the "significance of Constantinople" (ibid., p. 398), the latter implying that Russia is now the Third Rome.

Except for the statement "Long live the Third International" (which was not yet founded!) and some vague references to singing about the "brotherhood of peoples" and to revolution (ibid., pp. 397, 398), "Christ Is Risen" does not mention the Bolsheviks. Not a political person, Bely evidenced little interest in the empirical reality of the politicians. Assuming that the war was Russia's Golgotha, he trusted that the Revolution was her resurrection. Russia, to Bely, was a "green meadow"; not yet industrialized, she was innocent of sin. Through Russia, therefore, would begin the mystical renewal of the entire world.[15] True to the apocalyptic tradition, the etheric Christ appears amidst cosmic upheaval— whirlwinds, blizzards, comets. The "new eternal man," Bely once believed, was Kerensky; he never used this image to describe Lenin or Trotsky.[16]

Bely's 1917 essay *Revolution and Culture* demonstrates his conception of revolution as a primarily spiritual process and also makes very clear Bely's awareness of the differences between the Bolsheviks and himself. Critical of Bolshevik materialism, he proclaimed that not Marx and Engels but Nietzsche and Stirner are the true revolutionaries. Economic determinism, he insisted, bears no revolutionary spirit and the revolutionary leap from necessity to freedom will be accomplished, not through the operation of economic laws, but through art (*Revolution,* pp. 13, 19, 24–28). Comparing the proletariat to music, Bely regarded the first as the "class of classes," containing in itself the exit from the class-structured society; its "mission": to transform labor from a product to a process. (Elsewhere he referred to labor as abstract creativity.) Music Bely saw as the "form of forms"; its "mission": to transform the products of creativity, the abstract forms of art, into the depiction of the process of creativity itself. It is the "spirit of music" that motivates both the revolutionary and the artist. Their goal is not prosperity but a "new, unknown, never before existing, freely created world." That new world, that "Kingdom of Freedom" existing in the future, Bely believed is already here, though hidden, in the world of art; it will be reached through music. Music gave birth to all the arts; it is the "first sound" from the new world, the "will to it" (cf. Nietzsche's "will to power"), the "dove from the summit of the approaching Ararat," and it is also the "mathematics of the soul" (ibid., pp. 24–27; see also p. 7).

Bely was associated with the Scythians, a group of left Socialist Revolutionaries (populists, not Marxists) led by Ivanov-Razumnik who supported the Bolshevik Revolution for spiritual reasons. Ivanov-Razumnik differentiated between socialism as an economic system and Socialism [*sic*] as spiritual truth.[17] Aiming at spiritual revolution, Bely's socialism was of the Scythian variety; his social thought stressed the traditional populist categories of intelligentsia and *narod,* rather than the economically defined class categories of Marxism. Regarding the Bolshevik Revolution as a "revolutionary cleansing" (*Revolution,* p. 14) necessary to liberate humanity from materialism, capitalism, and the state, Bely considered the "liquidation" of old social forms a reflection of revolution rather than revolution itself, which he defined as the creation of new forms. According to Bely, the dictatorship of the proletariat, because it flows from conditions under capitalism, is the last stage of the old epoch; the new era lies outside history and bears no resemblance to bourgeois culture. "In this sense [social revolution] is not revolution; it is even bourgeois. The authentic revolutionary break, the real revolution, will come later—but here the curtain falls. The new social forms are not yet revealed to us in essence" (ibid., pp. 19–20). It seems that Bely regarded the Bolshevik Revolution as part of the "negative apocalypse" and expected a "positive apocalypse" to follow.[18] His reference to the "miracle of the birth of new life from the womb of revolution" recalls the apocalyptic image of the "Woman Clothed with the Sun" in the throes of childbirth, paining to be delivered (ibid., p. 14; cf. Rev. 12:2). The same eschatological tone is evident in his conclusion. In the union of revolution and culture, of the "star within us" (the divine I or ego of the Anthroposophists) and the comet without (revolution), said Bely, the biblical maxims "feed the hungry" and "not by bread alone" will both be fulfilled (*Revolution,* p. 28).

The prominence of apocalyptic imagery in Bely's work further evidences his apocalyptic orientation. In *At the Pass* (1, pp. 85–88), Bely speaks of the storm of fire already blazing on the earth that will burn out everything in us that is not fire (i.e., will leave only the soul). And fire, both spiritual and real, is a recurrent image in *Revolution and Culture* (pp. 6–7, 18). In addition to its general eschatological significance, fire has a special meaning in Russia, where the Old Believers burned themselves alive in their battle against the state, which they considered to be the Antichrist. Russian revolutionaries sometimes identified with them.[19] Cosmic upheaval is another prominent theme, as in the opening lines of *Revolution and Culture:* "Like an underground shock, smashing everything, appears the revolution, appears a tornado sweeping away forms . . . revolution recalls nature, storm, flood, waterfall: everything in it reaches 'beyond the limit,' all is extreme" (p. 5). And, recalling the apocalyptic significance of earthquakes, a few lines later Bely refers to the revolutionary lava on which green young sprouts will soon grow. Red, he says, is the color of revolution, while the color of culture is green (pp. 6, 7). Elsewhere, he states, "in explosion, catastrophe, and fire the old life falls to pieces . . . the new epoch [is being prepared]" (*Notes of an Eccentric,* 1, pp. 77–78). Repeated references to thunder and lightning also connote the apocalypse they portend (*At the Pass,* 1, pp. 86, 114–16; *Revolution,* p. 16). Similarly, Bely's fellow Symbolist Aleksandr Blok, who disapproved of Bely's mysticism but shared his hatred of modern civilization, also spoke of cosmic upheaval and regarded the task of Russian culture as being "to burn what must be burned," to turn the storm of Stenka Razin and Emelyan Pugachyov into a "volitional musical wave." [20] Like Bely, Blok was also associated with the Scythians; his eschatological symbolism, particularly with respect to music, provides an interesting counterpoint to Bely's.

Music, for both Bely and Blok, though in different ways, possesses eschatological significance. The philosophic tradition of Schopenhauer, Nietzsche, and Wagner (by which both Bely and Blok were influenced) which holds music as the language of the world will, the elemental, the Dionysian, embodies only one dimension of the "spirit of music."[21] Historically, music contains a religious dimension; and religiously, music implies harmony and redemption. In Medieval Europe music was considered the expression of the divine harmony ruling the world, linking heaven and earth in various mathematical combinations; and music is a prominent feature of most religious liturgies. For Bely and Blok, objecting to modern civilization, music provides a rival cosmology to the rationalistic, individualistic enlightenment and a bridge to the postapocalyptic world. Like the Socinians and Gnostics of earlier eras who considered music the language of mysticism, Bely and Blok opposed music to the written word and to the religious or secular authority—commandment, contract, or law—that the fixed written word implies.

"In the beginning," Blok wrote in his diary, "was music. Music is the essence of the world."[22] Distinguishing between "calendar time" and "musical time," Blok equated the latter with the eternal

rhythms of life and opposed the goal-directedness of modern civilization.[23] Bely, a believer in spiritual progress and cosmic evolution, was far more conscious of "calendar" or historical time. For
him, music was "the way" and "the life" (*Revolution,* p. 27). The
spiral, synthesis of a circle and a line and a symbol he used frequently (*At the Pass,* 3, pp. 67, 69, 74, 86), implies direction rather
than the endless cycles of nature. Unlike Blok, who detested all
form and structure and spoke approvingly of perennial flux, Bely
did expect new forms to develop; for him the chaos was temporary
(ibid., 3, p. 45). His statement that music is the "mathematics of
the soul" implies a faith in cosmic order. Furthermore, recalling
his earlier belief in the poet as magus, Bely believed music represented a direct plug into the creative processes of the universe, a
means of investing man himself with creative powers. Finally, in
a cosmos whose essence is sound, striking the right chord might
set in motion a series of vibrations leading to the Second Coming
of the Messiah. It is sound—the seven trumpets of the Apocalypse—
that brings on the convulsions of the Last Days, and it is sound
in the form of a "new song" that signals the new dispensation.
And only the pure are able to sing it.[24]

The "spirit of music" augurs glad tidings, a new era, a new
man, and a new society. Socially, it connotes a choirlike community,
a world orchestra, where differences blend and where the parts
work together with the whole; and used in this sense, it registers
opposition to individualism. In a largely illiterate society, as
Russia then was, music also connotes the end of class divisions
based on intellect and education, as the ability to read and verbal
ability in general become irrelevant. Through music, furthermore,
the ear of a people accustomed to the beautiful music of the Ortho-
dox liturgy might be gained. Thus results Blok's belief in the
coming "musical reconciliation" between intelligentsia and *narod,*
and Bely's desire to return to the sources of a true humanism in the
musical culture of the Renaissance.[25] For both Bely and Blok,
though again in different ways, the "spirit of music" signals liberation (both personal and social) from the dominance of the
analytical intellect. Speaking directly to the psyche, music evokes
new human qualities of creativity, beauty, and love. For Bely in
particular, music connotes the universal man, ideal of the Renaissance, synthesizer of art and science.[26] Thus through music, both
writers believed, the new era of social harmony and personal

integration begins. A new man—creative, spiritual, aesthetic, and loving—the very opposite of rationally calculating, egoistic, and utilitarian economic man, emerges from the crucible of revolution.

Speaking for Andrey Bely, the child Kotik Letaev says: "I am a sinner: with Mama I sin against Papa; with Papa I sin against Mama. How can I exist and: not sin?"[27] The product of a traumatically unhappy marriage, the young Bely was torn between his dogmatic and ultrarational father and his sensitive but hysterical mother, and these two opposing spirits remained for him symbols of the eschatological dualism of the world. He never ceased attempting to resolve the dualism through some sort of radical break from the existing order, and his apocalyptism constitutes a dramatic example of this tendency. The roots of Bely's apocalyptism, in other words, are psychological rather than social, and they can be found in what Bely himself called "the family apocalypse."[28]

As Bely grew older he tended to cast his apocalyptism in social and cultural terms. His perception of the very real social and cultural crisis of his time was deeply colored by his own personal crisis.[29] Events in the external world validated, reinforced, and extended his already existing apocalyptism. The social application of his apocalyptism, his espousal of a revolutionary resolution to conflict, also stems from a "profound sense of anarchical revolt."[30] That revolt was directed as much against his father as against the existing political and social system. Indeed, for Bely the two were one: the disease of the "bourgeois professordom" which infected his home was but a "symptom of the general intellectual disease of those times."[31] He hated bourgeois society for the same traits he resented in his father: coldness, abstract cerebralism, mechanism, joylessness, lack of love.[32] Bely's childhood experience, then, constitutes one of the factors in his desire for a spiritual revolution that would end authority, eliminate repression, and liberate the "spirit of music," which he equated with his mother.[33]

Romantic revolts are characterized by their insistence on the complete negation of the old in order to promulgate the new on the ashes of the old.[34] Bely's apocalyptic revolution is very much in this tradition. He was opposed to mere reform; practical attempts to improve social conditions simply did not interest him. The entire system had to be destroyed, so that humanity could be purified by going through the ordeal of blood, fire, and suffering. His anarchism enabled him to avoid the empirical problems of the political arena altogether and, though Bely did support *Vekhi,* he never shared the latter's emphasis on legality and economic progress. Opting for spiritual progress, he opposed industrialization per se, considered machines demonic, and made pointed remarks on their resemblance to skeletons (*Revolution,* p. 13; *At the Pass,* 1, p. 24). His hatred of materialism led him to condemn capitalism for the "fat bellies" it created (*At the Pass,* 1, p. 13), and it was perhaps his sense of guilt ("I am a sinner"), that drew him to the traditional Christian virtue of self-sacrifice, to the point of identifying with Christ and fantasizing about his own crucifixion.[35] For similar psychological reasons, Blok, also deeply affected by a sense of guilt, predicted the immolation of himself and his entire class and did not oppose it. It is too late for repentance, he said in 1910: "our sin, both individual and collective, is too great."[36]

Though neither Bely nor Blok joined the Communist party, both cooperated with the Bolsheviks; whether this was for reasons of survival or conviction is too complex an issue to discuss here. Suffice it to state that the incompatibility of their goals with those of the Bolsheviks soon became apparent. Blok died, disillusioned, in 1921. Bely lived on to 1934, remaining a loyal Soviet citizen to the end. But the Bolsheviks, not without reason, never regarded him as one of their own.

NOTES

1. See Revelation, especially chapters 6, 8, 9, 13, 16. See also Norman Cohn, *Pursuit of the Millennium* (New York: Harper, 1961).

2. Soviet scholars tend to argue that Bely's and Blok's abandonment of apolitical aestheticism for advocacy of social revolution stemmed from their recognition, around 1905, of the futility of the artist's attempt to insulate himself from social problems. See, for example, Tamara Khmelnitskaya, "Poeziya Andreya Belogo," introduction to *Poetry* (Moscow-Leningrad, 1966), pp. 5–6, who argues that the characteristic trait of the second generation of Russian Symbolists was their desire to leave the narrow confines of literary and aesthetic problems. See also V. Orlov, ed., *A. A. Blok–Andrey Bely, Perepiska* (Moskva: Izd. Gos. Lit. Muzeya, 1940), p. xxvi, for his view that these Symbolists felt the crisis of capitalist culture and sought an exit from the bourgeois world. While limitations of space prohibit discussion of the validity of this explanation

for other Symbolists, in Bely's case social problems (of which he was undoubtedly aware) were not the primary cause of his apocalyptism.

3. For a discussion of Merezhkovsky's views see B. G. Rosenthal, *D. S. Merezhkovsky and the Silver Age: The Development of a Revolutionary Mentality* (The Hague: Mouton, 1975).

4. *Prishedshy*, the drama on which Bely worked from 1898 to 1903, has an eschatological theme, as does his 1903 cycle "Vechny zov," dedicated, incidentally, to Merezhkovsky. See *Poetry*, p. 55 and John Elsworth, *Andrey Bely* (Letchworth: Bradda, 1972), pp. 10–44, for biographical detail.

5. Gerald Janecek, "Literature as Music: Symphonic Forms in Bely's *Fourth Symphony*," *Canadian-American Slavic Studies* 8, no. 4 (Winter 1974): 508.

6. Andrey Bely, "Apokalipsis v russkoy poezii," in *Lug zelyony* (New York: Johnson Reprint Corp., 1967), pp. 222–47 (quote is on p. 223). First published in the April 1905 issue of *Vesy*—i.e., after "Bloody Sunday" but before Russia's startling defeat by Japan at Tsushima and before the most turbulent phase of the revolutionary year—the essay expounds Bely's belief that disastrous events were about to occur and that these events are mere external reflections of the more important internal process, the universal struggle between cosmos and chaos. In the same essay he located the source of chaos in the East.

7. For a description of Steiner and his views see A. P. Shepherd's biography, *A Scientist of the Invisible* (London: Hodder & Stoughton, 1954).

8. Helene Hartmann, "Andrei Bely and the Hermetic Tradition" (Ph.D. diss., Columbia University, 1969), p. 26.

9. Orlov, *A. A. Blok . . .* , pp. 295–96.

10. Elsworth, *Andrey Bely,* p. 88.

11. Andrey Bely, *Na perevale:* vol. 1, *Krizis zhizni;* vol. 2, *Krizis mysli;* vol. 3, *Krizis kultury* (St. Petersburg: Alkonost, 1918–20); (the fourth volume *Krizis slova* was unavailable to me). Henceforth cited in the text as *At the Pass,* 1, 2, or 3.

12. Also Andrey Bely, *Revolyutsiya i kultura* (Letchworth: Bradda, 1971), p. 12. Henceforth cited in the text as *Revolution.*

13. "Rodine," in *Poetry,* pp. 381–82. Compare this with the earlier version "Otchayane" in *Poetry,* pp. 159–60.

14. "Khristos voskres" can be found in *Poetry,* pp. 385–402. See especially p. 401.

15. Elsworth, *Andrey Bely,* p. 92; Samuel Cioran, *The Apocalyptic Symbolism of Andrej Belyj* (The Hague: Mouton, 1973), pp. 101, 105.

16. Nicholas Berdyaev, *Dream and Reality* (London: Geoffrey Bles, 1950), pp. 224–25n.

17. R. I. Ivanov-Razumnik, *Aleksandr Blok: Andrey Bely* (St. Petersburg: Alkonost, 1919), pp. 164–65. See also pp. 28–118.

18. Cioran, *The Apocalyptic Symbolism* . . . , p. 2.

19. Emanuel Sarkisyanz, *Russland und der Messianismus des Orients* (Tübingen: J. C. B. Mohr [Paul Siebeck], 1955), pp. 76, 87–88, 134.

20. Aleksandr Blok, *Sobranie sochineny v vosmi tomakh* (Moscow-Leningrad: GIKhL, 1963), 7: 297 (diary entry for 7 August 1917).

21. For Blok see Rolf D. Kluge, *Westeuropa und Russland im Weltbild Aleksandr Blok's* (Munich: Otto Sagner, 1967), pp. 107, 202–6. For Bely see *At the Pass,* especially vol. 3.

22. Blok, *Sobranie sochineny,* 7: 360 (diary entry for 31 March 1919).

23. Ibid., 6: 101–2.

24. Rev. 5: 9, 14: 3, 15: 13.

25. See Blok, *Sobranie sochineny,* 6: 8, 9–20, 21–25, *passim.* Note especially his use of Christ as the symbol of the new man. For Bely see *At the Pass,* 3: 21–44.

26. A long-standing concern of Bely's was his attempt to synthesize art, science, and philosophy on the basis of a new epistemology to be achieved through symbolism in order to achieve organic unity.

27. Andrei Bely, *Kotik Letaev,* trans. Gerald Janecek (Ann Arbor, Mich.: Ardis, 1971), p. 157.

28. Cioran, *The Apocalyptic Symbolism* . . . , p. 6; "The Family Apocalypse," in ibid., pp. 26–42, especially pp. 32–38.

29. For this reason, Helen Muchnic, in "Russian Nightmares," *New York Review of Books,* 17 April 1975, pp. 35–36 claims that Bely cannot be taken seriously as a prophet and historian.

30. Cioran, *The Apocalyptic Symbolism* . . . , p. 40.

31. Ibid.

32. The father-son conflict is particularly obvious in *Petersburg.* See Vladislav Khodasevich, "Ableukhovy—Letaevy—Korobkiny" in *Literaturnye stati* (New York: Chekhov, 1954), pp. 187–218, for the argument that Bely's novels recapitulate his family situation.

33. Cioran, *The Apocalyptic Symbolism* . . . , pp. 37–38. As a child Bely was forbidden by his mother to speak to his father, a fact which may also account for his later emphasis on music rather than words; see Elsworth, *Andrey Bely,* pp. 7–8, for the importance of music in Bely's childhood.

34. Cioran, *The Apocalyptic Symbolism* . . . , p. 41. See also Bely, *Kotik Letaev,* p. 211 ("I don't like the world: in it all is—difficult and complicated").

35. Bely, *Kotik Letaev,* pp. 217–22. Bely's fantasies of self-destruction in *At the Pass* and *Notes of an Eccentric* may also evidence a desire for martyrdom.

36. Blok, *Sobranie sochineny,* 5: 434. Blok's resentment of his father and his identification of his father with modern civilization can be seen in his long poem "Vozmezdie" ("Retribution").

ROGER KEYS

THE BELY–IVANOV-RAZUMNIK CORRESPONDENCE

Although Andrey Bely was a prolific and often painstaking correspondent, very few of his letters have been published hitherto, either in their entirety or in extract. His copious correspondence with Blok is, of course, the major exception.[1] And his letters to Bryusov have recently been published in the Soviet Union.[2] A few items have been printed in periodicals (for example, Bely's letters to Sologub[3] and to Marietta Shaginyan[4]). But with rare exceptions these all date back to the period before the October Revolution (though Bely's letters to such major pre-Revolution correspondents as Metner and Morozova seem not to have been published at all). As for the letters which Bely wrote after 1917, the published material is even more thinly scattered.[5] It is in relation to this second and less fully documented half of Bely's creative career that the correspondence with R. V. Ivanov-Razumnik acquires unique significance.[6]

In his *Memoirs* Ivanov-Razumnik recounts the story of how he came to compile and annotate Bely's correspondence.[7] He was in exile in the town of Kashira at the time, a little over 100 kilometers from Moscow.

At this period (Autumn 1936) the State Museum of Literature under its director V. D. Bonch-Bruevich, was proposing to publish a volume of letters from Andrey Bely to Aleksandr Blok which the Museum had acquired from Lyubov Dmitrievna Blok.[8] I suggested to the Museum that I should prepare for publication Andrey Bely's letters to myself (200 letters covering the years 1913 to 1933, about forty printer's sheets). The Museum accepted my suggestion and twice authorized me to travel to Detskoe Selo (in December 1936 and April 1937, on both occasions for a month). . . . According to my contract I was required to submit the completed volume of fifty printer's sheets by the first of July 1937: forty sheets of text and ten of commentaries. I completed this task, which cost me seven months of unremitting labour, just in time and sent the results off on the very last day.

But, he goes on to observe, "the date of its ultimate appearance is quite another question." The situation is not very different today, when, thirty years after his death, Ivanov-Razumnik's political and literary reputation has still not been officially restored in the Soviet Union.[9]

Bely appears to have met Ivanov-Razumnik for the first time in Petersburg in September 1906,[10] probably at Vyacheslav Ivanov's "Tower" (*Beginning of the Century,* p. 324). This period—the climax of Bely's affair with Lyubov Dmitrievna—was a particularly difficult one in his life, and the meeting with Ivanov-Razumnik does not seem to have impinged upon him very much. It was not until six years later that their paths were to cross again, as a result of Blok's efforts to find a publisher for the novel *Petersburg.* The millionaire Mikhail Ivanovich Tereshchenko [11] and his two sisters had decided in the autumn of 1912 to set up a new publishing house, Sirin, with the aim of producing major new editions of certain of the Russian modernists. Blok, Remizov, and Ivanov-Razumnik were members of the editorial board, and although the latter may not have thought very highly of the earliest version of Bely's novel,[12] he began to correspond with the writer when Bely returned to Russia from Berlin in March 1913, soon after Sirin had decided to accept the novel for publication.[13] These earliest letters appear not to have survived. Bely eventually met Ivanov-Razumnik again at the office of Sirin on 11 May 1913.[14]

During the months that followed, Bely and his future wife, Asya Turgeneva, traveled extensively around Europe, listening to the lectures of the Anthroposophists' leader, Dr. Rudolf Steiner. In November and December of 1913, Bely finished work on the eighth and final chapter of *Petersburg,* and it is with the gradually deepening critical interest of Ivanov-Razumnik in the progress and significance of that novel that their correspondence may properly be said to begin.[15] In the first letter that has come down to us Ivanov-Razumnik had written, apropos of *Petersburg,* that "in spite of many 'buts' (especially lack of knowledge concerning revolutionaries) it gives me much joy, and I am intending to write about it at length." He was as good as his word and eventually published in 1916 the first of several essays on the novel, a long article entitled "East or West?" which derived some of its ideas from Bely's first and subsequent letters on the subject.[16] "Your opinion of my novel," Bely had written in December 1913, "is very valuable and dear to me, because my conception of it contained features having absolutely nothing in common with everyday life [*byt*], revolution, etc. And for that reason I willingly agree with you: in the novel there probably are very gross errors of fact in regard to everyday life, knowledge of milieu, etc. Revolution, everyday scenes, 1905, etc., entered the plot accidentally, unintentionally." He goes on to thank Ivanov-Razumnik once again for his thoughtful, and above all, helpful criticism of the novel: "I have always aimed to learn from criticism, but alas! until now I have learned little; people have either approved of me without giving reasons, or they have reviled me without giving reasons . . . and, to tell the truth, you don't gain very much from either abuse or praise." He returns to this theme two and a half years later in a letter posted from Dornach in June/July 1916: "Do you know that it [Ivanov-Razumnik's article] nearly moved me to tears: why—in my fifteen years of literary activity, this is the *first article* about me which has excited me and about which I can say that *criticism* not only reveals my intentions as an author but is even teaching me, opening the way ahead for me, making it easier for me to think about my future works."

A final postscript to this occurs in a letter of 18 November 1923, in which Bely responds with grateful enthusiasm to the two articles on *Petersburg* written by Ivanov-Razumnik in March-April of the same year and published in his book *Summits*.[17] "I was extremely touched, almost shaken by your work on the versions of *Petersburg,* remarkable as it is in its conclusions, so full of love for me, so thorough and painstaking; I read it and was astounded, almost shaken; and it seemed to me (this is not because you were writing about me) that with this article on *Petersburg* you are opening a completely new era in the science of literary criticism [v nauke o podkhode k khudozhestvennym proizvedeniyam]."

Ivanov-Razumnik's literary relationship with Bely began at an important turning point in Bely's own attitude to his closest friends, to literature, and to the world at large. As he noted several years later in an entry in his unpublished "Material for an (Intimate) Biography":

> In the first months of my initiation into Anthroposophy (May to December 1912 and January to October 1913) I accomplished something which was very difficult for me: I questioned all the paths I had followed hitherto. . . . I broke—because of the Doctor—with a number of friends (Metner, Ellis, S. M. Solovyov, Rachinsky, Morozova, . . .), I abandoned Russia . . . and to all intents and purposes retired from literature. . . . And yet in my heart the feeling was building up that "No, this is too much: I have been completely robbed by Anthroposophy; I have been deprived of my native land, poetry, friends, life, glory, wife, position in life. Instead of all this I am hanging about here in Dornach, at Asya's beck and call, known by nobody and looked upon by most people as some sort of 'naive Herr Bugaeff.' " It began to appear to me that, taking into account my literary name, my age and all of my writings, they might take a greater interest in me.[18]

The knowledge that one Russian critic at least accorded his work the serious and sympathetic attention it deserved was an important element in bolstering Bely's failing self-confidence at this time, and the warmth of his feeling for Ivanov-Razumnik was to grow steadily in the years that followed.

The period from 1917 to 1921 was a busy time for both writers, during which they collaborated almost continuously on a number of literary and cultural projects. Bely sympathized with Ivanov-Razumnik's Left Socialist-Revolutionary sentiments, though neither of them were party members, and he made extensive contributions to the *Scythians* collections envisaged by Ivanov-Razumnik at the end of 1916. The novel *Kotik Letaev* appeared in these publications,[19] and there are occasional discussions of Bely's progress on this work in the correspondence.[20] He was a frequent visitor at Ivanov-Razumnik's house in Tsarskoe Selo at this time, and it was there that he became acquainted with Klyuev, Esenin, Oreshin and others who sympathized with the "Scythian" cause. His letters from Moscow are full of vivid descriptions of the rapidly changing political scene and express clearly his own growing disillusionment with what he sees as an ever-deteriorating situation.[21] But above all, he is struck by the magnitude of events and the unparalleled possibilities for political, social, and spiritual transformation in Russia: "We are living in colossal times, we are not even able to 'take it all in,' we are living at only a hundredth part of the pace of time; time is outstripping us; it is almost impossible to catch up; it commands us imperiously; we are *counter-revolutionaries* not at our own behest, but at the behest of time which is rushing forward irresistibly" (letter of 27 July 1917).

In January 1919 several writers and thinkers, including Bely, Ivanov-Razumnik, and Blok, decided to found a research academy in Petrograd.[22] Various objections from official Bolshevik sources delayed its establishment, and the Free Philosophical Association or Volfila, as it came to be called, did not come into being until November 1919. In January 1920, Bely received an invitation from Ivanov-Razumnik to come to Petrograd and work in Volfila, which had begun to widen the scope of its activities. From February to June of the same year Bely was resident in Petrograd, living in the newly founded "House of the Arts" and immersing himself in the affairs of Volfila, giving many lectures and participating in numerous public debates. He returned to Petrograd in March 1922, continuing to work in Volfila until September and spending much of the summer at Ivanov-Razumnik's house in Detskoe Selo. Soon after he left Russia for western Europe, where he remained for two complete years.

The period from 1919 to 1923 is not very fully reflected in the correspondence. For part of the time Bely was in daily contact with Ivanov-Razumnik in Petrograd, while most of the letters dispatched from Moscow are brief and deal with practicalities. The months Bely spent in Berlin were a period of deep despair and mental prostration, although, as a letter of November 1923 reveals, he was by no means unaware of the encroachments on freedom of speech which were being made in Russia: "I knew a *very great deal* about conditions of life in Russia; and for that reason everything that you write about Volfila . . . I find even reassuring (alas! a 'melancholy' reassurance); but at the present time a flourishing Volfila seemed to me to be an abnormal phenomenon,[23] and this hasn't anything at all to do with the fact that in Russia now conditions of life are such and such, but because *throughout the whole world* now this is an evil period; everything that is revolutionary, free, new, has in the nature of things to disappear beneath the ground; and for that reason life in the catacombs is the natural existence for people who live by the rhythm of the future."

In the same letter he goes on to sound the themes which would characterize his personal life for the next ten years, until his death:

a gradual narrowing of horizons, both political and literary; increasing loneliness and an awareness of his own embattled position in Soviet society; the cherishing of a few, true friends; and recourse to private values as the only secure element in an adverse environment: "Externally my position is extremely unpromising; there is, of course, nowhere for me to publish my work, I am absolutely forbidden to express any opinions (on this score I possess extremely accurate information from people who have been speaking with Lebedev-Polyansky, the All-Russian censor) . . . but nonetheless I am tranquil; my life is a catacomb which is in being here and now [*osushchestvlyonnaya katakomba*]; I see nobody, go nowhere, I am cut off from all social milieux, there is nowhere for me to be published, I am forbidden to speak; and yet— I am not despondent because, *for all that,* the air in Russia is completely different. . . . Those I feel to be 'our' people are K. N. Vasileva, Nilender, S. M. Solovyov, Stolyarov. . . ." [24] In fact, from the point of view of literary publication, events did not turn out for Bely as badly as he had feared. From 1926 he was once again allowed to publish novels, travel notes, memoirs, and works of specialist literary criticism, though a possibly even larger quantity of writing (chiefly works dealing with the history and theory of culture and with Anthroposophical themes) remains unpublished and is hardly likely to appear under present circumstances. In a later letter of 8 February 1928, Bely remarks wryly, apropos of a suggested reprinting of *Petersburg: "Petersburg* wasn't passed by the censorship, but after she [Nikitina] [25] had spoken to Polyansky it was passed; for Polyansky said that a leopard *'can't change his spots,'* that anyway, according to him, I am such a hopeless case, that I am so *harmless,* for I've had my day and am living out my *hoary old age,* that publishing *Petersburg* with all its mysticism won't arouse temptations for anyone, so it might as well appear." But he goes on to remark of Ivanov-Razumnik: "You are obviously more dangerous, for even the fearless Nikitina suddenly took fright."

Ivanov-Razumnik was one of the happy (or not so happy) few— one of that small circle of intimate friends with whom Bely had contact in his final years and through whom he felt his life acquired meaning in the present. 1924 marks the beginning of an extensive series of letters, many of them several score pages long, in which Bely meditates unconstrainedly upon the nature of life and friendship; literature, and Anthroposophy; Symbolism and his own literary development; his work in progress; death and "the future that we won't see." [26] The tone of the letters—until 1930 at any rate—is reflective and unhurried. They coincide more or less with the six comparatively tranquil years that he spent with Klavdiya Nikolaevna Vasileva in their little cottage at Kuchino (seventeen versts from Moscow in the direction of Nizhny Novgorod). Many of these letters were sent "s okaziey," as suitable circumstances arose, and the opportunity that this afforded to circumvent both the censorship and the vagaries of the Soviet postal service, allowed Bely to be as candid as he wished. Though offering few confidences about his intimate, emotional life, Bely's letters to Ivanov-Razumnik of this period are spiritually and intellectually very frank. The degree of their sincerity may be judged from the following extract, taken from a letter of 11 March 1925:

> It grieved me terribly to learn that you destroy letters which you have written to me. I feel a kind of inner need, you see, for you to write to me about everything and in whatever way you like, even if it's in trans-sense language [zaumny yazyk]! . . . At times when living is difficult, when you write fitfully at night, the only sense that a correspondence has, is that it gives you the chance to keep a record of your consciousness from day to day, dissociating yourself from the subjectivism which is laid upon it by the passing *days* and *hours*. . . . Dear, dear Razumnik Vasilevich, do believe in me: and write to me about everything in any way you wish. It is very important for me to respond to you, respond with you and have you respond to me [*pereklikatsya so-klikatsya i otklikatsya*]. I shall be doing this, writing to you as best as I can, getting rid of everything that builds up inside me along with the chance detritus of events around us, because I believe in you; and you—*you must believe in me*. I am firmly aware that this conversation between us will carry on without interruption; let the very irregularity of our appeals to one another be a symbol of their *"permanence."* . . .

It is impossible within the confines of a short paper to do more than give a summary of some of the areas in which the letters either throw new light on Bely's experiences and beliefs or at least add significantly to information already in our possession. He describes his last meeting—and reconciliation—with Valery Bryusov in Koktebel after a break of twelve years.[27] He muses on the life and death of Gershenzon in 1925 [28] and later on the sufferings and achievement of Sologub.[29] He tells of the harsh conditions of life in Moscow [30] and contrasts them with the peace and privacy of

Kuchino.[31] Work on the *Moscow* novels,[32] his attempts at collaborating with Mikhail Chekhov on a dramatized version of *Petersburg*,[33] and his bitter disappointment at the outcome [34]—all this forms part of the content of the letters written in 1925 and 1926. For a personal evaluation of his literary development to date—given in the light of Anthroposophy—we can turn to Bely's long autobiographical letter of 1–3 March 1927, recently published in France.[35] Ivanov-Razumnik had written to him ten days earlier,[36] telling him of a publisher who wished to issue a bibliography of Bely's works, but only on the understanding that Ivanov-Razumnik would preface it with an introductory article entitled: "The Stages of A. Bely's Creative Work." To which Bely replied, in very characteristic fashion: "For me the theme of the stages of my writing cannot help merging with another theme: that of the stages of my life."

This more or less tranquil period of his life was to continue for a few years yet, although latterly the warm relationship with Ivanov-Razumnik began to cool somewhat. In his *Memoirs* Ivanov-Razumnik recalls a discussion on "dictatorship, collectivization, industrialization, [and] the 'building up of culture' " [37] which took place in December 1931 [38] between himself, Bely and a few guests. "Bely and his wife had spent the whole year with us. Our friendship was one of long standing, although lately we had found it impossible to agree on political matters and this had begun to darken it . . . ever since he had attempted in his book *Wind from the Caucasus* [*Veter s Kavkaza*, Moscow, 1928] to sing hosannas to the building of the new life without saying anything of the methods employed for that purpose." Ivanov-Razumnik had visited Bely in Kuchino three times, for a few weeks in April 1926, again in early September 1928, and for the last time in May 1930, when Bely was putting the finishing touches to his final novel, *Masks*. Bely had spent the months of May and June 1926 with his friend in Detskoe Selo, and was destined to find shelter in his house twice more. By 1931 the storm clouds were gathering for both writers. This is reflected in the laconic, factual quality of Bely's final letters (1931–32). Life in Kuchino had become unbearable for Bely and Klavdiya Nikolaevna for a variety of reasons, and on April 19 they left the village for good and moved in with Ivanov-Razumnik and his wife, Varvara Nikolaevna. In late May/early June 1931 several members of Bely's former Anthroposophical circle were arrested by the OGPU, including Klavdiya Nikolaevna and her legal husband, Pyotr Nikolaevich Vasilev. The latter were not released until July 2. On July 18 they formalized their divorce, and on the same day Klavdiya Nikolaevna and Bely were married at a register office in Moscow. In early September she was allowed to return to Ivanov-Razumnik's home in Detskoe Selo, provided she gave an undertaking not to leave that place and to stop seeing her Anthroposophical friends.[39] She and Bely remained with Ivanov-Razumnik until April of the following year, when they and their host were obliged to leave the house (it was being converted into an asylum for tuberculosis patients) and find other accommodation.[40] Bely and his wife moved to Moscow. Nine months later, on 2 February 1933, Ivanov-Razumnik was arrested in Detskoe Selo on a charge ostensibly relating to his former Left Socialist-Revolutionary background, and there began for him eight years of imprisonment and exile. He and Bely were never to meet again.

NOTES

1. *Aleksandr Blok i Andrey Bely Perepiska,* ed. Vl. Orlov (Moscow: Izd. Gos. Lit. Muzeya, 1940).

2. In *Literaturnoe Nasledstvo* 85 (Moscow, 1976): 327–427.

3. S. Grechishkin and A. Lavrov, "Andrey Bely. Pisma k F. Sologubu," *Ezhegodnik Pushkinskogo Doma na 1972 god* (1974): 131–37.

4. M. Shaginyan, "Desyat pisem Andreya Belogo (ot 1908 do 1928 goda)," *Novy Mir*, no. 6 (1973): 141–52.

5. For example, V. F. Khodasevich, "Tri pisma Andreya Belogo," *Sovremennye zapiski* 55 (1934): 256–70; "Pismo Andreya Belogo," [dated 11 November 1921, addressed to Asya Turgeneva, but never sent], *Vozdushnye puti* 5 (1967): 296–313; extracts from letters to M. Gorky in I. V. Koretskaya, "Gorky i Andrey Bely," *Gorkovskie chteniya,* (1968): 189–206; Nvard Teryan, "Pisma Andreya Belogo k A. M. Miskaryan," *Russkaya literatura*, no. 1 (1973): 155–58. For a detailed, though by no means complete, survey of Bely's "epistolary legacy," see K. Bugaeva and A. Petrovsky, "Literaturnoe nasledstvo Andreya Belogo" in *Literaturnoe Nasledstvo* 27–28 (Moscow, 1937): 634–36.

6. The originals of Bely's letters to Ivanov-Razumnik [real name: Razumnik Vasilevich Ivanov (b. 1878, d. 1946)] number 184 items in all and are dated between 1913 and 1932. They were given by Ivanov-Razumnik to the State Literary Museum in Moscow on 1 July 1937, along with two sets of copies and three sets of commentaries. The original letters are to be found at TsGALI, fond 1782 (Ivanov-Razumnik), ed. Khr. 4–23. There would appear to be no trace either of the typed copies or of Ivanov-Razumnik's commentaries in this archive. One set

of (unverified) copies was retained by Ivanov-Razumnik in his personal archive at Detskoe Selo, where they remained until the outbreak of war in September 1941. Ivanov-Razumnik has the following to say of his archive in his book *Pisatelskie Sudby* (New York, 1951), p. 11: "In the autumn of 1941 our small wooden house on the very outskirts of Tsarskoe Selo turned out moreover to be right on the front line. Its destruction began with bombs dropped from aeroplanes in August and September and ended with artillery shells in the winter of 1941–1942. When I visited the house for the last time, my library and archive were nothing but a heap of paper trampled on by soldiers' boots and scattered over the floors of all three rooms; now only the memory of the place remains. . . ." In fact, the archive did not perish entirely, as he feared. After the German troops retreated in 1944, Dmitry Evgenevich Maksimov (now professor of Russian literature at Leningrad State University) made his way to Ivanov-Razumnik's bombed-out house in Detskoe Selo and gathered up sheaves of manuscript and typescript material scattered all over the floor, as Ivanov-Razumnik describes. These he deposited at the Pushkinsky Dom (IRLI) in Leningrad, where they have remained to the present day. What has survived of the copies of Bely's letters (some 83 items in varying states of completeness, about two-fifths of the original typescript) is to be found at IRLI, fond 79 (Ivanov-Razumnik), opis 3, ed. Khr. 81. A set of Ivanov-Razumnik's commentaries to the letters does not seem to have been amongst the material rescued by D. E. Maksimov. Of Ivanov-Razumnik's letters to Bely, 88 are extant in the latter's archive at the State Lenin Library, fond 25, papka 16, ed. Khr. 6a and 6b. They cover the years from 1913 to 1929. Further letters written between 1919 and 1932 are at TsGALI (fond 53, opis 1, ed. Khr. 193). Only one of Bely's letters to Ivanov-Razumnik has been published in full, that of 1–3 March 1927. G. Nivat, "Andrey Bely: lettre autobiographique à Ivanov-Razumnik," *Cahiers du Monde Russe et Soviétique* 15, nos. 1–2 (Janvier-Juin 1974): 45–82. An extract from Bely's letter of 31 August 1921 was quoted by Ivanov-Razumnik in his book *Vershiny* (Petrograd: Kolos, 1923), pp. 109–10. Extracts from three letters were published by Vl. Orlov in his introductory article to the Blok-Bely correspondence, pp. xlviii, lv, lviii. (See note 1 above.) Part of another letter was apparently published in Armenian translation, in *Sovetakan Ayastan*, no. 1 (1960): 20–22.

7. P. S. Squire, trans., *The Memoirs of Ivanov-Razumnik* (Oxford: Oxford University Press, 1965), pp. 200–201. The original Russian text, *Tyurmy i Ssylki*, was published in New York in 1953. The passage referred to was actually written in September 1937 (see Squire, p. 190).

8. See note 1 above.

9. It should be said, however, that signs of a more balanced evaluation of Ivanov-Razumnik's work as a literary and social critic in the period before the Revolution are visible in the recently published article

by M. G. Petrova "Estetika pozdnego narodnichestva" in *Literaturno-Esteticheskie kontseptsii v Rossii kontsa XIX-nachala XX v.* (Moscow: Nauka, 1975): 156–69.

10. See "Material k biografii (intimnoy), prednaznachennoy dlya izucheniya tolko posle smerti avtora," written 1923, at TsGALI, fond 53 (A. Bely), opis 2, ed. Khr. 3, sheet 53.

11. M. I. Tereshchenko (1888–1958) was to become minister of finance and minister of foreign affairs in the Provisional Government.

12. That is, chapter 1 and part of chapter 2 of the so-called Nekrasov version of *Petersburg* (nine printer's sheets); cf. Blok's diary entry for 15 February 1913 in A. Blok, *Sobranie Sochineny v vosmi tomakh,* ed. Vl. Orlov (Moscow-Leningrad: GIKhL, 1960–63), 7: 220: " ['Sirin'] very much dislikes the beginning of the novel (*Petersburg*) in the form in which it has been set up by Nekrasov." In the entry for February 16 (ibid.) he mentions "Ivanov-Razumnik's unfavourable attitude to A. Bely."

13. *Petersburg* was published in Sirin almanacs No. 1 (1913), No. 2 (1913), and No. 3 (1914). In a letter sent from exile to the critic A. G. Gornfeld on 8 May 1934, Ivanov-Razumnik recalls his hostility to the philosophy which he found implicit in *Petersburg.* "All the same: when I received the manuscript [of the novel] in 1912 and read it through, I was extremely grieved not to be able to print it in *Zavety* (there wasn't enough money); to make up for this I made every effort to ensure that it would be published in *Sirin*—and this cost me (and Blok) a great deal of trouble. What is the explanation? The novel is antipathetic, yet I myself try to arrange its publication as well as I can? There is no mystery here, of course, for 'great art' exercises its own compulsion." (TsGALI, fond 155, opis 1, ed. Khr. 321: quoted in *Literaturno-Esteticheskie kontseptsii . . .* , p. 168.)

14. See entry in K. N. Bugaeva, "Andrey Bely. Letopis Zhizni i tvorchestva" at GPB, fond 60 (A. Bely), ed. Khr. 107.

15. Ivanov-Razumnik's first letter is dated 8 November / 25 November 1913. Bely's reply was sent in December 1913 from somewhere in Germany.

16. "East or West?" appeared in *Russkie Vedomosti,* 4 May 1916.

17. R. V. Ivanov-Razumnik, "K istorii teksta 'Peterburga' " and "Peterburg," *Vershiny* (Petrograd: Kolos, 1923), pp. 89–101, 105–71. Ironically, this was to be the last book which Ivanov-Razumnik managed to get published in his own lifetime, with the exception of literary commentaries, editorial work, etc. No work of his of any kind has appeared in the Soviet Union since 1930.

18. Entry for April 1914, sheets 78–79. Bely's relationships with both Blok and Bryusov had already cooled long before this.

19. Chapters 1–4 published in *Skify,* Sbornik 1 (St. Petersburg, 1917); conclusion published in Sbornik 2 (1918).

20. See especially Bely's letters of 20 November 1915 and 23 June 1916.

21. See especially Bely's letters of 16 June and 27 July 1917; 27 February 1918; 17 November [?] 1923; 6 February 1924.

22. See A. Bely, "Volnaya filosofskaya assotsiatsiya," in *Novaya russkaya kniga*, no. 1 (Berlin, 1922): 32–33. See also "Rakurs dnevnika" (1899–1930), at TsGALI, fond 53, opis 1, ed. Khr. 100. Quoted in Bugaeva, "Letopis zhizni i tvorchestva."

23. See A. Bely, "Pochemu ya stal simvolistom . . . ," 1928, at TsGALI, fond 53, opis 1, ed. Khr. 74, section 14. "In 1922 it [Volfila] was obliged to reduce its activity, and in 1924 it was forced to cease its existence."

24. All Anthroposophists: Klavdiya Nikolaevna Vasileva (1886–1970), later to become Bely's second wife; Vladimir Ottonovich Nilender (1883–1965), poet and literary critic, a friend of Bely's from their early "Argonaut" days; Sergey Mikhaylovich Solovyov (1885–1943), Symbolist poet and translator, one of Bely's oldest friends; Mikhail Pavlovich Stolyarov, a member of the Anthroposophical circle and deputy president of the Moscow branch of Volfila.

25. E. F. Nikitina, organizer of the Moscow publishing house Nikitinskie Subbotniki, which published several of Bely's works, including the novels *The Baptized Chinaman* (two editions 1927, 1928), *The Moscow Eccentric* (1927) and *Moscow in Jeopardy* (1927). The reprint of *Petersburg* referred to in the letter appeared in 1928.

26. Letter of 3 October 1927.

27. Letter of 8 December 1924.

28. Mikhail Osipovich Gershenzon (1869–1925), literary critic and philosopher. See letter of March 1925.

29. Letters of 25 December 1927 and 7–10 February 1928.

30. Letter of March 1925.

31. Letter of 27 September 1925.

32. Letter of 27 September 1925.

33. Letters of 27 September and 19 October 1925.

34. Letters of 6 and 18 March 1926.

35. See note 6 above.

36. Letter of 20 February 1927.

37. Squire, *Memoirs*, pp. 103–4.

38. Ivanov-Razumnik had written "Dec. 1930" in error.

39. See the following letters to Ivanov-Razumnik: 3 July, undated, 19 July, and 31 August 1931.

40. See the letter from Bely to Aleksey Sergeevich Petrovsky of mid-March 1932, at GPB, fond 60, ed. xp. 56, published in *Novy Zhurnal* 122 (New York, 1976) 159–62.

THOMAS R. BEYER, Jr.

THE BELY–ZHIRMUNSKY POLEMIC

Andrey Bely, the brilliant apologist of Russian Symbolism and one of its most ardent and capable polemists, asserted most emphatically in his study, *Rhythm as a Dialectic*, that he was a "formalist prior to the formalists in Russia" (p. 28). Although Bely's book has been largely ignored or dismissed by later critics, his assertion has been echoed by several noted literary historians. Thus, for example, Oleg Maslenikov in *The Frenzied Poets: Andrei Biely and the Russian Symbolists* (Berkeley: University of California Press, 1952), p. 81, declared that Bely's first investigations of the formal aspects of verse in *Symbolism* "laid the foundation for the Russian formalist school of criticism. . . ." Contemporary scholars have often repeated or paraphrased the statement of Maslenikov, such that it has become a generally accepted cliché.[1] Although few if any question the validity of the claim, there still has been no comprehensive study of Bely's influence on Formalist poetics, nor of the relationship which existed between Bely and those whom he considered his legitimate offspring.

A few scholars, it should be noted, have devoted attention to the issue of Bely's influence on Formalist writings. Victor Erlich in *Russian Formalism: History–Doctrine*, 3d ed., Slavistic Printings and Reprintings (The Hague: Mouton, 1969), p. 38, briefly examines the historical role of Bely in the evolution of formal literary criticism and concludes that "in spite of their deficiencies Bely's studies in versification were an important milestone in the development of Russian scientific poetics." Erlich, however, concentrates on the uniqueness of Russian Formalism, a view which the Formalists themselves were eager to espouse and uphold; consequently his remarks on Bely are limited to a reiteration of their comments. More recently, Ewa M. Thompson in *Russian Formalism and Anglo-American New Criticism* (The Hague: Mouton, 1971) provides a more balanced evaluation of Bely's philosophical and theoretical principles which inspired the Formalists.

While both Erlich and Thompson offer valuable, though admittedly incomplete, information on Bely's impact, neither focuses specifically on the Formalist reception of Bely. More significantly, neither mentions Bely's lengthy explanation of his own position vis-à-vis his critics. This neglect to include or consider Bely's opinion is symptomatic of the general failure of Bely to attract serious scholarly attention as a literary critic. Notwithstanding the continuing applications and implications of Bely's pioneering efforts, there remains this lacuna in the history of Russian literary criticism. Essentially little has altered since 1953 when Kiril Taranovski lamented the fact that "today the contributions of Bely to the science of verse have already begun to be forgotten." [2] Bely himself was disturbed by what he considered a conspiracy of silence on the part of the Formalists concerning his role in the formulation of their new aesthetics and methodology. This so-called silence constituted one of the major issues raised in the controversy, which had as its starting point Viktor Zhirmunsky's celebrated *Introduction to Metrics* (1925).[3]

In his examination of the history of Russian poetics Zhirmunsky provided the most comprehensive discussion and criticism of Bely's *Symbolism* to that time. His survey was the first to examine in some detail the new scope of scientific poetics created by Bely's pioneering work. Previously, *Symbolism* had evoked only one serious analytical review when it had first appeared: Valery Bryusov's highly antagonistic "On a Single Question of Rhythm" (1910).[4] The fifteen-year interval between publication and objective evaluation was indicative of *Symbolism*'s continuing importance and impact on literary studies; but more important, the new evaluation pointed to the incomplete and inconsequential quality of the criticism previously directed at Bely. Such criticism as had existed was largely confined to passing references, allusions, or footnotes employed by apologists of Bely seeking to declare their affinity to his work, or by his detractors, chiefly the Formalists, seeking to pronounce unconditionally the independence and novelty of their own efforts.

Zhirmunsky avoided the obsequiousness of the first, meticulously granting recognition to Bely in those areas where deserved, and the protestations of the second, carefully refraining from labels and unsupported allegations. Describing the growth of the Formalist school in his article, "Formprobleme in der russischen Literaturwissenschaft," the critic had written: "Die formale Methode ist in der russischen Wissenschaft zuerst bei der Behandlung *metrischer Fragen* angewandt worden. Begründet wurde hier die neue Richtung durch die Arbeiten des Dichters *Andrej Belyj* über den russischen vierfussigen Jambus." [5] Zhirmunsky continued in *Introduction to Metrics* his tradition of conscientiously assigning to Bely his rightful position as one of the initiators of formal literary studies, while opposing Bely's theories and practices on what he considered to be matters of substance. Thus Zhirmunsky tempered his praise by noting that although Bely was the first to make the necessary applications for the study of rhythmic deviations (*otstuplenie*), he was not original in his discovery of this phenomenon. In summarizing his opinion of *Symbolism* Zhirmunsky affirmed: "It is impossible not to recognize the outstanding significance of Bely's works for the study of Russian verse" (*Introduction to Metrics,* p. 40).

The author's praise was counterbalanced with his objections to Bely's research. First, Bely's diagrammatic method was limited to unstressed syllables where stress was expected in the iambic line. These tabulations, according to Zhirmunsky, provided an inaccurate representation of the data because of the total disregard for verse and stanza delineations. Second, Bely had relied on 596 lines of poetry as the basis for his statistics; a quantity judged by the critic to be insufficient. Third, he attacked Bely's frequent practice of offering both subjective and prescriptive statements, which for Zhirmunsky were indicative more of personal preference or inclination of Symbolist poets than of empirical reality. Finally, Zhirmunsky expressed dismay at Bely's haphazard, inconsistent, and often confusing use of terms to describe his data. Although Zhirmunsky's objections appeared to have some merit, they have had little effect on the later practitioners of Bely's methods. The insistence upon the separation of poems into stanzas has been ignored in the major computations of Boris Tomashevsky and Kiril

Taranovski.[6] In addition, Bely's own computations based on only 596 lines of verse per poet have achieved new credibility in the much more comprehensive and definitive studies of Taranovski.[7] Finally, the attack on Bely's terminology pales when viewed in light of Tomashevsky's own complaint of "terminological arbitrariness" (*terminologichesky proizvol*) in the field of scientific poetics.[8]

Zhirmunsky's assessment of *Symbolism* was restrained, well organized, and for the most part a judicious appraisal; nevertheless, it became the referent for Bely's impassioned response in *Rhythm as a Dialectic.* In this work the author offered a refinement of his older techniques, a proposal for a new mathematical study of verse, and an attempt to clarify and define his own opinion of and relationship to the Formalist school. Bely ignored the essence of Zhirmunsky's criticism, only briefly refuting the charge of careless terminology. Instead he chose to denounce all of his detractors in an embittered and often ironic tour de force reminiscent of his style during the first decade of this century, when he had clashed with the "mystical anarchists." Apparently not content with the numerous accusations and vilifications interspersed throughout his text, Bely included an afterword aimed at discrediting the entire Formalist movement and in particular Viktor Zhirmunsky.

Bely contended that he had been engaged in studies of formal aspects of poetry long before the appearance of the Formalists. Relying on the historical sequence of events to justify his claim, he noted that his article on the "Principle of Form in Aesthetics" (1906) [9] was one of the earliest attempts to initiate a formal approach to literary analysis at a time when "Prof. Zhirmunsky was merely . . . a schoolboy" (p. 29). Bely then suggested that his readers consult bibliographical evidence if they doubted his declaration of primacy in the field: "from 1910 (year of publication of *Symbolism*) until 1928 in the place where nothing had stood there grew a monumental library written for the most part by formalists . . . " (p. 38). Bely's argument is convincing even today. One need only inspect any respected study, such as the work by Edward Stankiewicz and Dean S. Worth, *A Selected Bibliography of Slavic Linguistics,* vol. 2 (The Hague: Mouton, 1966), pp. 398–401, to ascertain that *Symbolism* chronologically precedes the voluminous literature devoted to questions of Russian metrics and rhythm in the twentieth century. Having established himself as a forerunner of formal criticism, Bely quickly disavowed any mutual borrowing from the later writings of the Formalists. While conceding that they had made significant advances in the area of nomenclature for the classification of poetic phenomena, he insisted that they had added little to the study of rhythm as he had first proposed. In order to insure the distinction between his own work and that of the Formalists Bely supplied the word "real" (*realno*) (p. 20) to characterize his own investigations. Furthermore, he suggested that the Formalists who had accused him of mysticism were themselves unscientific because they refused to seek or even to admit the existence of some "principle" in their studies.

On the basis of Bely's perception of his role in the history of formal aesthetics it is not difficult to understand his dismay and consternation, which he subsequently translated into contempt toward his calumniators. Convinced that his own contributions to the field had been intentionally ignored, he offered the following sarcastic reply:

> A surprising thing occurred: Andrey Bely had already begun in 1910 that which others went on to develop; and he then vanished into silence. These others, under the guise of "criticism" of Bely's absurdities have usurped from him his point of departure, and the not-too-distant, nice guy Bely thanked them and bowed to them in silence.
>
> The story of how poor Bely "futilely endeavored" for ten years to construct his "little work" on rhythm would make a rather interesting historico-cultural document on caste mores; for 100 years there had been no professors of "metrics" in Russia; and a poor poet, in the absence of a "professorate" began to cleanse the Augean stables of their filth; the place was made clean; and suddenly there appeared an excessive quantity of professor-"describers," . . .
>
> It is not good to be the cleaning man for another's filth; you leave soiled: on the cleansed spot arrive *good-looking* gardeners, and they will not allow you near the gardens. You . . . stink. . . . (pp. 43, 44)

In spite of the exaggerated tone of the excerpt, there was considerable truth in the allegations. Although the Formalists referred to Bely more than to any other critic, their comments were always equivocal, extending praise in one sentence and revoking it in the next. Thompson correctly commented on these inconsistencies in Formalist writings, noting that "their denunciations of Bely sometimes sound too emphatic to be credible." [10] Thus Boris

Eykhenbaum in his historical sketch of the Formalist movement admitted: "Naturally, such books as A. Bely's *Symbolism* (1910) meant immeasurably more to the younger generation than monographs without principle by historians of literature. . . ." In the same article he attacked Bely and the other Symbolists for their "subjective esthetic and philosophical theories." [11] Boris Tomashevsky, whose own studies owed an obvious debt to investigations by Bely, could not deny the critic's historical primacy; but he attempted to illustrate his own originality with the unproven assertion that "the material for my article on iambic tetrameter was developed over a year before the publication of A. Bely's book, *Symbolism*, which initiated a new epoch in the study of Russian verse." [12] These brief examples indicate the quandary in which the Formalists found themselves. Their own works showed such a marked similarity to those of Bely that they could not avoid mention of him; but they consistently refused to dignify *Symbolism* with serious scholarly criticism, preferring instead to utter repeated disclaimers of any significant influence on the part of Bely.

Corresponding to his belief in a conspiracy of silence directed toward him, which he considered had deprived him of an address for rebuttal, Bely filed a more serious accusation: "you took from me all rights to interfere in that field of studies which I had initiated before you, . . . from 1910 until 1928 I did not have an opportunity to publish my works on poetics . . . *without interference*" (p. 43). The author presented no evidence to confirm that his adversaries had excluded him from the arena of formal literary investigations. An examination of Bely's bibliography does, however, confirm an inexplicable absence of writing on literary themes during the years he mentioned. The only notable exception is a series of four articles which Bely had published in *Gorn* (*The Forge*) between 1918 and 1920 when he had been allied with the Proletkult.[13] Bely had, of course, published prolifically during his years in Berlin and only slightly less after his return to the Soviet Union; writings in this period were confined to poetry, novels and memoirs, with no investigations of literary form.[14] Many reasons may be offered for this silence, including Bely's lack of attention to aesthetics because of other endeavors. A case against the Formalists may exist if one considers that the market for literary studies of a strictly formal nature was obviously limited and at the same time overwhelmingly dominated by the Formalists, who welcomed no work by Bely in their own publications. Consequently there is some indication to suspect that Bely's complaint was not totally unfounded.

Bely's final indictment was his most vicious: Zhirmunsky and, by association, the Formalists were guilty of plagiarism. Bely noted that already in 1910 and 1911 his Rhythmical Circle had refined and corrected the inconsistencies first presented in *Symbolism*. He then claimed a "complete and pitiful concurrence" of his own revised system with that presented by Zhirmunsky in *Introduction to Metrics*. Bely alluded to his *Register*, the record of substantive corrections to *Symbolism*, which Zhirmunsky had failed to mention "in case he had become acquainted with our *Register* of 1911, which had some distribution from hand to hand; indeed, the work on registration had been given life by me; if we accidently coincided, then why did Prof. Zhirmunsky who personally attended my course in the Leningrad *House of the Arts* in 1920, at which I mentioned more than once my mistakes of transcription in *Symbolism* (if my memory does not betray me—also referring to the *Register*),—why did he not find time to express his observations to me at that time" (p. 243). It is impossible to resolve this issue without access to the *Register* or to Zhirmunsky's notes of the period, if indeed copies of these materials exist. What is most striking is the maliciousness of the charge which clearly expressed Bely's almost hysterical reaction to his critics.

Zhirmunsky did not allow this challenge to his integrity pass without comment. His reply was contained in a searing review entitled "Apropos the Book *Rhythm as a Dialectic*." [15] The author displayed his own talents as a polemicist first softening the blow and lulling Bely with a somewhat exaggerated restatement of his earlier opinions: "I have always considered it unjust to forget the debt of gratitude in regard to the author of *Symbolism*, as have done several representatives of the new literary studies in the heat of polemical alienations . . . " (p. 203). He then offered his condolences and pity to Bely for most of his statements and vigorously denied that he had come in contact either with the *Register* or with any reference to improvements on the data in Bely's work. Instead he opened a counteroffensive by claiming that Bely had raised no objections to Zhirmunsky's own work in 1925 when it had been discussed at a meeting of writers and critics. Zhirmunsky concluded his arguments with a spiteful allusion to Bely as "the well-known Muscovite mystic Boris Bugaev" (p. 208), a rejoinder to Bely's sarcastic use of "Professor" Zhirmunsky. After this review the conflict apparently ended never being mentioned again in print although both Zhirmunsky and Bely continued to work in the field of poetics after this time. Bely in a review article "Poema o Khlopke," *Novy Mir* 11 (1932): 229–48, returned to the methodology of *Rhythm as a Dialectic* but failed to comment on Zhirmunsky's article. Interestingly, Bely was extremely generous with his praise for some of the Formalists, particularly Boris Eichenbaum and Viktor Vinogradov, in his posthumously published scholarship entitled *Gogol's Craft.*

The controversy was unfortunate because of the childish attitude displayed by both participants, but also because Bely's work failed to attract attention on its merits. Although little was proven by the polemic, the writings involved constitute a valuable historical record of the intensity of emotion raised by the question of Bely's relationship to the Formalists. Always a controversial figure, whether as aesthetic theorist, novelist, or memoirist, Bely aroused the same love–hate response in his literary investigations. Perhaps due to the often caustic character of the writer, his critical writings have not attracted serious scholarly review. Although the history of Bely as a literary critic still remains to be written, there can be little doubt concerning the lasting quality of his contributions to the study of poetics. Perhaps more than any other work, *Symbolism* has had a continuing impact on the study of Russian verse, as is evident in ongoing research by Kiril Taranovski and James Bailey.[16] Thus while many of Bely's statements in his own defense may be viewed in perspective as hyperbolic, he is still more highly regarded today than most Formalists were ever willing to admit.

NOTES

1. Cf. Marc Slonim, *From Chekhov to the Revolution: Russian Literature 1900–1917* (New York: Oxford University Press, 1962), p. 195: "His [Bely's] works on Symbolism, on the principles of Russian prosody, on rhythmics in poetry, all laid the foundations for a special branch of formal criticism . . ."; R. H. Stacy, *Russian Literary Criticism: A Short History* (Syracuse: Syracuse University Press, 1974), pp. 136, 137: "his [Bely's] early pioneering experiments and studies had already laid the foundation for important areas of formalist poetics."

2. Kiril Taranovski, *Ruski dvodelni ritmovi I—II,* Posebna izdanje No.

217, Otdelenje literature i jezika No. 5 (Beograd: Srpska akademija nauka, 1953), p. 353.

3. *Vvedenie v metriku,* Voprosy poetiki No. 6 (Leningrad: Academia, 1925).

4. "Ob odnom voprose ritma," *Apollon* 11 (1910): 52–60.

5. Viktor Zhirmunsky, "Formprobleme in der russischen Literaturwissenschaft," *Zeitschrift für Slavische Philologie* 1 (1925): 130.

6. Taranovski, *Ruski dvodelni* . . . , and Boris Tomashevsky, *O stikhe* (Leningrad: Priboy, 1929).

7. See Tables 2, 3, 4 from Taranovski, *Ruski dvodelni* . . . .

8. Tomashevsky, *O stikhe,* p. 95.

9. A. Bely, "Princip formy v estetike," *Zolotoe runo* 11–12 (1906): 88–96.

10. Ewa M. Thompson, *Russian Formalism and Anglo-American New Criticism* (The Hague: Mouton, 1971), p. 14.

11. Boris Eichenbaum, "Teoriya 'formalnogo metoda,' " in *Literatura: Teoriya, kritika, polemika* (Leningrad: Priboy, 1927), pp. 119, 120.

12. Tomashevsky, *O stikhe,* p. 326.

13. These include one review in *Gorn* 1 (1918): 83–85; one article on prose rhythm, "O khudozhestvennoy proze," *Gorn* 2–3 (1919): 49–55; and two on poetics, "O stikhakh Aleksandrovskogo," *Gorn* 1 (1918): 79–81; "O ritme," *Gorn* 5 (1920): 47–54.

14. Those articles which did appear on Andreev, Blok and Khodasevich are of an aesthetic-philosophical nature and do not belong in the corpus of Bely's works on aspects of literary form.

15. Viktor Zhirmunsky, "Po povodu knigi 'Ritm kak dialektika': Otvet Andreyu Belomu," *Zvezda* 8 (1929): 203–8.

16. In addition to the work of Taranovski already cited see his *Ruski četvorostopni jamb u prvim dvema decenijama XX veka* (Beograd: Južnoslovenski filolog, 1955–1956) and "Chetyryokhstopny yamb Andreya Belogo," *International Journal of Slavic Linguistics and Poetics* 10 (1966): 127–47. James Bailey has continued the work of Bely and Taranovski in "The Evolution and Structure of the Russian Iambic Pentameter from 1880–1922," *International Journal of Slavic Linguistics and Poetics* 16 (1973): 119–46.

CONTRIBUTORS

GERALD JANECEK is Associate Professor of Russian at the University of Kentucky, translator of Bely's novel *Kotik Letaev,* and author of four articles on Bely's prose.

GLEB STRUVE, born in Saint Petersburg and educated at Oxford, is Emeritus Professor of Slavic at the University of California, Berkeley, and author of *Russian Literature under Lenin and Stalin: 1917–1953* and *Russian Literature in Exile.* Among other major publications, he has coedited the collected works of Gumilyov, Mandelstam, Akhmatova, Klyuev, and Zabolotsky.

ZOYA YURIEFF is a graduate of Barnard College and received her M.A. and Ph.D. degrees from Radcliffe. She is Professor of Slavic Literature at New York University, member of editorial boards of *Novy Zhurnal* and *Forum,* and author of *Joseph Wittlin* and numerous articles.

CHARLOTTE DOUGLAS is a specialist in modern Russian theories of literature and art. Her articles have appeared in the *Structurist,* the *Russian Review, Art Journal, Russian Literature Triquarterly, Art in America,* and elsewhere. Recently she spent a year in the Soviet Union gathering material for a book on early twentieth-century art.

HERBERT EAGLE is Associate Professor and Chairman for Slavic Languages at Purdue University. His publications on Russian and Czech literature, theory of verse, and the semiotics of literature and cinema have appeared in *Semiotica, Books Abroad, Modern Fiction Studies, Russian Literature Triquarterly, Rus-*

sian Language Journal, Dispositio, Germano-Slavica, and *Film Studies Annual.*

SAMUEL D. CIORAN is Chairman of the Russian Department at McMaster University, Hamilton, Ontario, and author of numerous translations and articles on Russian Symbolism and of the first monograph on Bely in English, *The Apocalyptic Symbolism of Andrej Belyj.*

NINA BERBEROVA, born in Saint Petersburg, left Russia in 1922 as the wife of Vladislav Khodasevich. She lived in Paris from 1925 to 1950, when she came to the United States. She has taught at Yale, Princeton, Pennsylvania, Columbia, and Indiana universities. Her publications include an autobiography, *The Italics Are Mine,* and short stories, novels, biographies, and criticism.

HELENE HARTMANN-FLYER was born in Saint Petersburg and educated in Finland and Paris. After a successful business career in the United States, she earned B.A., M.A., and Ph.D. degrees from Columbia. She taught Russian language and literature at Columbia and at Hunter College. She is working on a book about Bely.

JOHN D. ELSWORTH was educated at Saint John's College, Cambridge, and the University of Moscow. He teaches at the University of East Anglia, Norwich, England, and is author of *Andrey Bely,* the first biography of Bely written in English. He has published several articles on Bely, including "Andrei Bely's Theory of Symbolism" in *Forum for Modern Language Studies.*

ROBERT P. HUGHES is Associate Professor of Slavic Languages and Literature and of Comparative Literature at the University of California, Berkeley. He is the author of *Ideas and Images of Music in Russian Poetry* and articles on Fet, Nabokov, Blok, Khodasevich, and Mandelstam; and is working on a translation of Bely's memoirs of Blok.

GEORGE KALBOUSS, who received his Ph.D. from New York University, is Associate Professor at Ohio State University. He is a specialist in Russian Symbolist drama and is also interested in techniques of teaching Russian.

STANLEY J. RABINOWITZ holds a Ph.D. from Harvard (1975) and is Assistant Professor of Russian at Amherst College. A specialist on Fyodor Sologub, he is author of "On the Death of a Poet: The Final Days of Fyodor Sologub," in the *Russian Literature Triquarterly,* and has been working also on Chekhov and Pasternak.

ARTHUR LEVIN is Associate Professor of Russian History at the University of Calgary, Canada. His publications include several articles on M. O. Gershenzon as well as translations of M. I. Tugan-Baranovsky's *The Russian Factory* and V. Lvov-Rogachevsky's *Russian-Jewish Literature.*

BERNICE GLATZER ROSENTHAL holds a Ph.D. in Russian history from the University of California, Berkeley, and is Associate Professor of History at Fordham University. She has written *D. S. Merezhkovsky and the Silver Age: The Development of a Revolutionary Mentality* and numerous articles and book reviews on Russian intellectual history and the history of Russian women.

ROGER KEYS is Lecturer in Russian at the University of Saint Andrews; he taught at the New University of Ulster from 1974 to 1977. He has published selected letters of Andrey Bely to A. S. Petrovsky and E. N. Kezelman in *Novy Zhurnal.* He is working on a study of Bely's place in the development of Russian modernist fiction during 1900 – 1914.

THOMAS R. BEYER, Jr., received his Ph.D. from the University of Kansas. He has published "Belyj's *Serebrjanyj golub':* Gogol in Gugolevo," in *Russian Language Journal.* He is Assistant Professor of Russian at Middlebury College.

INDEX